ECONOMIC COMMISSION FOR LATIN AMERICA AND THE CARIBBEAN

SUSTAINABLE DEVELOPMENT: CHANGING PRODUCTION PATTERNS, SOCIAL EQUITY AND THE ENVIRONMENT

UNITED NATIONS
ECONOMIC COMMISSION FOR LATIN AMERICA AND THE CARIBBEAN
Santiago, Chile, 1991

LC/G.1648/Rev.2-P
May 1991

UNITED NATIONS PUBLICATION

Sales No.: E.91.II.G.5

ISBN 92-1-121166-2

CONTENTS

Page

Foreword 9

Chapter I: THE WORLD ENVIRONMENT: THE CURRENT
                CHALLENGES AND THEIR BACKGROUND 13
                1.   Towards the third millennium 13
                2.   The environment in the context of changing production patterns
                      with equity 14
                3.   The long road from Stockholm to Rio 16

Chapter II: THE SUSTAINABILITY OF DEVELOPMENT:
                BEYOND NATURAL CAPITAL 21
                1.   Introduction 21
                2.   Implications of the approach 25
                3.   Micro and macroeconomic equilibria 27

Chapter III: ECONOMIC AND ENVIRONMENTAL POLICIES 29
                1.   Introduction 29
                2.   Major areas of environmental policy 29
                3.   Relationship between economic policies and the environment ... 34
                4.   Macroeconomic policy and its environmental impact 38
                5.   Sectoral and microeconomic policy 44
                6.   Problems of co-ordination of public policies 47

Chapter IV: POPULATION AND NATURAL RESOURCES 49
                1.   Population, the environment and resources 49
                2.   Use of the region's natural resources 54
                3.   Management of natural resources 63

Chapter V: POVERTY AND SUSTAINABLE DEVELOPMENT 65
                1.   Level of poverty 65
                2.   Population, poverty and the environment 67
                3.   Indigenous peoples, poverty and the environment 70
                4.   Poverty and capital formation 73
                5.   The relationship between natural capital formation and poverty .. 75
                6.   Technology and poverty 75

Chapter VI: TECHNICAL PROGRESS, COMPETITIVENESS
                AND SUSTAINABLE DEVELOPMENT 77
                1.   Introduction 77
                2.   The convergence of international competitiveness,
                      technical progress and sustainable development 77
                3.   Consequences for Latin America and the Caribbean 78
                4.   Technology, competitiveness and natural resources:
                      relative position of Latin America and the Caribbean 80

5.   Technology, competitiveness and environmental sustainability:
      The energy system   82
6.   Industrialization, enterprises and environmental sustainability ...   87

Chapter VII: INSTITUTIONS AND SUSTAINABLE DEVELOPMENT   95
1.   The nature of institutional capital   95
2.   Organizing for sustainable development   100
3.   Environmental administration and management   101
4.   The international and regional legal framework   101

Chapter VIII: FINANCING AND SUSTAINABILITY   109
1.   Introduction   109
2.   Financial capital and natural resources   109
3.   Justification for special financing   111
4.   Conditionality and additionality in external financing   113
5.   New instruments: debt-for-nature swaps   114
6.   Nature and styles of future investment   120
7.   Financial policy: implementation of a strategy   120
8.   An increase in investment capacity   121

Chapter IX: ENVIRONMENTAL SUSTAINABILITY, INTERNATIONAL
               CO-OPERATION AND THE GLOBAL LIST OF ENVIRONMENTAL
               PRIORITIES   123
1.   Environmental sustainability and international co-operation   123
2.   Negotiation of global environmental problems   125

Chapter X: SUMMARY AND PROPOSALS   131
1.   The United Nations Conference on Environment
      and Development   131
2.   Development and environment from the regional perspective ...   132
3.   The commitments needed   134
4.   Criteria and principles   135
5.   Some suggestions for formulating a regional position   137
6.   Preparatory activities for the United Nations Conference   142

BOXES AND TABLES
Box   II-1   Shortening of the useful life of reservoirs   23
          II-2   Forces giving rise to the environmental deterioration
                  of the Amazon basin   24
          II-3   Towards sustained agricultural development   25
Box   III-1   Changing production patterns and environmental conservation:
                  mining enterprises in Chile   31
          III-2   PETROBRAS   32
          III-3   Pesticide subsidy policies   35
          III-4   Effects of urban expansion on the city of Lima   36

	III-5	Cotton in Central America	37
	III-6	Economic policies that encourage deforestation	39
	III-7	Air pollution in Santiago, Chile	43
Box	IV-1	Effects of increased water demand on large cities	51
	IV-2	Rationalization of urban transport in Mexico City	52
	IV-3	Reclamation of salinized soils in Peru	56
	IV-4	Waste water disposal alternatives	58
	IV-5	Deregulation and the Fisheries Act in Chile	61
Table	IV-1	Latin America and the Caribbean: land use	55
Box	V-1	Poverty in Latin America: spread and coverage	66
	V-2	Floods in Metropolitan Buenos Aires in 1985	69
	V-3	The vicious circle of peasant poverty in the Peruvian highlands	71
Box	VI-1	Projects in PEMEX's ecological package	79
	VI-2	The environmental activities of Petróleos de Venezuela, S.A.	84
	VI-3	Environmental impact of different energy sources	85
	VI-4	Corporación Venezolana de Guayana and environmental protection	93
Table	VI-1	Latin America: percentage distribution of the sales of the 10 leading enterprises in selected countries, 1989	81
	VI-2	Selected OECD countries and Latin America: energy-intensity trends	83
	VI-3	Latin America: general data on selected large Latin American enterprises, 1989	91
Box	VII-1	The Environmental Sanitation Technologies Company (CETESB)	97
	VII-2	Institutional reforms in Colombia	99
	VII-3	Mexico: Federal Sea Act	103
	VII-4	Guatemala: Tikal National Park	105
Box	VIII-1	Global Environment Fund	112
	VIII-2	Debt-for-nature swaps: the case of Bolivia	117
	VIII-3	Debt-for-nature swaps: the case of Costa Rica	118
	VIII-4	Debt-for-nature swaps: the case of Ecuador	119
Table	VIII-1	Latin America and the Caribbean: value of external debt paper in the secondary market	114
	VIII-2	Latin America and other developing regions: debt-for-nature swaps	116

FOREWORD

In March 1990, the secretariat of the Economic Commission for Latin America and the Caribbean (ECLAC) placed before the Governments of its member States a proposal for the development of the countries of Latin America and the Caribbean in the 1990s and beyond.[1] That proposal contains a set of guidelines which can be adapted to the particular situation of the countries of Latin America and the Caribbean. It seeks to promote changes in the production patterns of the region within a context of growing social equity, and it also expressly incorporates the environmental and geographico-spatial dimension into the development process when it states: "what is needed is ... to reverse the negative tendencies towards the depletion of natural resources and the increasing deterioration through contamination and global imbalances, and ... to take advantage of the opportunities for making use of natural resources on the basis of research and conservation".[2]

The present document has a dual purpose. On the one hand, it seeks to delve more deeply into ways of incorporating the environmental variable into the development process: that is to say, into the process of changing production patterns with equity. In this respect, taking as a basis a number of previous studies by the secretariat which deal with different aspects of this topic,[3] this issue is examined here from the point of view of development, with emphasis on some of the central concerns of the above-mentioned study on *Changing Production Patterns with Social Equity*.[4] At the same time, this document forms part of the preparatory activities for the United Nations Conference on Environment and Development to be held in mid-1992, the specific aim being to provide sound bases and guidance for the discussions at the Regional Preparatory Meeting for that Conference to be held by ECLAC in Mexico City in March 1991.

The United Nations Conference gives the community of nations a chance to reappraise the way in which governments and societies are tackling two of the most pressing tasks of mankind as we stand on the threshold of the coming millennium. The first of these is to offer a decent standard of living to all the inhabitants of our planet, which will call for a very considerable and sustained effort, especially in the developing nations, where in most cases around two thirds of the population cannot even satisfy their basic needs. The second task is to ensure that further economic growth takes place within an environmentally sustainable context, for there is a growing awareness of the magnitude of the frequently irreparable damage caused to the physical and natural environment of mankind both by the excesses associated with prosperity and the shortcomings linked with poverty. Both the excesses and the shortcomings are related to the development style which has taken for granted that natural capital is infinite. Until quite recently, there has been little effort to avoid squandering, polluting or degrading it.

The Regional Preparatory Meeting organized by ECLAC is being held at a relatively early stage in what should be seen as an ongoing process. This document therefore concentrates on some salient aspects which the secretariat considers to be essential for the environmentally sustainable development of Latin America and the Caribbean, leaving their more detailed elaboration for later stages, as progress is made towards the harmonization of criteria within each country, between the countries of the region, and between those countries and the rest of the nations participating in the United Nations Conference. In other words, this document represents a first approach to the task of linking Latin American and Caribbean development with the environment: a task which will assuredly be the subject of many subsequent efforts. It also seeks

9

to provide background information to help adopt the position of the countries of the region with regard to the agenda of the United Nations Conference.

This document is based on six central ideas which form the unifying threads of its different chapters. The first idea is that we have now left behind us the controversies of bygone years in which it was claimed that there is some kind of conflict between concern for the environment and the objective of development. Although such a conflict often does arise, especially at the microeconomic level, there can be no doubt that concern for the environment is now perfectly legitimate and amply justified in both developed and developing societies. This is particularly true in the case of Latin America and the Caribbean, whose economies are based fundamentally on the exploitation of natural resources, many of them vulnerable to irreversible degradation. Thus, those responsible for formulating the economic policy of the region must incorporate among their key variables that of environmental sustainability, not only in order to meet the needs of coming generations, but also as a vital element for ensuring sustained growth for the benefit of the present generation.

Secondly, and in view of the foregoing, it is obvious that both the origins and the consequences of environmental problems are different in the developing countries (where they are frequently associated with situations deriving from a lack of resources) from those encountered in developed societies, where they are associated with high levels of consumption and even with the outright squandering of resources because of their abundance. Thus, ecological and environmental problems take different forms in these two different types of societies.

Thirdly, it is considered that man's relation with nature begins at the level of the individual, subsequently passing through the levels of the community, the district, the region, the country, the ecological systems of common interest to more than one country, the continent and the world. There can be no clear-cut distinction between local, national and global phenomena, as they all influence each other. Consequently, this document deals with both the domestic effort to

incorporate the environmental variable in the development process and the international effort to solve common problems through co-operation.

Fourthly, it is held that within the context of the many links that exist between development and the environment, it is vital to understand the need for the sustainability of development within a broad context which goes beyond mere concern for the world's natural capital. Thus, it is held that the achievement of sustainable development helps to secure a dynamic balance between all the forms of capital or assets that take part in the national and regional effort, be they human, natural, physical, financial, institutional or cultural.

Fifthly, it is argued that the incorporation of concern for the environment within the development process calls for a systemic effort which also involves the type of economic policies followed, the management of natural resources, technological innovation, broad participation by the population, education, institutional consolidation, investment and research.

Finally, it is held that international co-operation must not limit itself to tackling environmental problems in an isolated manner. Thus, as the development effort cannot be separated from protection of the environment and many environmental problems are the result of phenomena linked to conditions of underdevelopment, international co-operation must seek to promote development and protection of the environment in an integrated manner: in other words, it must seek environmentally sustainable development. It can therefore be seen that the 1992 United Nations Conference provides an opportunity to look anew at various items related with international economic co-operation, this time perhaps from a fresh perspective.

The various topics dealt with in the document are presented in line with the thematic layout of the above-mentioned proposal on *Changing Production Patterns with Social Equity*. Thus, among other aspects, the present document examines the mutual links between environmental sustainability and macroeconomic policy; natural resources; changing production patterns; poverty; development of concerted strategies; financing; and international co-operation. Specifically, the document has the following 10 chapters: chapter I sets forth concern with the environment as a future challenge and describes, by way of background, the work already done at the global level in this respect. Chapter II defines sustainable development and shows that it must be viewed in a manner that goes beyond considerations limited to natural capital. Chapter III describes the nature of the relations between economic policies, natural resources and the environment. Chapter IV presents a diagnosis of the current situation as regards natural resources and the human environment in the region. Chapter V analyses the main relations between poverty and the environment. Chapter VI analyses the role that must be played by technology in the achievement of changing production patterns with social equity and environmental sustainability. Chapter VII sets out the basis for a new institutional structure with regard to the environment, the objectives that should be pursued in the management and organization of sustainable development and their relation with political systems and legislation. Chapter VIII proposes suitable financial policies and financing arrangements for sustainable development. Chapter IX links the international co-operation agenda with the topic of sustainable development, and finally, chapter X contains a summary and a set of proposals.

Notes

[1] Economic Commission for Latin America and the Caribbean (ECLAC), *Changing Production Patterns with Social Equity* (LC/G.1601-P), Santiago, Chile, March 1990. United Nations publication, Sales No. E.90.II.G.6.

[2] *Ibid.*, p. 14. See also pp. 134-137.

[3] See, for example: ECLAC, *El medio ambiente como factor de desarrollo. Prefactibilidad de proyectos de importancia ambiental y de interés económico* (LC/G.1549-P), Estudios e informes de la CEPAL series, No. 75, Santiago, Chile, February 1989 (United Nations publication, Sales No. S.89.II.G.6); *Report of the Seminar on Environmental Impact Assessments as an Instrument of Environmental Management. Situation and Prospects in Latin America and the Caribbean* (LC/L.519), Santiago, Chile, November 1989, and *Elements for an Effective Environmental Policy* (LC/L.581(Sem.56/5)), Santiago, Chile, August 1990; *Indicadores económico-ambientales para las cuentas nacionales* (LC/R.876(Sem.54/5)), Santiago, Chile, March 1990; ECLAC/UNEP, *Avances en la interpretación ambiental del desarrollo agrícola de América Latina* (LC/G.1347), Santiago, Chile, May 1985 (United Nations publication, Sales No. S.85.II.G.4), and *Estilos de desarrollo, energía y medio ambiente. Un estudio de caso exploratorio* (E/CEPAL/G.1254), Santiago, Chile, July 1983 (United Nations publication, Sales No. S.83.II.G.24).

[4] For various reasons, the document does not attempt to deal with all the important issues involved. One obvious but deliberate omission is the link between drug eradication and sustainable development, since this topic will be the subject of a special study to be undertaken by the ECLAC secretariat in the next few months.

Chapter I

THE WORLD ENVIRONMENT: THE CURRENT CHALLENGES AND THEIR BACKGROUND

The real challenge of economic development does not refer to the speed at which a country grows, but the level of well-being it can attain while growing more rapidly.

1. Towards the third millennium

Today, on the threshold of the third millennium of the modern era, Latin America and the Caribbean are facing an enormous challenge in the economic and social sphere: the attainment of integral development and the need to ensure the sustainable management of natural resources and the environment. The first of these aspects has long been part of the aspirations of the region. The second, however, has gradually been incorporated into the core of the development debate in recent years.

Latin America and the Caribbean stand at an historic crossroads. This situation calls for changes in production patterns which –within a context of political democracy, economic openness, and reshaping of the role of the State in order to facilitate greater participation by society as a whole– will give fresh vigour to the economies while at the same time providing new bases for the attainment of greater equity. The efforts in this direction could be frustrated, however, unless there is rational management of natural resources and the environment (the natural capital). This is a challenge which calls for very considerable efforts at the national, regional and global levels.

The region is entering the 1990s against a more democratic and participative political background. In this context, environmental issues are a growing concern of the people and communities affected, as they seek to exploit the available resources in order to raise their standards of living or improve living conditions in the physical spaces they occupy. The challenge is not so much that of improving the quality of life of the population at the cost of their standard of living –a dilemma faced in particular by the developed countries– but rather to improve the standard of living in an environmentally sustainable manner. This involves recognition of the fact that alterations in the human and natural environment are an underlying fact in the development process, so that the topic of the environment cannot be absent from the minds of those responsible for guiding that process.

The rational management of the world's natural capital is a necessary condition for achieving economic growth and sustainable improvements in the standard of living of the population. This natural heritage or capital is of fundamental importance in achieving changing production patterns with equity. The region has already entered upon a stage in which the indiscriminate and abusive exploitation of the existing resources will soon be reflected in serious checks on development.

Thus, the region is now on the threshold of a number of environmental problems which, if not corrected, will adversely affect the productive capacity of the economies. The countries producing agricultural goods, for example, depend on the management of natural resources such as soil, water, vegetation and the climate. These elements are already beginning to suffer considerable changes which are having a progressive effect on the quality and quantity of agricultural products.

The relations between growth, equity and environmental sustainability are extremely complex. On the one hand, the transformation of natural resources into goods is essential for growth and the raising of living standards. Thus, for example, the expansion of the water supply is what makes it possible to maintain the growth of human settlements. On the other hand, however, economic development processes affect the quality of the environment. An example of this is air and water pollution, which reduces the capacity of ecosystems to provide the community with vital goods and services.

The United Nations Conference on Environment and Development offers a unique opportunity to systematically tackle the problem of attaining environmentally sustainable development. Among the priority issues to be dealt with are the following:

– It is necessary to achieve a dynamic balance between all the forms of capital involved in the effort to secure sustainable development. Laying the foundations for sustainable development is an issue that goes beyond the mere rational management of natural capital.

– Economic policies are not neutral or even-handed with regard to the use of natural resources. It is necessary to recognize and appraise the effect of these policies on natural capital in order to ensure that the efforts to change production patterns with equity also meet the requirement for sustainability.

– Technological progress helps economies to grow, but it must be guided towards the reduction of negative impacts or the generation of positive impacts on natural capital.

– People and communities are the basic objective of development, and sustainable development is incompatible with the continued existence of poverty. Consequently, overcoming poverty is an indispensable condition for the achievement of sustainable development by the region.

– It is essential to take account of the institutional aspects of sustainable development. Thus, there must be a suitable structure of incentives, legislation and measures for the management and organization of productive activities. This structure must facilitate the fulfilment of the specific tasks of the public and private sectors, as well as participation by the population as a whole.

– Financial policies and the instruments for their implementation must be placed at the service of sustainable development. New financing instruments must be suitably adapted to the realities of the region, including the long period of stagnation of the 1980s.

Moreover, the topic of environmentally sustainable development provides an opportunity for reappraising the list of priorities in international co-operation in all its aspects.

2. The environment in the context of changing production patterns with equity

As already noted in the Foreword, the reflections on the environment presented in this document have a dual purpose. The first aim is to examine in greater detail ways of incorporating the environmental variable into the development process: a question which was only dealt with in its broad lines in the above-mentioned proposal for changing production patterns with equity.[1] In this respect, it outlines a suitable economic and social approach in environmental matters, analyses the implications of some policies, and puts forward proposals on the institutions and reforms needed for achieving sustainable development.

Its second purpose is to offer guidelines to facilitate the discussions of governments and non-governmental organizations in the preparatory process which will culminate in the United Nations Conference on Environment and Development, with emphasis on those aspects considered to be particularly important for the countries of Latin America and the Caribbean, both from the point of view of incorporating the environmental dimension into the development strategies of each country and with regard to the way these issues fit into the context of international co-operation.

Mention may be made, at this point, of some of the main concepts around which the proposal for changing production patterns with equity is constructed. Before doing so, it is worth noting, as the secretariat pointed out at the time, that this proposal does not pretend to offer a single universal recipe. Instead, it seeks to give a set of guidelines that can be adapted to the particular situations of the different countries.

The central idea of the proposal, around which all the others revolve, is that changes in production patterns must be based on the deliberate and systematic incorporation of technical progress, within the context of greater international competitiveness, in order to achieve increasingly high levels of productivity.

Secondly, emphasis is placed on the systemic nature of competitiveness, as reflected in the network of linkages between each enterprise and the educational system, the technological, energy and transport infrastructure, labour relations, the system of public and private institutions and the financial system.

Thirdly, changes in production patterns cannot be merely the result of creating a suitable stable macroeconomic climate or applying a policy of "correct prices". Coherent and stable macroeconomic management is of fundamental importance, but it is not enough on its own: it must also be combined with sectoral policies.

Fourthly, one of the key elements in changing production patterns is the removal of hermetic sectoral divisions. Thus, industrialization must go beyond the narrow sectoral framework in which it has often been dealt with hitherto and must be linked with the primary and services sectors in order to integrate the productive system and further the growing homogenization of levels of productivity.

Fifthly, the proposal assigns just as much importance to equity as to changes in production patterns, maintaining that these two concepts are mutually supportive. Thus, it is held that sustained growth based on increasing competitiveness is incompatible with the continued existence of shortcomings with regard to equity, although it is recognized that the latter cannot be corrected without sustained growth.

Sixthly, the proposal assigns major importance to Latin American and Caribbean integration and intraregional co-operation, since these can make a vital contribution to the consolidation of changes in production patterns.

A seventh point made is that the formulation and application of economic strategies and policies must take place in a democratic, pluralistic and participative context. Within this democratic context, the process of consensus-building on the strategies to be followed, understood as the establishment of a set of long-range explicit and implicit agreements between the main actors in national society and the State, will necessarily be of decisive importance.

The eighth point made is that there must be a process of renovation with regard to the style of State intervention: it is considered desirable that State action should be concentrated on strengthening competitiveness based on the incorporation of technical progress and the continued evolution towards reasonable levels of equity and environmental sustainability.

Finally, it should be noted that the relationship between the proposal for changing production patterns with equity and the issue of the environment is not limited to what was expressly stated on the full incorporation of the environmental and geographico-spatial dimension into the development process. It must be emphasized that each and every one of the concepts detailed here is part of the background to the reflections of the ECLAC secretariat presented in this document.

3. The long road from Stockholm to Rio

3.1 *How this issue came to be included in the United Nations agenda*

From the end of the war until the early 1970s, great efforts were made all over the world to stimulate economic growth. The achievement of such growth involved the rapid accumulation of various forms of capital, especially those considered to be scarcest, such as physical and financial capital. Technological progress was taken as the symbol of this process of change, but in contrast there was a tendency to underestimate the importance of the other forms of capital: human, natural, institutional or cultural.

In the early 1970s, however, various of these postulates began to be questioned. The problems of underdevelopment and poverty, which were difficult to solve, clearly required fresh approaches. Against the background of these changes, various organizations in the world began to question the basic hypothesis that natural capital was by its very nature abundant. Thus, the Club of Rome came to the conclusion that natural capital was scarce and that the accumulation of physical and financial capital, such as industries, could further deteriorate the existing natural capital. The environmental issue gradually entered the collective conscience of mankind, above all in the industrialized countries.

One of the most important milestones in this period was the Panel of Experts on Development and Environment held at Founex, Switzerland from 4 to 12 June 1971, at which a document was prepared on the state of the human and natural environment of the planet. This document became one of the bases for the United Nations Conference on the Human Environment held in Stockholm in 1972, which issued a Declaration and Plan of Action for the Environment containing 109 specific recommendations.[2]

Both the Founex document and the proposals emerging from the United Nations Conference touched upon normative aspects of fundamental importance for the developing countries. The first problem examined was that of the human environment, with particular attention to the problem of poverty, and the aspects covered included housing, water, health, hygiene, nutrition and natural disasters. In this context, it was clearly stated that environmental problems called for changes in production patterns. It was noted, however, that although economic growth was very necessary, it did not of itself guarantee lasting welfare for the population. In order to achieve that, it was necessary to attain other social goals.

One of the aspects dealt with in detail was the relation between development and the environment. A specific distinction was drawn between two types of problems: those due to insufficient development, and those which were a consequence of development. Special emphasis was placed on the latter, since it was expected that most of the nations in the world would be entering upon a rapid industrialization process. In this respect, the main objective defined was to attain the benefits of development in each sector with a minimum of adverse secondary effects.

Another salient aspect was that of international trade. It was noted that it was very likely that environmental rules would emerge in connection with the growth of international trade, and this would be likely to cause changes in the competitive position of various countries through changes in the comparative production cost structures. It was emphasized, however, that these environmental considerations could also benefit some regions of the world because of the relation between natural capital and synthetic products and the degree of influence of foreign capital.

With regard to environmental policies, it was held that these should be an integral part of the general development strategy. Consequently, it was maintained that the developing countries should redefine their goals, establishing minimum environmental standards and formulating a macroeconomic, general and sectoral environment policy, and that suitable techniques should be elaborated for including the environmental factor in the appraisal of development projects.

Mention was also made of the need to change the traditional approaches to project evaluation, such as cost-benefit analysis. It was also considered necessary that a more appropriate concept should be developed of the notion of "opportunity costs", to include external spatial and temporal effects. It was considered, however, that it would be practically impossible for the countries to plan and evaluate their investments, policies and reforms adequately, because of the precarious nature of the existing information.

As a necessary condition for the formulation of an environmental strategy, it was considered necessary to make various institutional reforms (including reforms in legislation). It was recognized, however, that it was still too early to state categorically what those changes should consist of.

With regard to international relations, both the Founex meeting and the report of the United Nations Conference on the Human Environment stressed the need for a start to be made on the evaluation of the position with regard to international co-operation, external trade, external financial aid, technology transfer and the rules applied by the industrialized countries.

Finally, there was an awareness that environmental problems manifested themselves with different characteristics and contents in developed and developing societies, and that many problems were peculiar to the particular national and even local conditions. At the same time, it was recognized that although the environmental dimension –an issue which knows no frontiers– could unite nations around the task of solving common problems, it also had the potential for dividing them into groups consisting of the main polluters and causers of environmental deterioration, on the one hand, and those directly affected by the consequences of those phenomena on the other.

3.2 ECLAC's treatment of the issue from 1971 onwards

All the foregoing discussions naturally also had a Latin American and Caribbean expression, reflected *inter alia* in the documents prepared and meetings sponsored by the Economic Commission for Latin America and the Caribbean and the United Nations Environment Programme (UNEP). Thus, in 1971 ECLAC organized a meeting

as part of the preparatory activities for the 1972 United Nations Conference, at which it was noted that the low level of development of the countries contributed to the deterioration of the environment and it was also indicated that the development problems of the region were perhaps more closely linked to those of the environment than in any other developing region in the world.[3]

With regard to the environmental situation in the region, four main areas were identified: human settlements, natural resources, environmental pollution, and international-level problems. Another important concern was the incorporation of environmental problems into national development policies. The use of planning was recommended as a necessary means of achieving the desired environmental objectives. Emphasis was also placed on the need to tackle a large number of problems affecting human settlements in both urban and rural areas. In urban areas, it was recommended that protection should be given to human settlements weakened by the constant deterioration in the environment (e.g., air and water pollution). In rural areas, spatial and human settlements planning was directly related to the prevailing land tenure systems (latifundios and minifundios).

The problems of energy and the rational management of water and mineral resources assumed special importance. In most cases, details were given of the negative effects of pollution due either to the results of production processes or to inappropriate waste management and disposal policies. It was emphasized that these problems should be dealt with in an integral manner in the formulation and execution of development policies.

In the following years, these issues were developed much more fully both inside and outside ECLAC.[4] Even so, however, in the field of specific actions the efforts made in the last two decades to improve the environmental situation in Latin America and the Caribbean have been far from satisfactory, as governments have concentrated their energies on other issues, mostly of a short-term nature. The actions taken with regard to the environment have been characterized by great diversity both in the political, institutional and juridical approaches and in the energy with which they have been pursued.

3.3 Recent developments

In the last few years, there has been further progress in the world debate on the sustainability of development, and this progress has also been reflected in Latin America and the Caribbean. The greater emphasis given to this issue seems to be associated primarily with the deterioration of specific environmental problems, such as concern over energy and mineral resources and environmental pollution. The debate has also been accompanied by discussions on such aspects as technological change, international trade relations and changes in consumption patterns.

At the same time, the debate has been broadened to take in such issues as the interdependence of countries and regions, the effects caused by production processes and the various forms of trade. There has been wider recognition of the magnitude of the various forms of interdependence, and in certain respects development and population growth have shown that *there is no such thing as ecological environmental independence in the world*, so that desertification in Africa, deforestation in the Amazon region and the pollution of the seas are all problems with worldwide implications. Likewise, the conservation of certain resources, the protection of flora and fauna and of the tropical forests, and the defence of the natural and cultural heritage are no longer seen as the exclusive concern of particular countries.

Thus, there have been important changes in the perception of the links between development and the environment. The first of these is connected with the emergence of an awareness of the finite nature of the total resources of our planet. This has led to growing concern over the problems created by development. Whereas traditional economics dealt mainly with problems of resource allocation, new problems are now arising due to the unremitting pressure being exerted on the stock of existing natural resources.

The second change in perceptions concerns the much greater importance now assigned to relations between countries in respect of such global natural resources as the air, the ozone layer and the oceans, whose deterioration affects both the developed and the developing countries, regardless of the political frontiers between them.

The third change is that the issue of the environment is now seen to go beyond the question of mere "environmental protection". There is seen to be a close relation between economic efficiency and the quality and quantity of natural, institutional and cultural capital.

Finally, there is a growing –albeit as yet insufficient– awareness that natural resources and the environment are capital goods whose life extends beyond that of our own generation. Consequently, quite apart from the question of their exploitation, there is increasing interest in obtaining the maximum added value without negatively affecting the stock of such goods.

In short, everything indicates that a good deal of progress has been made since the 1972 United Nations Conference in contributing to an increasing awareness of the relation between environmental issues and development. The maintenance of the natural heritage of the region has come to be a fundamental element in the determination of the standards of living that can be attained.

This renewed interest in the links between development and environment is also reflected in the decisions adopted by the United Nations General Assembly, culminating in the decision to hold the United Nations Conference on Environment and Development in 1992.[5] In 1987, for example, the World Commission on Environment and Development, co-ordinated by Ms. Gro Harlem Brundtland, issued its pioneering report entitled *Our Common Future*, which was officially welcomed by the United Nations General Assembly.[6] The concern of Latin America and the Caribbean in this field was reflected in the Latin American and Caribbean Commission on Development and Environment, organized by the Inter-American Development Bank and the United Nations Development Programme, with the support of the Economic Commission for Latin America and the Caribbean and the United Nations Environment Programme. This Commission, which was made up of a number of leading personalities from the region in this field, issued a report entitled *Our Own Agenda*[7] which, *inter alia*, offers the bases for a sustainable development strategy.

In the same connection, mention may be made of the holding in October 1990 of the Seventh Ministerial Meeting on the Environment in Latin America and the Caribbean, sponsored by the United Nations Environment Programme, at which the countries adopted the Action Plan for the Environment in Latin America and the Caribbean. They also expressly agreed that that Plan should be considered a "working document" both for the Regional Preparatory Meeting organized by the Economic Commission for Latin America and the Caribbean and for the United Nations Conference on Environment and Development.[8]

Today, as we begin the preparatory activities that will culminate in the United Nations Conference on Environment and Development, there are organized movements calling for the consideration in that international forum of such issues as world climatic change, the destruction of the ozone layer, pollution of the seas, destruction of tropical forests and the consequences this will have on biodiversity, acid rain, changes in water quality, and many other such matters. In the discussion of these topics, there is a clear awareness that the scope of sustainable development goes beyond the merely ecological aspects. In this respect, the relation between development and environment is now seen to be of a systemic nature.

Notes

[1] ECLAC, *Changing Production Patterns with Social Equity, op. cit.*

[2] See *Report of the United Nations Conference on the Human Environment*, Stockholm, 5-16 June 1972 (A/CONF.48/14/Rev.1), New York, 1973. United Nations publication, Sales No. E.73.II.A.14.

[3] See ECLAC, *The human environment and economic development in Latin America* (ST/ECLA/Conf.40/L.2), Santiago, Chile, 1971.

[4] For a summary of this, see Osvaldo Sunkel and Nicolo Gligo (eds.), *Estilos de desarrollo y medio ambiente en la América Latina* (Mexico City, Fondo de Cultura Económica, two volumes, 1981).

[5] See, for example, resolutions 42/184 (International Co-operation in the Field of the Environment), 42/186 (Environmental Perspective to the Year 2000 and Beyond), 42/187 (Report of the World Commission on Environment and Development), 43/196 (United Nations Conference on Environment and Development), and 44/228 (United Nations Conference on Environment and Development).

[6] See General Assembly resolution 42/187, para. 1.

[7] See Latin America and the Caribbean Commission on Development and Environment, *Our Own Agenda*, Washington, D.C., Inter-American Development Bank (IDB) and United Nations Development Programme (UNDP), 1990.

[8] See United Nations Environment Programme (UNEP), *Final Report of the Seventh Ministerial Meeting on the Environment in Latin America and the Caribbean* (UNEP/LAC-IG.VII/4), Port of Spain, 23 October 1990, pp. 11-12. Annex II contains the Action Plan in question.

Chapter II

THE SUSTAINABILITY OF DEVELOPMENT: BEYOND NATURAL CAPITAL

Whereas traditional growth theory sought to determine the optimum speed of capital formation, more modern approaches focus on the sustainability of development and seek to determine what kinds of capital need to be formed and for how long.

1. Introduction

At a time when the countries of the region are still striving to attain a reasonable level of growth and social equity, a new dimension of development has come to the fore: sustainability. Although the World Commission on Environment and Development has proposed a definition of the concept,[1] no consensus yet exists as to its meaning or implications, despite the fact that the terms "environmental sustainability" and "sustainable development" are employed in almost all the more recent writings on development strategy. This chapter will not attempt to lay to rest the controversy surrounding this subject, but it will explore its most relevant aspects.

A wide range of examples can be cited of areas in which the sustainability of development is a concern. A few such examples are the following:

The analysis of the long-term consequences of economic policies, investments and institutional reforms;

The evaluation of different development styles' impacts on the well-being of future generations;

The identification of non-traditional capital goods (fish, forests, soils) with a view to their incorporation into the evaluation of development or resource allocation schemes; and

The recognition of the pivotal role played by natural capital or heritage in providing important benefits to society.

The studies conducted in the region have approached the issue of sustainable development from two different angles. *The first focuses on the environmental dimensions of economic and social development.* In this case, the foundations of sustainable development are primarily expressed in certain conventions or "working rules" which constitute a specific approach to the analysis of the subject. The most orthodox of these working rules define sustainable economic and social development as an activity which does not violate certain laws of nature. If these laws are contravened as a result of the over-exploitation of some resource, then a process of environmental degradation will be set in motion which, in some cases, may be irreversible.

This line of thinking is not new. The literature of the sciences of biology, physics and chemistry has been making valuable contributions to its development for many years now. In fact, the concept of sustainability, in its most elemental form, comes from the biological sciences. Thus, the procedure used for assessing the conservation or abuse of a resource calls for the adaptation of these working rules to the natural patterns and characteristics of the resource in question. These types of assessments give rise to specific recommendations concerning such aspects as a resource's optimal use, acceptable forms of exploitation, levels of investment, etc. In the case of renewable natural resources, these working rules include the recommendation that use rates should not exceed a given "critical zone" in the flow of the resource because higher use rates could lead to its eventual disappearance. This critical zone is referred to as the "maximum sustainable yield" or "maximum use capacity".[2] In other cases these rules entail a recommendation that a resource's productive capacity should be restored, which is, given the cost of the necessary technology, generally an extremely expensive undertaking.

The agreements reached among specialists as to a given resource's levels of sustainability vary depending upon the quality and quantity of the existing information, the extent of knowledge about the resource in question, and the way in which exogenous phenomena that affect it are evaluated.

"Exogenous" phenomena are all those which operate outside the framework of the above-mentioned working rules. Hence, for example, the human population is an exogenous phenomenon because it does not follow the natural pattern of the resource as such. Nonetheless, as is well known, it is precisely the human population itself which is the primary subject of development. Examples of specific activities to which these working rules have given rise include forest conservation programmes, the closure of grazing areas and the protection –sometimes regardless of the cost– of the productive potential of these resources. The institutional manifestation of such activities is often sizeable, as in the case of the creation of departments of forestry management which, in some instances, constitute veritable armies of forestry-resource defence forces. This also occurs with respect to other resources such as fisheries, and in both cases these types of activities usually place a heavy burden on the fiscal budgets of countries deciding to use such options.

As a greater awareness of the need for the public to participate in development emerges, these orthodox working rules become less relevant. It is no longer possible to continue to believe that economic potential invariably runs counter to conservation. This is far more than just a political issue. The survival of existing resources is at stake. This new focus on sustainability tends to become increasingly complex, however, as other working rules which influence resource management and use are introduced, such as those relating to the participation of the citizenry, policies and institutions. Under such circumstances, in order to achieve sustainable development we will have to succeed in reconciling the two types of working rules –those that focus solely on the resource itself, and those which combine that focus with considerations relating to the participation of those who use the resource.

The second approach addresses the question of sustainability by analysing development in terms of space and time. This focus is reflected in much of the work being done in the region, such as, for example, studies to ascertain why certain investment projects deteriorate or disappear before the end of the estimated life of the project as calculated during the design stage [3] (see box II-1).

This topic is not new to the region either, since the region has had ample experience with development initiatives that have failed for reasons that go beyond the natural and environmental capital involved. These failures have, *inter alia*, been due to an absence of suitable institutions, shortcomings on the part of the human capital involved, a policy of incentives that works against sustainability, or a lack of the necessary physical and financial resources to sustain the development effort.

A review of these two concepts of sustainable development reveals a number of noteworthy points, some of the most valuable of which are the following:

The phenomenon of sustainability cannot be understood solely at the microeconomic level because, as has become evident during the past two decades, sustainability largely depends on sectoral and macroeconomic factors. For example, the external debt burden tends to cause support to be withdrawn from long-term environmental programmes due to the shortage of fiscal resources which it engenders.

The ability to sustain a development activity depends on the level and performance of other activities within the economy. The achievement of a sustainable level of development therefore requires a recognition of the intersectoral, national and international linkages that are involved; the simple fact that ecosystems do not conform to man-made boundaries is enough to demonstrate the need to consider these relationships. This is also true of air pollution, marine pollution, the depletion of the ozone layer and the greenhouse effect.

This second general observation relates to various dimensions of the issue. One such dimension is brought out by the fact that an evaluation of levels of sustainability must go beyond the specific activity in question. What is being evaluated is not a natural resource or a specific environmental variable but rather a dimension that relates to an entire set of development activities (see box II-2). Hence, intra- and inter-sectoral relationships are more important than they were portrayed as being by traditional economic thinking. Forestry policies are one example: although such policies may have been designed and implemented for the purpose of achieving a sustainable form of development, experiences in the region have shown that if these policies are accompanied by policies aimed at expanding the agricultural frontier, it will be virtually impossible to protect forest resources. Similarly, a policy designed to control air pollution in a city by rationalizing automobile use and transport in general may be undermined by another policy which dispenses with environmental standards in an effort to promote industrial development.

The analysis and evaluation of the sustainability of development should figure as one of the main topics of discussion in the dialogue between lending nations, continents, and international institutions and the countries of the region. This dialogue is likely to revolve around the following aspects: i) the relationships between external investments and the various economic

FORCES GIVING RISE TO THE ENVIRONMENTAL DETERIORATION OF THE AMAZON BASIN

The main environmental impacts of the agricultural settlement of the Amazon basin are the result of the destruction of the forest in the areas of dry land within the basin and of subsequent attempts to introduce inappropriate agricultural crops, practices and methods in the areas that have been cleared.

In assessing the environmental impact of this process, it is necessary to distinguish between the activities of small-scale farmers (homesteaders participating in land settlement projects, squatters) and those of large-scale agricultural projects.

a) *The impact of small-scale farming*

Generally speaking, small-scale farmers use slash and burn agricultural methods to grow subsistence crops; the impact of this method of farming on the environment depends on the population density of the area in which it is used. The natural fertility of the soil decreases sharply two or three years after the land has been cleared, whereupon the farmers abandon their plots and go on to clear and settle other, more remote tracts of land. The forest grows back on the abandoned plots, but if the pressure of the population is intense, the amount of time they lie fallow will be shorter and they will be farmed more intensively, and the soil will therefore not have a chance to recover. This is what has happened in a large part of the area along the agricultural frontier.

b) *The impact of large-scale agriculture*

In the early 1980s the average area of approved projects (which ranged from 4 000 to 200 000 hectares) was 27 300 hectares. Most of the projects of the Development Agency for the Amazon Region (SUDAM) call for the clearing of extensive tracts of land which are then planted with grasses suitable for grazing. The way in which this programme has functioned has permitted the clearing of such land regardless of meat prices and the market conditions for these products. In addition, due to the limited supervisory powers of the authorities, most of the livestock-raising activities which have been introduced are not suited to the ecological conditions of the newly-cleared areas.

The difficulties encountered by many livestock-raising projects have chiefly stemmed from the fact that the methods and practices developed in the central and southern zones of the country are inappropriate in the Amazon basin. One of the main problems lies in the fragility of the soil in the basin, which, once exposed, is subject to rapid deterioration unless special precautions have been taken when clearing the land.

The increasing importance of land in the investment portfolios of large-scale enterprises, the provision of credit on attractive terms for investment in the Amazon basin, the low taxes levied on capital gains, and the minimal extent of oversight and control of land acquisition have together given rise to a speculative demand unparalleled in the history of Brazil.

Source: Mueller, Charles (1983), "El estado y la expansión de la frontera agrícola en la Amazonía", *Expansión de la frontera agropecuaria y medio ambiente en América Latina*, ECLAC/UNEP, Madrid, International Centre for Training in the Environmental Sciences (CIFCA), 1983.

activities; ii) the role played by what might be called "non-traditional forms of capital", which are not necessarily quantifiable but which are nonetheless essential, such as the institutional setting, the natural resource base or natural capital, and cultural assets; iii) the role of the "time" variable and how it affects medium- and long-term decisions; iv) the legitimacy of certain types of economic appraisals which are based on stocks of physical and financial capital and their rates of return; v) a systematic quantification of external and indirect impacts; and vi) a number of other aspects which are difficult to quantify in monetary terms.

Taking these assessments into consideration, on the basis of the work done by ECLAC and other international bodies, it can be asserted that *sustainable development requires a dynamic balance among all the forms of capital or assets involved in the countries' economic and social development effort* so that the resulting use rate for each form of capital will not exceed its own reproduction rate, taking into account the substitutive or complementary relationships existing among them. The most important forms of capital include human capital (where people also constitute the subject of development), natural capital, institutional capital (decision-making systems), cultural capital, physical capital (infrastructure, machinery and equipment, etc.) and financial capital.

This view of sustainable development, which focuses on the need for a dynamic balance among all the forms of capital involved, highlights a series of elements which are necessary in order to succeed in changing production patterns with social equity. One of the chief such elements is the possibility of placing environmental issues within the setting of development so that development and environment become two dimensions of a single, indivisible reality (see box II-3).

2. Implications of the approach

An historical review of the allocation of different types of capital to the development effort reveals a number of major stages in the economic evolution of the region. Traditional theories of economic growth emphasized, in practice, just one dimension of development: the optimum amount and speed of capital formation.

Box II-3
TOWARDS SUSTAINED AGRICULTURAL DEVELOPMENT

Various studies have shown how the use of policy instruments often distorts the opportunity costs of natural resources and consequently encourages their neglect or over-exploitation.[*] Such instruments as subsidies, prices, taxes and credit systems affect the structure of incentives that economic agents most deal with, thus influencing their behaviour and indirectly affecting the rate of environmental degradation and, in particular, the problems of sustained agricultural development. The decisions of economic agents which result in the inappropriate use of resources and the inefficiency of many agricultural practices are due to the natural tendency to seek to further short-term interests in the light of the "wrong signals" given by the economic policies in question.

The paragraphs below describe how the use of policy instruments such as prices, subsidies, credit and taxes has a direct or indirect influence on the use of natural resources. An analysis is then made of some constraints on the correction of these distortions and the many policy recommendations which have emerged in past decades.

Experience of three sectoral policies

Prices and subsidies: The policies followed by many countries of the region with regard to prices and subsidies have led to inefficiency and resource allocation problems.[**] In some cases these policies have discriminated against the agricultural sector in favour of urban activities, with the result that big farmers have increased their production on more extensive lines, with a lower labour/land ratio, which seems to have led to an increase in rural poverty and environmental degradation. In other cases, subsidies for the production of basic grains have contributed indirectly to the deterioration of natural resources by encouraging the use of marginal areas where agricultural practices are not, generally speaking, sustainable. Moreover, although these subsidies were designed to relieve rural poverty, their main beneficiaries have been the big farmers,

since it is they who have access to the land. In the case of Haiti, for example, import restrictions artificially kept up the prices of grains such as maize and beans, until 1985, thus encouraging their production to the detriment of coffee, which was subject to a high export duty. This policy indirectly accelerated soil erosion, since coffee bushes hold the soil in place better than the cultivation of such grains.

Land taxes: In a large number of countries of the region, land taxes had not given the right signals to encourage a form of land use in keeping with sustained agricultural development. The evidence indicates, for example, that these taxes have not served to promote agricultural activities other than extensive livestock-raising, which uses big areas of more fertile land and exerts pressure on the use of marginal land, thus accelerating ecological deterioration. Generally speaking, the region's experience with these taxes has not been very satisfactory, either from the point of view of tax revenue or as instruments to bring about the proper management of natural resources. On the one hand, the evidence indicates that the high rates of inflation suffered by many countries in recent years have significantly eroded the tax base, so that the proportion of government income coming from this source has gone down from 15-20% to 1-2%. On the other hand, the traditional difficulties in applying direct taxes, together with the rather unsuccessful attempts to increase tax rates in rural areas, have caused the very possibility of the effective reassignment of resources through such instruments to be called into question.

Credit policies: The distortions created by credit policies in the region have been analysed on numerous occasions. On the one hand, policies designed to provide subsidized credit for agricultural activities have helped to distort the opportunity cost of resources, thus resulting in the misuse of the latter. The evidence indicates, for example, that the granting of subsidized credits for the development of livestock-raising in countries

---

such as Brazil and Costa Rica has encouraged the expansion of a non-sustainable form of agriculture which has contributed to the deterioration of the tropical forests. At the same time, however, difficulties in gaining access to agricultural credit, whether subsidized or not, can also be an obstacle to sustained development. This has been indicated as one of the serious problems in Haiti, where it is estimated that only 10% to 15% of the rural population has access to institutional credit, thus limiting investments which could increase agricultural productivity.

* Robert Repetto, *Economic Policy Reform for Natural Resource Conservation*, Environment Department Working Paper No. 4, Washington, D.C., World Bank, 1988; G. Foy and H. Daly, *Allocation, Distribution and Scale as Determinants of Environmental Degradation: Case Studies of Haiti, El Salvador and Costa Rica*, Environment Department Working Paper No. 16, Washington, D.C., World Bank, 1989; and Hans P. Binswanger, *Brazilian Policies that Encourage Deforestation in the Amazon*, Environment Department Working Paper No. 19, Washington, D.C., World Bank, 1989.

** Based on "Sustainable Agricultural and Rural Development in Latin America and the Caribbean", Regional Document No. 3, FAO/Netherlands International Conference on Agriculture and the Environment, 8-12 October 1990.

This concern with rapid capital formation led to the expansion of the capacity for its formation, based on the hypothesis that there was a shortage of physical capital (infrastructure, bridges, roadways, hydroelectric plants, etc.) and of financial capital. Accordingly, until the 1970s development activities were aimed in this direction.

The other side of this hypothesis was that all other forms of capital were in abundant supply. Obviously, however, the sustainable development cannot be thought of solely as a function of the quantity and quality of natural capital. To do so would lead to a repetition of the same mistakes as those inevitably engendered by the approaches which sought to "optimize" physical and financial capital. An extreme example of the outcome of this type of thinking is provided by programmes designed to develop certain types of natural resources, such as those which have been implemented to protect native forests in countries that have very meagre supplies of human, institutional or financial capital. In such cases, the result is almost always the same: the development effort cannot be sustained.

An examination of experiences with a large number of projects designed to improve environmental conditions leads to the conclusion that the crucial elements in determining sustainability are always, in essence, human and institutional factors.[4] Consequently, environmental sustainability hinges on systems for assigning property rights and tenancy, economic and social incentives, economic and resource management and the roles of the different actors in the system, such as the State, businesses, communities of various types, and people.

With respect to the question of financing, it is important to remember that environmental programmes are usually long-term plans, and as such require financing over longer periods than those provided for within the context of administrative cycles. A lack of financing produces severe distortions in terms of the achievement of such programmes' proposed objectives, as will be discussed in depth in chapter VIII.

As noted earlier, a basic requirement of a strategy for achieving sustainable development is that all forms of capital should be represented, and it is therefore important to ascertain where imbalances exist, whether in natural or other forms of capital. No targets of any sort will be achieved if no natural capital is available, but the same thing will also occur if there is a partial or total lack of some other form of capital. These types of imbalances are illustrated in the boxes included in this chapter (see boxes II-1, II-2 and II-3).

As may be seen from these specific examples, the central question asked by traditional growth theory is not enough to lay the foundations for sustainable development. A different approach is needed, and different questions must therefore be asked. One of these is the following: *What types of capital should be formed or increased and for how long?* Whereas the traditional approach emphasized the rate of capital formation, this question basically refers to the optimum composition of capital formation, and thus opens up the possibility of a more detailed analysis of the trade-offs among growth, social equity and sustainability.

This focus on the relationships among various forms of capital underscores aspects which are usually overlooked or underestimated. This is especially the case in appraisals of the economic efficiency of physical or financial capital, which generally disregard the fact that the economic efficiency of such capital depends on the quantity and quality of the other forms of capital (human and natural capital) and institutional and cultural resources. The ECLAC secretariat regards these relationships as one of the pivotal issues to be considered in the negotiations leading up to the United Nations Conference to be held in Brazil in 1992. It is essential that an understanding of these relationships be attained by that time, since they will constitute the basis for the formulation of plans of action which will be in keeping with the realities of the region.

The most important types of relationships among the various forms of capital are those of *complementarity and substitution*. Most of the differences of opinion as to how sustainable development is to be achieved are related to differing ideas about the degree of complementarity and substitutability existing among natural capital, institutional capital and the remaining forms of capital.

Although technological progress opens up the possibility of increasing the substitutability of various forms of capital and their rates of reproduction to some extent, as the evaluation of the region's experience progresses it is becoming apparent that the degree of substitutability is extremely low, especially when it is a question of

conserving biological or cultural diversity. In the worst of cases, natural resources are irreplaceable; in the best of cases, they can only be rebuilt at a very high cost.

3. Micro and macroeconomic equilibria

The *microeconomic dimension* comes into play when a given activity falls within the immediate boundaries of the resource in question. In this case, economic agents have a direct relationship with the environmental or natural resource system. The link between economic agents and natural resources does not pose a problem in the region, since it is generally recognized. The problems arise when it is a question of understanding how natural ecosystems function and the nature of their relationship with economic systems. Unfortunately, the amount of information we have about these relationships and the extent to which they are monitored are negligible, and as a result certain circumstances go unrecognized when the time comes to take decisions.

It is at this point that the *macroeconomic dimension* becomes highly important, since the activities of the individual agents of development should all be directed towards the social and economic objectives of the nation concerned. Moreover, a balance between the micro and macro levels may increase the possibility of ensuring that the country's economic policy will take both present and future generations into consideration.

The materialization of this macroeconomic dimension is brought about by means of changes in policies and investment strategies, and through institutional and social changes. Environmental macroeconomics is a new field which is beginning to take on great importance precisely because its aim is to achieve a rational articulation of sustainable development strategies.

Notes

[1] "Sustainable development is development that meets the needs of the present without compromising the ability of future generations to meet their own needs." See *Our Common Future*, Oxford, Oxford University Press, 1987, p. 43. See also, *Our Own Agenda, op. cit.*, pp. 44-45.

[2] See such classic works on the subject as S.V. Ciriacy-Wantrup, *Resource Conservation: Economics and Policies*, Berkeley and Los Angeles, University of California Press, 1952; "The economics of environmental policy", *Land Economics*, vol. 47, No. 1, February 1971; Vernon L. Smith, "Economics and production from natural resources", *The American Economic Review*, vol. 58, No. 3, part 1, June 1968; and G. Hardin, "The tragedy of the commons", *Science*, vol. 162, No. 1243-8, 1968.

[3] ECLAC, *Report of the Regional Seminar on Environmental Management and Large Water Resource Projects* (E/CEPAL/L.262), February 1982.

[4] Examples include integrated rural development projects concerned with highland farming which include a component on soil, water and forest conservation, such as those which have been conducted in almost all the Central American countries; agricultural-terrace rehabilitation projects in the Andes; and numerous environmental clean-up projects in large and medium-sized cities of South America and Mexico.

Chapter III

ECONOMIC AND ENVIRONMENTAL POLICIES

If sustainability requires a dynamic equilibrium among all the forms of capital that contribute to the development effort, then a sound policy would be one that would promote such a balance, so that the improvement of the environment would lead to economic and social development.

1. Introduction

The impact of economic policies on the environment and natural resources is neither symmetrical nor neutral. Such policies have primary and secondary effects and externalities which must be duly recognized and evaluated. While the origin of these effects is varied, they all influence the behaviour of the economic agents involved in the use of these resources. Typical examples of these policies are those concerning changes in interest rates which affect the lead time of investments and therefore their rate of economic return; reallocation of fiscal resources and credit, which can alter the entire incentive structure; and devaluations of local currencies, which have an effect on the rate at which non-renewable natural resources are tapped.

On the other hand, a wide range of existing environmental policies do contribute to the achievement of sustainable development. The objective of these policies may be to reduce the rate of use of one or more resources, or to improve the direct protection of the environment. Examples abound: taxes on contaminating agents, modification of the property rights to a forestry or fishing resource, subsidies for technological changes that reduce pollution or controls for protecting against overgrazing in zones with fragile plant cover, among many others.

Since economic and environmental policies interact in the most diverse ways and mutually affect each other, it is important for this interaction to be consistent. One of the principal tasks facing the region in this decade, in fact, is to incorporate the environmental dimension into economic policy and planning. This incorporation of the environmental dimension should be achieved through macroeconomic instruments, such as structural adjustment programmes (national and sectoral), public investment and expenditure programmes and investment projects. Similarly, educational and public awareness efforts should incorporate environmental issues as a major component of equitable and sustainable development.

2. Major areas of environmental policy

The scope of environmental policies exceeds local or sectoral economic boundaries. There are three major areas of environmental policy which are of particular importance: i) personal and social consciousness-raising and education, ii) sectoral and national investment and iii) technology. Since the technological dimension of sustainability will be dealt with in chapter VI, this section will examine only the first two, as well as other specific environmental policies.

2.1 *Personal/social awareness and education*

Increasing the awareness of the general public is a necessary pre-condition for the success of any development effort. In the absence of a proper understanding of the role played by nature in the well-being of individuals and the community, environmental actions are doomed to failure. It is in the national conscience –that amalgam of individual levels of awareness– that options are established and the most important priorities are set for development and the environment. A strong social conscience promotes consensus, increases the commitment of all agents participating in development and permits greater participation by the citizenry (see box III-1).

The individual and collective conscience has been a major protagonist in the history of development, and the importance of campaigns of persuasion to mobilize the population is a well-known theme. The power of "public opinion" has thus begun to modify the conduct of certain sectors that pollute air and water. Another expression of the importance of environmental awareness is the success of non-governmental organizations (NGOs) in organizing and mobilizing communities for sustainable development. These promote participation and consciousness-raising at the community level, thus achieving objectives of development which bilateral and multilateral organizations have not been capable of achieving. This is particularly true when the actions of NGOs take place within a favourable setting created by the general and regional measures adopted by the State. On the other hand, the absence of co-ordination and complementarity between public and private organizations, or conflict among them, have been the root causes of many failures.

The educational system, particularly at the primary level, is an important tool for modifying the values and conduct of the society *vis-à-vis* its natural resources. The socialization of these values among youth, together with the active participation of the latter in the design and execution of sustainable development, are the most effective means of ensuring the achievement of established developmental goals for the benefit of those sectors of the population –young people– who will be most affected by the deterioration of the environment.

The increasingly important role of women in the protection of resources also deserves mention here. Through them, the family and the community participate in environmental strategies. They constitute, moreover, a key element of the social conscience of the general public.

2.2 *Investment policies*

National investment policies provide the basis for the equilibrium among all the forms of capital that participate in development. These policies, which generally emerge within their sectoral ambit, define the forms of accumulation in the short and long term (see box III-2).

They promote the creation of a climate that stimulates private and public investment. In order for this to happen, however, it is essential to recognize that natural and environmental resources are forms of capital and, as such, should also receive investments.

One way of incorporating essential elements of sustainable development is through national investment and public expenditure programmes. The formulation and review of such programmes represents a unique opportunity for determining whether there is a general balance among all forms of capital. Environmental and natural resource management programmes should be incorporated at this level. Their incorporation will depend on the different investment options that exist, on the perception of the net benefits to be received and on the economic criteria that will be used to select and evaluate these investments.

The criteria used to decide on a given investment, are not, however, generally subject to adjustment programmes. In practice, financial institutions evaluate investments on the basis of a certain anticipated level of opportunity cost. The only exceptions have been those investments directed towards education and public services. Hence investment programmes in the area of the environment have clearly suffered, partly on account of the physical impossibility of

Box III-1

CHANGING PRODUCTION PATTERNS AND ENVIRONMENTAL CONSERVATION: MINING ENTERPRISES IN CHILE

The process of introducing technology for environmental monitoring in copper-works shows how the processes of changing production patterns have interacted with environmental conservation criteria in Chilean mining enterprises. In the 1980s, Chile increased its capacity for smelting concentrates from about 1.9 million tons a year in 1980 to 3.4 million tons in 1989. This achievement was the result of a policy to increase investments in State-owned mining, in which emphasis was placed on expanding the installed capacity by making operational improvements and introducing new fusion technology for the purpose of strengthening the performance of Chilean copper on international markets by increasing production and reducing costs.

The main advantages of the new fusion technology (the Outokumpu flash furnace, a modified Teniente convertor operating with oxygen-enriched air) were greater efficiency and lower energy consumption than those associated with conventional technologies (reverberatory furnaces). The new technology was for the most part incorporated without taking environmental conservation criteria into consideration and as a means of supplementing the reverberatory furnaces, which are still in operation (under various conditions of environmental control) in the six existing foundries.

Because production patterns were changed only under the impetus of economic factors associated with the profitability of the copper industry, and also because there was little awareness of the environmental impact of the mining industry or much desire to monitor compliance with environmental quality standards, it seemed reasonable not to invest in total technological renovation but rather in an approach in which old and new technologies were mixed, since in that way the marginal investment needed to expand production capacity was kept down to a minimum.

However, the increase in copper production was accompanied by a considerable rise in the emission of pollutants (sulfur dioxide and particles) from foundries and caused the levels of pollution in nearby farm regions and populated areas to soar. This gave rise to disputes with the farm sector and with communities, one of which was resolved in 1987, when the people of Chañaral (10 000 inhabitants) won a suit brought against the National Copper Corporation of Chile (CODELCO), the leading copper producing enterprise in the world. The Chañaral case provides an indication of what a force citizen pressure can be in identifying policies aimed at environmental control and introducing technologies for ensuring such control in the Chilean mining industry.

The new management of CODELCO-Chile has made it a strategic objective of the company to be a world producer of copper which operates with low costs while accepting its ecological responsibilities. In the case of the foundries, this means the gradual incorporation of environmental control technologies, which will usher in a number of changes in the production patterns of the copper industry in the 1990s.

The most reasonable environmental conservation criterion in Chilean foundries is that of applying different environmental regulations for existing plants than for new units. New foundries are to be required to utilize technology which, while commercially viable, ensures that environmental quality controls will be applied more diligently. As for existing units, the levels for the emission of pollutants set for them are to enable them to meet national standards of air quality within a reasonable period of time. Since this may mean very different levels of emission for foundries in different geographical locations, the control of emissions will not necessarily require that the production patterns of all units be changed, since in some cases merely incorporating environmental control technology in existing equipment will be enough to keep within the standards set.

This environmental conservation policy will have certain significant consequences for Chilean foundries. First, plans to reduce emissions will be implemented in practically every foundry, which will mean investing in environmental control technologies (primarily for the plants which produce sulfuric acid), in new fusion technology and in engineering, studies and analyses. Second, fresh investments made for the purpose of increasing the smelting capacity of existing units must be preceded by an analysis of the environmental impact of the project showing that the changes in production patterns to be made will lie within the parameters of environmental conservation. Third, thanks to investments made in various sulfuric acid plants, the country will stop importing this input in 1993 and will be able to produce a higher proportion of copper at a lower operational cost by using hydrometallurgical technologies. Finally, since 95% of the present smelting capacity is controlled by State enterprises, the new policy would provide a strong incentive for executives, professionals and workers to improve the environmental management of these undertakings.

Box III-2

PETROBRAS

Brazilian Petroleum Inc. (PETROBRAS), with annual sales totalling nearly US$15 billion, has been one of the largest firms in Latin America for a number of years now. Despite its standing, however, the company's performance in terms of environmental control and protection used to be quite lackluster; its investments in environmental equipment and controls had not kept pace with the expansion of its production and its increasing levels of activity, and the firm therefore lacked the capability to reduce the risk of accidental spills and of a progressive degradation of the environment in the areas where its various fuel production and distribution activities are conducted. In fact, until a few years ago, the protective measures taken by the firm were limited to the bare minimum required by law and, even in this respect, it received numerous complaints from State environmental protection agencies regarding a failure to meet environmental standards.

In recent years, however, PETROBRAS has been making an increasingly determined effort to remedy this situation, despite the fact that it, along with most public utility companies in Brazil, has been experiencing budgetary difficulties. Its initiatives in this connection have focused on organizational matters and investment plans as well as the pursual of specific environmental research and development programmes.

At the organizational level, there has been a noteworthy increase in exchanges of expertise and in collaboration among the 12 industrial complexes of PETROBRAS located throughout the country.

PETROBRAS has two branches which have specifically been placed in charge of environmental matters: the Leopoldo Américo Miguez de Mello Research and Development Centre (CENPES) and the Superintendency for Environmental Safety (SUSEMA). The latter, which is attached to the Office of the President, is primarily concerned with the institutional relations of PETROBRAS. In addition, each technical department has an Advisory Office for Environmental Safety (ASSEMA) which serves to promote a decentralized management of environmental affairs in each industrial complex. The firm's regularly scheduled personnel training programmes include modules on the preservation of the environment. Mention should also be made of the recently created Advisory Office for Industrial Protection (APIN), a subsidiary unit of PETROBRAS Distribuidora S.A., which is responsible for addressing problems related to safety and the environment in the industry.

The amount of funding allocated for investments in environmental controls has risen steadily in recent years. Projects representing a total investment of US$330 million are currently under way in areas such as the treatment of liquid effluents; solid waste incineration; the monitoring and treatment of gas emissions; the recovery of sulphur, water and crude oil; waste treatment and disposal; electrostatic particle precipitation; the use of vacuum chambers to improve drainage systems; and the separation of by-products by means of horizontal centrifuging.

The fact that these investment projects depend on the firm's general budget for their financing has frequently occasioned delays in their implementation. The establishment of a separate budget for environmental preservation initiatives has been proposed as a means of preventing such delays and protecting environmental projects from the frequent cuts in the general budget necessitated by the present economic situation.

Simply to comply with existing environmental regulations, investments totalling nearly US$150 million are planned over the next five years. It is estimated that such investments would represent between 7% and 10% of the total cost of establishing any new industrial complex.

In the field of research, CENPES has recently conducted specific programmes in a variety of areas:

– The establishment of standards for the biodegradation of petroleum wastes by means of land-farming techniques;

– Bioassays for the treatment of liquid effluents;

– Studies on the biological treatment of liquid effluents (in co-operation with the Environmental Sanitation Technologies Company (CETESB));

– Experimental measurements of emissions of liquids and gases;

– Networks for monitoring environmental quality in the areas influenced by the activities of oil refineries;

– The development of products which do less harm to the environment (diesel oil, gasoline, desulphurized fuels);

– Reforestation programmes in the vicinity of the Cubatão refinery, and the reclamation of despoiled areas in the São Mateus mine.

Now, however, because the firm is temporarily unable to send technical missions abroad on a regular basis, as it had in earlier years, and given the calculating the economic rates of return, and also because of the lack of symmetry between the intertemporal origin of benefits and the allocation of costs. This subject will be dealt with in greater detail in chapter VIII, which deals with financing and sustainability.

Finally, investment policies and programmes should be evaluated on the basis of their contribution to the sustainability of economic development. The lesson to be drawn from many completed projects is that negative external effects could have been avoided if, in addition to the traditional economic appraisal, there had been rigorous institutional and environmental impact studies.

2.3 *Other environmental policies*

A wide range of specific environmental policies also exists. These are designed to regulate access to natural resources and their use and to eliminate certain effects which are prejudicial to development.[1] A difference is noted between these two aspects only to define the areas of institutional decisions involved in this subject. In practice, these policies constitute an indivisible "package" of instruments. Some of these policies affect the behaviour of economic agents in the allocation and distribution of their resources. In this regard they are similar to the economic policies discussed above. Examples might include taxes on polluters, or subsidies for those adopting clean technologies. In both cases, these instruments will change the relative prices or net earnings of the affected parties.

Other policies modify the prices of inputs and products that affect the environment, i.e., by setting minimum or maximum prices for environment-related goods or services not traded in traditional markets, by instituting taxes or subsidies that change the use rates of mineral resources or by taxing or subsidizing land in order to alter its allocation or productivity.

However, environmental policies have tended to favour the use of instruments for the direct regulation of resources at the expense of indirect economic instruments. Examples include closed seasons for fishing; zoning for the exploitation of forestry resources; exploitation quotas for resources in danger of depletion; production quotas for polluting products; and protection of certain areas, such as native forests, flora and fauna, in order to preserve ecological diversity.

Rights of access, as in the case of national parks, represent a type of policy frequently used. In other areas of the economy, such as the forestry sector, entrance fees are complemented by regulations governing lumber prices and logging. Mention should also be made of so-called "regulations". Generally speaking, environmental policies are regulatory in nature, i.e., they set standards for measuring the behaviour of economic agents. Of the plethora of regulatory instruments in the region, a substantial number are not enforced despite being part of the legal system.

Lastly, policies governing property rights and restrictions also affect environmental policy, since there is a significant number of cases in which the performance of economic and social agents largely depends on tenure systems. Where property rights do not exist, or are not properly exercised by their public or private holders, it is impossible to control the exploitation of a natural resource, since the user will be motivated to exhaust the potential rent from the resource rapidly, thereby depleting it. This fact produces a chain reaction: when an agent exploits a resource, others will follow his example, thus setting off a race to capture the potential rent from the resource. In most countries, property rights generally do not exist with regard to irrigation water, ocean fishing and land allocation.

3. Relationship between economic policies and the environment

A complex interrelationship exists between economic and environmental policies, which may be characterized schematically through a conceptual and practical framework that illustrates how certain economic policies which have been implemented in the region over the past two decades have affected the environment. This makes it possible to identify the most important relationships between economic and ecological systems; it also helps to identify criteria for the formulation of policies, and permits the establishment of a system to evaluate these policies in terms of the sustainability of development.

The link between economic policies and the environment is illustrated by the following factors:

i) availability of stock of a particular resource;

ii) flow of benefits which it is expected will be derived from a given resource;

iii) spatial distribution of economic and social activities;

iv) land allocation and use (a topic which because of its importance will be dealt with separately);

v) incentives for investing and reinvesting in a resource;

vi) behaviour of economic agents in terms of the "rent" to be derived from a resource;

vii) comparative and absolute advantages in international trade;

viii) redistribution and equity at the national, regional and local levels (all environmental problems involve redistribution);

ix) effectiveness of economic and environmental policy instruments;

x) time preferences (intertemporal use of a resource); and

xi) the availability of domestic resources.

The direct influence of all or each one of these factors in sustainable development will depend on particular situations. Various examples exist in the region of economic policies with contradictory objectives. For example, while the coefficients of comparative advantages may suggest that a country should export a given industrial product, the external effects of the pollution associated with this product may suggest the opposite. Certain export-promotion policies may thus reduce the effectiveness of environmental policies. In other cases, however, policies aimed at improving economic efficiency actually lead to sustainable development. This would be true, for example, in the case of the removal of subsidies on pesticides or other contaminating inputs, which would help to enhance economic efficiency while at the same time cleaning up the environment (see box III-3).

It is useful to elucidate some of the relationships between economic and ecological systems. Three of them are particularly noteworthy in view of the magnitude and frequency of their secondary effects and externalities in the region, and also because they are important in evaluating national policies. These are *land use, investment and reinvestment incentives* and *the effectiveness of economic and environmental policy instruments*.

With respect to *land access and use*, note should be taken of its pressing importance to the agricultural and urban sectors, and to a lesser degree to coastal resources. Changes in economic policies –such as the establishment of systems of relative prices which enhance the efficiency of the farm sector– lead to profound changes in land use. In view of the multifaceted nature of this resource, its peculiar characteristics will determine its productive capacity within the framework of a given space and time. Thus, for example, idle land will be incorporated into cropland as a result of variations in the relative price of certain products, or significant changes in the alternative use of soils. One of the sectors most affected by these

Box III-3

PESTICIDE SUBSIDY POLICIES

Many governments often provide direct or indirect subsidies for the production and sale of pesticides through tax exemptions, sale at prices below costs, access to foreign currency and credits on favourable terms, among other mmechanisms. Although these subsidies represent heavy outlays for governments, and in spite of the evidence of the harmful effects on health and the environment caused by the abuse of pesticides, there are still not enough systematic studies analysing the economic and environmental impact. Some of the questions connected with pesticide subsidy policies are set forth below.

Economic and environmental aspects

Estimates on pesticide subsidies carried out in respect of a group of nine developing countries showed that in 1982 the average level of subsidy came to 44% of the total retail cost of these products. In Honduras, Colombia and Ecuador, the level of the subsidy was 29%, 44% and 41%, respectively, representing a total annual subsidy of nearly US$70 million in Colombia, US$14 million in Ecuador and US$12 million in Honduras. In the case of the latter country, for example, this means a per capita cost of US$3 per year.*

Subsidies for pesticides take various forms. Thus, for example, importers of pesticides or of their ingredients can buy foreign exchange at a lower cost, enjoy favourable import duties, and also receive some tax exemptions.

The subsidy policies affect the decision-making process of farmers. By reducing the cost of pesticides, these subsidies encourage farmers to use more chemical products more frequently than if they were comparing the benefits with the non-subsidized prices. These subsidies also discourage pest control by methods that do not depend so heavily on chemicals, as well as discouraging the development and promotion of methods which could prove to be more effective.

Moreover, by promoting increased use and perhaps even abuse of pesticides, these policies increase the possibility that –through their secondary harmful effects on health and the ecological balance– these products may damage society as a whole. Such risks, needless to say, do not enter into the calculation of private costs and benefits. In this respect, various

studies indicate that in Central America indiscriminate use of pesticides is one of the most serious problems with regard to health and environmental pollution. In many agricultural areas, especially in the cotton-growing regions on the Pacific coast, the levels of application of pesticides even exceed those recommended by the manufacturers themselves, so that in 1977, for example, an average of 6 kilogrammes of pesticides per hectare were being used in this area.

The levels were particularly high in El Salvador and Guatemala, and it is estimated that in the latter country a total of 80 kilogrammes of insecticides are used annually on each hectare of cotton, which represents an extraordinarily high figure by world standards. Likewise, it is estimated that in 1975 El Salvador used 20% of the entire world production of parathion, representing an average of 5.15 kilogrammes per hectare harvested. Finally, excessive pesticide use in Central America has been responsible for serious contamination of the human and animal population. Numerous cases of poisoning of human beings (especially agricultural workers) have been reported, and there are many indications of excessive levels of pesticide residues in samples of milk and meat, together with contamination of the land and water resources.**

Final comments

Although pesticide subsidies involve heavy costs for governments in terms of lost income and direct budgetary outlays, there have been few systematic appraisals of the benefits of these policies and the desirability of their continuation. In many cases, there is a shortage of precise information on the real effectiveness of these subsidies and their impact on resource use and production. Moreover, the question arises of whether there may not be less costly alternatives for pest control and other ways of increasing agricultural production and profitability. Finally, the benefits which a generous subsidy policy may at present be providing for agricultural production should also be appraised in the light of their impact on such variables as health and the environment.

---

*Based on Robert Repetto, *Paying the Price: Pesticide Subsidies in Developing Countries*, World Resources Institute Research Report, No. 2, Washington, D.C., World Resources Institute, 1985.

**H. Jeffrey Leonard, *Natural Resources and Economic Development in Central America*, New Brunswick: Transaction Books, 1987.

changes is forestry where, in order to profit from price increases, thousands of hectares of forests are cut or burnt down. In many cases, it is impossible to recover these soils for any kind of productive activity.

The big cities in the region tend to suffer from a shortage of land, frequently because of poor regulation of the real estate market. This leads to all kinds of problems in formulating human settlement policies that are environmentally sustainable. Moreover, where there are deficiencies in the rights to land ownership and in the quality of land registers, an irrational competition takes place for the occupation and use of these lands. This situation has a significant impact whose consequences are paid by the lowest-income strata of the population. Furthermore, the lack of planning of basic

services leads to prohibitive costs for the execution of infrastructural works requiring major investments, which only serves to exacerbate the vicious circle (see box III-4).

With respect to the *investment and reinvestment incentives*, it is worth noting in the first place, that most approaches conceive of natural and environmental resources as consumer goods and not as investments. This approach results in the rapid degradation of natural capital. It should come as no surprise, then, that the countries of the region, on the basis of market signals, have increased the rate of extraction of their resources. Land is a case in point: in many areas there is no interest in maintaining it, and even less in increasing its fertility. What typically happens is that land, once exploited, is

---

Box III-4

EFFECTS OF URBAN EXPANSION ON THE CITY OF LIMA

The city of Lima serves as a dramatic example of the problems in terms of water supplies and the availability of farmland which are created by uncontrolled urban growth. The city lies in the two valleys –veritable oases within the coastal desert– formed by the Rímac and Chillón, and to a lesser extent the Lurín, rivers. From 1535 to 1920, when Lima had a population of about 200 000, the city covered scarcely 10% of the valleys' total estimated area of 32 000 hectares. Between 1920 and 1964, the amount of unoccupied land which was devoted to agriculture decreased from 29 067 hectares to 27 275 hectares (84.6% of the valleys). Between 1964 and 1979, when Lima's population reached the four-million mark, urban sprawl cut the figure to just 9 064 hectares. Today, virtually no farmland is left (less than 8 000 hectares), the irrigation system has been abandoned, and, along with it, the practice of watering the city's public parks.

The city's explosive growth and the loss of prime farmland have been accompanied by alarming changes in the area's surface water and groundwater systems as a result of the heavy demands placed upon them. Between 1970 and 1979, Lima's consumption of surface water climbed from 6.8 m^3/sec to 11 m^3/sec. The valleys' agricultural zones, which required 6.5 m^3/sec, also served as a recharge

area for the groundwater aquifer, but they have since ceased to perform that function. Since the Rímac River provides scarcely more than 15 m^3/sec, by 1979 there was already a deficit of 1.5 m^3/sec. This shortfall was covered by pumping as much as 9.5 m^3/sec of groundwater when the river was low. Today, the average level of the water table is 20 metres lower than it was when this practice was begun.

By 1979 the city was aware that a crisis was brewing. The only option was to bring water from the Mantaro river basin, which is located approximately 150 kilometres from the capital city at about 4 000 metres above sea level. Unfortunately, the main channel of the Mantaro River is severely polluted by the tailings that have accumulated over the years along its bed and in the ponds that empty into it, and this made it necessary to design systems to draw off water from its tributaries. However, the high cost of the project (which has been further increased by the need to build special works for the catchment of unpolluted water), coupled with the complications created by the country's economic situation, has thus far thwarted efforts to complete its construction. In consequence, Lima suffers from serious water shortages which it is not going to be able to solve in the short term.

Source: Axel Dourojeanni, "Gestión de recursos hídricos en el Perú: Restricciones y soluciones", *Debate Agrario*, No. 4, Lima, October-December 1988.

abandoned. The same occurs with many other ecosystems (see box III-5).

Moreover, the *effectiveness of economic and environmental policy instruments* is minimal in very low-income areas. Where economic policies are designed to maximize their impact on the market, they cease to be relevant for those living on the periphery of that market. More finely tuned

---

Box III-5
COTTON IN CENTRAL AMERICA

The development of the cotton industry in Central America shows how the overabundance of financial capital (intensive application of insecticides, fertilizers, machinery and equipment, as well as investment in infrastructure) subjected the natural capital (land) to intensive exploitation which, in addition to reducing its yield, had a series of severe external effects. In such a situation, the country's Integrated Pest Control Programme was able to help to establish a more balanced relationship between the various forms of capital required by this crop.

In 1940 cotton was mainly consumed domestically and exported occasionally when prices were particularly attractive. Over the years, however, this product has become one of the principal export items of Central American countries, particularly Nicaragua, El Salvador and Guatemala.

The land was fertile, the rainy season made irrigation unnecessary and the dry season permitted the cotton to ripen: thus, the natural conditions were ideal for its expansion. To this advantage was added an abundance of cheap labour. However, the humidity and heat of the region also favoured the proliferation of insects which could not be controlled using traditional chemical compounds, since the tropical rains rapidly neutralized their effect, resulting in low yields or the intensive application of chemicals, thereby reducing profits.

The discovery of DDT in 1939, however, revolutionized the situation: insoluble in water and practically insensitive to the sun, it was ideal for application on the Pacific coast of Central America. This situation led to the rapid expansion of the cotton industry, at a time when favourable prices prevailed on the international market.

Generally speaking, the process of financial capital formation began with the application of new technologies, and then extended to the use of fertilizers and machinery at the same time as physical capital was being formed through the construction of roadways.

However, after four or five years of insecticide use, soil fertility declined, leading to the application of fertilizers. In view of the flatness of the coastal land, the fertilizers were spread by tractors, whose introduction was facilitated by favourable credit conditions. Thus, in the late 1960s and early 1970s the main cotton-producing departments (provinces) in El Salvador and Nicaragua were using 50% and 90% of the tractors in the entire country, respectively.

Financial capital formation during the 1950s and 1960s was facilitated by channelling resources, at subsidized interest rates, either through development institutions or commercial banks –with special facilities granted by the Central Bank–, which furthered the expansion of a crop which, by its very nature, requires a high credit component. Multilateral and bilateral financial institutions, for their part, supported the construction of an extensive network of roadways which enabled the plantations to have access to equipment and inputs and facilitated the transportation of cotton to ports. In this way a complementary relationship developed between financial and physical capital.

The clearest evidence of a profoundly unbalanced process of capital formation was probably the application of insecticides. With the passage of time, pests developed that were resistant to DDT, to toxaphene and similar compounds, and new pests appeared. In response, different varieties and greater quantities of pesticides were applied. This coincided with a drop in cotton prices on the international market and with an increase in production costs, owing to the oil crisis. Over the past decade, the reduction in the international price of cotton was aggravated by severe financial imbalances and devaluations which made even further cuts in the profitability of this product.

In contrast with the investment in inputs, equipment and infrastructure, the deterioration of natural capital was accelerated for a number of reasons. Firstly, the control of insects required cotton plants to be removed at the end of the harvest –during the dry season– by plowing the soils, thereby leaving the soil vulnerable to wind erosion. Further, in preparing for sowing, the land was plowed in the rainy season, thus creating the risk that rainfall and run-off water might cause further erosion on an even greater scale. Finally, cotton tended to make particularly intensive use of nitrogen, phosphorous and other soil nutrients. Rivers and mangrove swamps were also polluted by wastes and pesticides.

The problems resulting from international price fluctuations, new pests and increasing cost of applying insecticides lead to sharp declines in exports in some years during the 1960s and 1970s. In the 1980s, however, the crisis in the cotton sector in Central America, which was also associated with financial imbalances and political turmoil, was particularly acute, as illustrated in the following table.

COTTON EXPORTS

(Thousands of quintals)

	1983	1985	1988
Guatemala	1 214.1	1 253.6	638.1
El Salvador	769.7	513.8	20.3
Honduras	64.8	111.0	16.1
Nicaragua	1 726.0	1 460.0	765.5

Source: Central American Monetary Coucil, *Statistical Bulletin, 1988*, San José, 1989.

The problem of sustainability is evident: for the four countries taken together, production fell in 1988 to a little over one third (1 440 000 quintals) of its level five years previously (3 774 600 quintals).

One response to the problem created by the increasing use and cost of pesticides and fertilizers has been the Integrated Pest Control Programme. This is a system aimed at optimizing the control of pests while taking into account economic and ecological factors, and based on a scientific knowledge of the crop and of its pests and natural enemies, as well as its economic and social rationality, including incentives and restrictions deriving from the economic, political and social regulations and values.

The Programme included: a) prohibition of the use of synthetic pesticides; b) return to the use of organic pesticides such as calcium and lead arsenate; and c) the introduction of biological methods of control, including the elimination of a second crop (the likelihood of reproduction of certain pests would otherwise increase), the establishment of uniform dates for sowing, the distribution of the natural enemies of pests (particularly other insects) and the interspersed sowing of other crops such as maize and wheat to facilitate the development of populations of natural enemies of pests. Seven years after the launching of the Programme, the application of pesticides (mineral and natural) had been reduced to a little over two per year, cotton pests had been virtually eliminated and both the production and quality of cotton had increased.

intervention policies need to be designed for such cases, including policies on income and income redistribution and direct intervention policies such as the regulation of tenure and the classification of property rights.

Finally, if there is some lesson to be learnt from this situation, it is that there is an infinite number of relationships between economic policies and natural resources, and that these need to be more carefully studied. The region, however, does not have enough background information on this subject, owing to the absence of scientific research and the complexity of certain ecosystems. Getting down to the task of comprehensive research into these links is another challenge to be faced by the region in the present decade.

4. Macroeconomic policy and its environmental impact

Macroeconomic policies are generally evaluated according to their impact on the main economic aggregates, i.e., according to the primary or direct effects of such policies. At the same time, macroeconomic policies lead to significant secondary or indirect effects. By way of example, investment in one sector of the economy may attract idle resources from another sector. Or a specific investment may lead to technological innovation (see box III-6).

These indirect effects of macroeconomic policies are felt at certain levels –either productive or environmental– which are outside the institutional framework of those who originally designed and applied the policies. In other words, the impact of certain policies is felt by certain countries, sectors or forms of capital which were not taken into account in deciding how resources would be allocated. The Systems of National Accounts, for example, do not consider natural resources as capital goods subject to depreciation.

Variations in the supply of natural capital, or the availability of natural resources, are another aspect to be considered. Economic policies affect the stock and exploitable flow of resources, especially since they modify the comparative advantages of exploitation. Thus, an export promotion policy, for example, stimulates the exploitation of mineral, fishing or forestry resources. This attitude cannot be criticized as long as there is a management policy which rationalizes the use of the resources both spatially and temporally. This pattern of exploitation and the corresponding changes in the "availability of stock" are a key aspect of a policy that seeks to promote sustainable development.

Box III-6
ECONOMIC POLICIES THAT ENCOURAGE DEFORESTATION

The problems of deforestation in Latin America and the Caribbean are the subject of growing international attention, since the region has 57% of the tropical forests of the world and at the same time the highest rate of deforestation (1.3% per year) of the developing world. Attention has been centred in particular on Brazil, which has 30% of the world's tropical forests and where, according to different studies, the deforestation process affects between 1.7 and 8 million hectares per year. Although these figures cover a very wide range and the real magnitude of the problem is little known, there is sufficient evidence to state that in certain regions deforestation is taking place at a considerable rate.

There are many factors which play a part in deforestation in tropical areas, although it is not known exactly how many, and although the way some of them operate is as yet little understood. The expansion of small-scale agriculture, commercial lumbering and extensive livestock-raising are considered to be some of the main factors in question. In addition, there are others which are perhaps even more complex, such as poverty, inequitable land distribution, low agricultural productivity, and the incentives given by some economic policies to activities which harm the environment. The purpose of this note is to explore the last-named aspect.

Over the last 25 years, a development policy has been undertaken in the Amazon region whose execution has included big highway construction programmes to link the region with the north-west and south, the application of colonization schemes, and the provision of fiscal and credit incentives for agricultural and industrial development. Generally speaking, the evidence indicates that on the whole these policies have played an important part in the process of deforestation by encouraging activities which have contributed to the destruction of the tropical forests.

Fiscal incentives

The integration of the Amazon region with the rest of Brazil began in the mid-1960s with the completion of the highway linking Brasilia with Belém, at the mouth of the Amazon. This highway, plus the attractive land prices, encouraged the inflow of immigrants. In order to attract private enterprise into the region —one of the objectives of what was termed "Operation Amazon"– there was an increase in expenditure on infrastructure, involving the construction of roads, airports and telecommunications, and a package of fiscal and credit incentives was designed.

One of the most attractive measures was the 1963 fiscal incentive for investment, which offered corporations the possibility of obtaining up to 50% credit against their income taxes on condition that the resulting saving was invested in projects in the Amazon region, which must be approved by the Development Agency for the Amazon Region (SUDAM). Up to the end of 1985, nearly 1 000 projects had been approved, 631 of them for the livestock-raising sector. Of these livestock-raising projects, 75% were carried out in the Southern Pará and Northern Matto Grosso regions.

The development of livestock-raising in these two subregions has involved heavy costs. On the one hand, the expansion of livestock-raising seems to be the main cause of deforestation and environmental deterioration, while on the other hand the livestock-raising projects have not helped to generate jobs.

Furthermore, in spite of the heavy subsidies given by SUDAM to livestock-raising projects (some US$700 million) only a few of these projects have produced encouraging results. In this respect, the evidence seems to indicate that the subsidies or the capital gains due to the appreciation in land values are the only factor that make livestock-raising activities profitable in this zone. It has also been noted that many of these projects were undertaken solely because of the availability of fiscal incentives. Finally, the studies all agree that in this region livestock-raising is not only not economically profitable but also appears to be the least viable alternative from the point of view of its impact on soil erosion.

Credit subsidies

Another factor which has apparently played an important part in the process of the deforestation of the Amazon region, especially outside the Southern Pará and Northern Matto Grosso regions, is the availability of subsidized rural credits. Just as in the case of the fiscal incentives, these credit subsidies affect the decisions of the economic agents by increasing the domestic rate of return on investment and ultimately serve to encourage the development of activities which would never be undertaken if the credits were offered at market prices.

The volume of subsidized credit for the northern part of the Brazilian Amazon region increased almost 10 times in real terms between 1974 and 1980. Most of this credit went to crop farming, but the livestock-raising sector was also favoured. Although the shortage of data on the size of ranches, output and productivity, as well as the diversion of agricultural credits to other uses, make it difficult to calculate the exact effects these measures have had on the behaviour of farmers and ranchers in the Amazon region, it is estimated that at all events they facilitated the acquisition and subsequent deforestation of enormous areas of land.

In 1987, the policy of subsidized credit was eliminated and it is estimated that this measure will have positive effects in the long run. Paradoxically, however, in the short term the lack of subsidized credit has had some harmful results, since the lack of facilities for buying fertilizers, herbicides and other inputs has led many farmers to take up activities that are even more damaging to the forests, such as slash and burn agriculture.

---

* Based on Dennis J. Mahar, *Government Policies and Deforestation in Brazil's Amazon Region*, Washington, D.C., World Bank, 1989.

Furthermore, from the spatial perspective of development, macroeconomic policies are not neutral. On the contrary, they frequently lead to significant spatial modifications. This is the case, for example, of policies that modify patterns of employment and migration, or those that affect the location and degree of the urban or rural concentration of industries. This spatial dimension of sustainable development must be taken into account in the management and improvement of the environment. Note should be taken of the tremendous impact of road construction on the advance of the agricultural frontier and of how improvements in urban transport systems affect the growth of cities.

Finally, these policies have crowding-out effects on the activities of various sectors. These secondary impacts are related to the fact that priorities in the allocation of resources are set at the macroeconomic level in such a way that, in many cases, environment-related activities are displaced. For example, the priority of repayment of the external debt must be respected, thus necessitating a reduction in fiscal expenditures and consequent restrictions on budgetary allocations. Finally, those activities whose benefits are long-term, such as reinvestment in soils and forests, among others, are eliminated. In an institutional sense, this crowding out of certain activities most seriously affects those that require resources from the current account budget (for example, counterpart funds for the execution of externally funded projects). This is especially the case with environmental projects, which often contain a strong current-expenditure component.

On the other hand, they affect only slightly or not at all those activities that are financed exclusively from external sources.

The nature of a country's economic policy has a major impact on two key variables in the management of natural and environmental resources: the modification of time preferences and attitudes towards risk and uncertainty.

The first refers to the way in which economic and social agents take decisions regarding consumption or investment, or to the greater –or lesser– utilization of natural resources. The options will depend on the nature of economic policies and on the general state of the economy. Thus, in low-income population groups there is a greater propensity towards immediate consumption, an even higher than usual rate of exploitation of certain natural resources and frequently a neglect of investment in or conservation of these resources. In such cases, conservation policies must be incorporated into an overall poverty-fighting policy. At the same time, in the higher-income groups or countries whose consumption patterns are highly intensive in the use of polluting energy sources and the generation of waste, it is essential to design policies aimed at reorienting consumption patterns and development styles.

The second variable, relating to risks and uncertainties, and largely neglected by the authorities responsible for programming and executing development policies, is related to anticipated perceptions, attitudes and values *vis-à-vis* medium- and long-term benefits and costs. The nature of the uncertainties will vary, depending on technological innovations, changes of preferences in consumption and investment and changes in national economic policy. For example, economic agents affected by changes in economic policy will evaluate the levels of uncertainty in such a way as to prefer to obtain immediate benefits rather than postponing them. Uncertainty is an economic force which affects decisions about conservation and attitudes towards saving or consumption. As a general rule, insofar as economic agents perceive greater risks, they will exploit natural resources up to the maximum limit permitted by their economic and commercial capacities. This situation has led to the severe depredation of available resources in those instances in which economic policies and the level of activity have proven to be unstable.

4.1 External effects of policies

Economic and social policies are designed and implemented so as to have specific effects on the course of development. However, these policies often produce effects totally unrelated to their original objectives. These external effects (externalities) are the result of imperfections in markets and market valuation systems; short-sightedness in decision-making (emphasis on the short term or on immediate activities); problems relating to the allocation of property rights and to the access and use of resources; or other factors inherent in the economic and social system, such as a design which failed to take into account the possible negative environmental impacts, or specific initial circumstances in the short-term or development phase which constitute structural obstacles to overcoming environment-related problems.

In several countries of the region, industrialization policies have produced a high level of unanticipated external environmental pollution. In such cases, the market for industrial products through supply, demand and price-setting tends to consider only the value of the use of the product, with neither the consumer nor the producer paying for the costs of pollution. In the long run, this cost will be borne by the society as a whole.

As mentioned previously, a number of external effects are due to insufficient control over property rights and the use of resources. In areas where regulatory systems do not exist, or are poorly defined, economic agents will be motivated to derive the potential income from those resources as quickly as possible. In Latin America and the Caribbean, this is usually the case in the fishing and forestry sectors.

In other cases, the cost of regulating the application of pollution standards or monitoring individual economic agents may be greater than the expected benefit. The consequence of this situation is that economic agents contaminate and degrade resources in the absence of efficient and sound economic mechanisms for regulating their exploitation.

These externalities have led to the formulation of large-scale economic development policies. Two of them are relevant to the region: State intervention and the privatization of resources. The first has been criticized, *inter alia*, for its inefficiency and prohibitive management costs; and the second, which was used in attempting to resolve the problem of efficiency, was the object of bitter criticism owing to its short-sighted approach to the functioning of the market. In both cases there are merits and limitations.[2]

Another type of externality is related to the effects of the policy adopted by some countries on the environmental variables of others. For example, fluctuations in international exchange and interest rates affect resource allocation and economic behaviour throughout the world, not just in the major industrial countries. A similar phenomenon occurs as a result of other policies, such as those pertaining to agricultural subsidies, trade restrictions, energy generation and use and the disposal of toxic wastes, and even as a consequence of educational and cultural policies which encourage certain consumption patterns and development styles that are highly polluting and wasteful of natural resources throughout the planet. This type of externality turns the issue of the developing countries' progress into a problem that affects not only these countries but also the entire international community.

Where significant externalities exist, there will be more than enough reason to incorporate them into the agenda for government action in support of development. The region has a plethora of illustrative examples, including deforestation, erosion, desertification, salinization, mismanagement of highly productive land, urban pollution (see box III-7), deterioration of water quality, excessive solid and liquid wastes, destruction of biological diversity, deterioration of river basins, depletion of coastal resources, poverty and squalor, and destruction of natural and cultural capital in indigenous areas.

If policies for managing natural and environmental resources are not implemented, it will be very difficult to alleviate the negative impact of externalities and constitutes one of the major problems facing the region. Formulating such policies is therefore one of the major challenges of this decade.

4.2 *Structural adjustment and environment*

In the past, structural adjustment programmes have rarely included environmental considerations. Stabilization policies, moreover, necessarily place emphasis on short-term problems where changes in relative prices tend to be detrimental to environmental considerations. This is particularly true where programmes enhance the valuation of current benefits, and reduce that of future costs. In the 1980s, the region adopted short-term programmes which were accompanied by recessionary trends. In the early phase, from 1982 to 1983, there was an urgent need to generate trade surpluses in order to finance the net outward transfer of resources. Subsequently, it became necessary to control the inflationary upsurges which were exacerbated by the attempt to transfer enough resources domestically to make debt payments and by the devaluations brought about by the adjustment process.

In practice these short-term approaches were reflected in policies whose effects were quickly felt, such as attempts to reduce investment expenditure and to conserve the national heritage. It was thus more acceptable to consume natural assets at a faster rate than to devote resources to their conservation and growth. Recessionary policies, such as those resulting from fiscal adjustment, had a negative impact on long-term programmes, such as environmental programmes. Consequently, in the stabilizing phase of adjustment, it is difficult to introduce environmental programmes unless these are accompanied by changes in production patterns and contribute to faster growth.

In the case of long-term programmes, however, it is essential to incorporate the environmental dimension into development. Examples of long-term reform include the following: trade liberalization; fiscal reform which leads to control of public expenditure and more tax revenue; rationalization of the State apparatus, including its role in the areas of regulation and distribution; increased savings and national investment, including progressive liberalization of capital markets; and policies for changing production patterns which promote greater efficiency in the use of resources, including natural resources. All of these reforms may have a significant impact on the sustainability of development. Trade incentives alter comparative advantages, increasing the profitability of both traditional and non-traditional exports. To the extent that these advantages are based on non-renewable resources, it will become increasingly important to correctly record in their cost accounts the "amortization" funds corresponding to non-renewable resources. This involves a higher gross rate of reinvestment, in both absolute and intertemporal terms, and suggests that a tax should be imposed on the production of non-renewable resources, which could be applied to exports of such resources in the short term.

Finally, it should be noted that international prices do not always reflect the true opportunity cost of natural resources or the cost of the services provided by the environment. The reason for this lies in the externalities. This should lead planning

Box III-7
AIR POLLUTION IN SANTIAGO, CHILE

The Metropolitan Region of Santiago, Chile, is rapidly becoming one of the most highly polluted urban areas in the world. The degree of air and water pollution in this area may be taken as a warning of the harmful effects which certain deregulatory practices and the application of inappropriate regulations may have.

The Metropolitan Region has a population of 5.1 million inhabitants, representing 40% of the country's population while occupying only 2% of the continental territory of the country. Its population density is 334 inhabitants per square kilometre, in contrast with the average of only 17 inhabitants per square kilometre for the country as a whole.

The topography and climate of the area favour the accumulation of polluting particles and gases over the city, particularly during the winter months. Another problem is that recently there has been a dramatic increase in the emission of polluting gases from stationary and mobile sources. During the past few years, the levels of concentration of toxic elements in the atmosphere have far surpassed international health standards. In 1988, 300 000 additional cases of bronchopulmonary diseases were recorded by the medical-care centres of Santiago (53 000 cases of bronchopneumonia; 40 000 of obstructive bronchitis; 110 000 cases of flu, colds, pharyngitis and similar diseases) caused primarily by atmospheric pollution.

To illustrate the severity of this problem, it may be noted that in the past three years the number of private automobiles in Santiago increased by 10% each year to reach a total of nearly 450 000 units in March 1990. The number of public mass transport vehicles doubled between 1980 and 1988, rising from 6 000 to 12 000 vehicles, as a result primarily of the transport deregulation policy adopted by the authorities at that time. Under this policy, owners were free to set fares, enter the public transport sector, determine their routes and decide on the number of vehicles to be assigned to each line and on the frequency of the runs. This led to a state of affairs characterized by an enormous concentration of the flow of public vehicles on the most profitable routes from the point of view of private enterprise, with an extraordinarily low rate of passengers per vehicle and a slow traffic flow, which increased the emission of polluting agents. This situation became worse when permission to import used parts (including engines) was granted by government decree, since much of the increase in the total number of motor vehicles, especially those used for public mass transport, was based on the use of old, highly polluting engines.

A study carried out in 1985 noted that 71% of the respirable particles in the air came from vehicles with diesel engines (nearly all of which are found in the public mass transport sector).* In

measurements made during the winter of 1989, it was found that the indexes of carbon monoxide were three times as high as the international environmental standard, while those of respirable particles were over nine times higher than that standard.

In view of the severity of the problem, the argument in favour of complete deregulation began to lose force. Thus, towards the end of the term of the preceding administration some restrictions were introduced in a half-hearted manner, which turned out to be inadequate and ineffective, as shown by the fact that instead of disappearing, the problem continued to grow worse.

In March 1990, the new democratic Government designed a plan to eliminate pollution through the application of the following three instruments:

a) A master plan relating to medium- and long-term policies and action, including an environmental education information programme; the establishment of mandatory emissions standards, covering the short, medium and long terms, for each branch of activity, and of arrangements for monitoring compliance with them; an epidemiological vigilance programme; the modernization of the public mass transport system and the discouragement of the use of private automobiles; measures aimed at managing traffic in such a way that the road infrastructure can be used more efficiently; and regulation of the use of roads by vehicles engaged in mass transport.

b) A package of immediate and short-term measures designed to remind sectors which emit polluting substances to begin to take action to reduce those emissions as provided for in the long-term policy. Measures in this package include the creation of municipal public information offices; the registration and licensing of passenger services (lines) engaged in public mass transport; the prohibition of the installation of used engines and parts in public mass transport vehicles; the setting of emissions standards for imported vehicles; the rationalization of the parking of motor vehicles in downtown Santiago; the establishment of regulations relating to fuel quality and the monitoring of compliance with them; action to ensure that the metro is used to its best advantage; and the initiation, after a study has been carried out, of a programme aimed at the reduction of emissions by stationary industrial sources.

c) An emergency plan to be implemented when the air-quality indexes (gases and particles) reach a certain point. The plan provides for a number of stages of action as, for example, the immediate removal from circulation of 2 600 buses, the placing of restrictions on vehicular traffic and on the operation of large stationary sources of polluting substances and the reduction of the level of activity of some sectors in order to decrease the demand for transport.

The efficiency of all these measures remains to be seen. They represent a combination of the application of direct regulations, the use of market mechanisms, and citizen participation and action. The situation which emerges in winter 1991 will be the proving ground of their effectiveness.

---

* See Comisión Especial de Descontaminación de la Región Metropolitana, Programa de descontaminación ambiental del Area Metropolitana de Santiago, Santiago, Chile, April 1990 (table entitled "Caracterización físico-química material particulado").

and development offices to re-examine the traditional coefficients of comparative advantages, nominal protection and effective protection. This is an area which should be the subject of specialized studies aimed at producing concrete empirical evidence to rigorously justify changes in each case.

5. Sectoral and microeconomic policy

5.1 Links between sectoral and environmental policies

Evaluation of the impact of policies on the sustainability of development is an essential activity within the design and execution of development projects and programmes. Traditional economic ex ante appraisal is therefore inadequate. An examination must be undertaken, inter alia, of why environmental policies have not had the expected results in the region. One of the principal reasons has to do with the origins of these policies, which were generally designed in developed countries and therefore respond to the situations encountered there. In many cases, therefore, the cost of their implementation in the countries of the region is very high in terms of effectiveness and equity. This is the case, for example, of those policies which assume the existence of efficient markets in areas related to land, or to property rights. It is also true where specific behaviour is expected from certain economic agents who, on account of their low income levels, are excluded from the operation of the market.[3] The effectiveness of these policies is even further reduced when they are applied in areas in which the costs of implementation are higher than the anticipated benefits.

Another reason for the failure to accept environmental policies is related to the organizational foundations of regional development. This is the case, for example, of community organizations in rural areas or of the physical and economic spaces occupied by industrialization and urbanization processes.

Environment-related interventions have also been poorly received at the macroeconomic level. This is partly explained by the evaluation techniques used: investments, policy changes and institutional reforms are difficult to evaluate on traditional economic bases. Although in most cases the costs are known, it is difficult to identify the benefits. This is as a result of a tendency to refrain from attaching an economic value to the goods and services provided by the environment and natural resources. Economic appraisal is also significant in the area of bilateral and multilateral financing. Projects that do not demonstrably have a suitable economic rate of return are not financed by investment and development banks. Very few environmental programmes have thus been financed in recent decades.

This brings us to a key question for the formulation and execution of economic and environmental policies: what are the main criteria for appraising proposals that seek to clean up the environment and enhance the effectiveness of natural resource management? These criteria should no doubt be multidimensional, covering technical, economic, institutional, political and social aspects.

It should also be recalled here that environmental changes have economic consequences, while economic fluctuations have an impact on the environment. It is this interrelationship which should guide the evaluation of policies. Examples include the progressive scarcity of natural resources and of goods and services provided by the environment; natural resources exploited as if they were consumer goods and not investments, thus leading to their depletion and depredation; toxic wastes deposited in human settlements, affecting people's health, among other things.

The deterioration of environmental systems has a concrete economic cost. At the same time, their conservation and improvement bring considerable benefits in terms of the greater availability of resources –greater biodiversity– which means more options for development.[4] Generally speaking, it may be said that the most universal manifestation of the policies to be evaluated consists of the change in the productivity of economic and ecological systems. In the case of the economy, this change occurs through modifications to the cost functions or alterations in the structures of factor demand.

It is difficult to design environmental policies which affect only natural capital. But the sustainability of development requires that a dynamic balance be achieved between the various forms of capital that participate in efforts aimed at economic and social development. For this reason, it is necessary to consider as positive not only those policies aimed at directly enhancing natural capital, but also those which can improve the environment and the socioeconomic situation. The evaluation of these policies requires an estimation of the cost and potential benefits not only of improving environmental quality but also of the other economic and social activities affected by the policies under evaluation.

The acceptance of this principle also requires that consideration be given to the economic cost of implementing such policies. An investment or policy which minimizes costs is important, since countries of the region suffer from a great scarcity of financial and fiscal resources. This criterion, which will become increasingly important as the region's environment continues to deteriorate, is also crucial because environmental deterioration in the developed countries is making increasingly strict environmental standards necessary there. Stricter standards mean that policies must be more efficient, and an important element of this efficiency is the cost of applying them.

In order for the minimum cost criterion to be effective, however, there is a need for clearly defined environmental standards. There can be no policy of sustainable development without a more detailed knowledge of the acceptable limits of exploitation of ecosystems. The establishment of these standards is essential to development and is even more important in those cases where direct intervention is selected. However, *one of the main problems in the region is the lack of sufficient information to establish adequate environmental standards.* Incentives for scientific and technological research in all relevant fields are needed if this situation is to be improved.

Finally, in choosing policy-selection criteria, note should be taken of the pronounced differences –and in some cases dichotomies– between economic *"allocation"* and *"incidence"*. Experience shows that in most cases the impact of environmental policies on the allocation of resources is limited to those economic agents which are not greatly affected by the environmental changes that these policies seek to correct. One example is the case of an industry which pollutes a given location in which the agents taking the decisions concerning the location do not live, and hence do not directly suffer the consequences of their own decisions.

5.2 *Measuring the environmental impact of projects*

The systematic application of methods of economic appraisal in selecting and evaluating policies related to the environment has generally left much to be desired in the countries of the region. This is of even greater concern if account is taken of the significant progress made in the conceptualization of this subject. In reviewing the progress made, one recognizes a series of important aspects related to the planning and execution of investment projects, institutional reforms and economic and environmental policies.

In the initial phase environmental impacts were evaluated as a residual aspect of development. Subsequently, World Bank loans required the prior undertaking of Environmental Impact Assessments (EIA). These assessments, however, were undertaken virtually at the end of the project cycle and therefore played a minimal role in the reformulation of investment projects. As the effectiveness of (EIAs) diminished, the need arose to evaluate the economic prices –shadow prices– that were used to determine the allocation of resources before the project or policy was fully elaborated. As a result of this situation, many economists proposed a modification of the traditional concept of "opportunity cost". Today the modified concept is used to evaluate the trade-offs between development, equity and the environment. In its original form, this concept included only the notion of marginal production costs, evaluated through the use of economic prices.

Four additional elements were added to this initial conceptualization of operational costs, namely, spatial and intertemporal externalities, irreversibilities, natural disasters, and biological diversity. Considerable progress has been made in all of these areas. A good many manuals exist that illustrate how to incorporate spatial externalities into the evaluation process. These external factors include environmental impacts on upper river basins, from such activities as logging and, in lower river basins, sedimentation in hydroelectric dams.

Regarding intertemporal externalities, progress has been somewhat slower owing to the nature of the problem, which is related to questions of intergenerational allocation. Part of the complication lies in the nature of decisions, such as the need to deal with very long-term problems; another difficulty is the implicit (or explicit) questioning of the central objectives of traditional economic evaluation, which requires the development of analytic approaches other than cost/benefit analyses.

Some progress has been achieved with respect to irreversibilities and natural disasters, despite the lack of information and the limitations imposed by probabilistic models of evaluation. In most cases, the evaluation of disasters imposes a discipline on the demarcation of complex probabilistic events, such as responding to the question: "What is the likelihood of a flood or earthquake"? Nevertheless, considerable progress has been made in integrating hydrological and climatic models with economic models.

Lastly, biodiversity imposes a framework of analysis which is rarely incorporated into economic evaluation. Despite the considerable progress made in areas related to individual species within this diversity, models for the evaluation of biological diversity as a whole are very recent.

However, it is not enough to incorporate the above elements, since the success of environmental projects also depends on the macroeconomic context. Thus, certain projects that have received an excellent appraisal tend to fail during their execution phase because of a lack of well-designed policies.

This situation has led to two major changes in approaches to economic evaluation: firstly, there has been some interest in introducing the environmental dimensions of development at the macroeconomic level, and, secondly, the need to formulate environmental and national resource strategies at the country level has been identified. As a first step, it has been recognized that natural resources must form an integral part of national accounts, and although this is a new approach, a number of countries of the region have already shown some interest in it. The second change is related to the need to incorporate the dimensions of sustainable development into economic management programmes, including structural adjustment, medium- and long-term investment and public spending programmes.

The most significant conclusion that may be drawn from the above is that it can no longer be argued that there is a shortage of economic evaluation methods for environmental projects. If there is insufficient knowledge of these methods in the region, the next step will be to offer training in how to use them in public administration.

6. Problems of co-ordination of public policies

Since actions to promote sustainability must go beyond sectoral frontiers, it is important to improve efficiency in the co-ordination of policies. In the area of public administration, a rational approach would be to i) reduce the substantial costs inherent in isolated decision-making processes in sectors that are heavily interdependent, and ii) restructure the traditional co-ordination systems used by governments to implement their economic and environmental policies.

The design and implementation of public policies without taking into account the interaction among them in certain areas does not lead to optimal results. In practice, however, various spheres of government decision-making operate as if interdependencies did not exist. For example, the public sector responsible for macroeconomic balances, particularly with regard to finances, is restricted by legal regulations governing the period of applicability of budgetary policy. By limiting themselves to such a restrictive time horizon as the fiscal year, economic decision-makers tend to ignore the tax system and public spending and investment patterns that are associated with the use and availability of natural resources over the medium and long term. Moreover, by adopting the traditional assumption that the supply of freely available natural resources (air, rivers, lakes and seas) is infinitely elastic, the Government loses sight of the notion of scarcity. This means that the budgetary practice of establishing fiscal incentives, subsidies and tax policy overlooks the distinction between renewable and non-renewable resources.

Other reasons for the lack of co-ordination are i) the thematic variety and technical complexity of the specific problems of each area, and ii) the lack of information available to specialists in respect of basic problems, theoretical frameworks and methodological approaches in the contiguous area. Fortunately, this situation is beginning to change, albeit slowly and imperfectly, owing to the perception on the part of leading groups that benefits can be derived from greater integration between the socioeconomic and environmental spheres.

Despite the establishment of co-ordination between these two spheres of public action, obstacles may nevertheless arise and should be provided for. Firstly, government sectors responsible for the fiscal/economic and environmental spheres may have different views as to the priority that should be attached to what are perceived as competing objectives. Secondly, there may be differences in relation to the instruments considered most suitable for achieving specific objectives of environmental policy. Frequently, the teams responsible for the preservation of the environment tend to attach greater importance to the setting of standards and regulatory measures than to the alternatives favoured by the fiscal and economic sectors, such as taxes, subsidies, rates of use, prices, and public tariffs. Thirdly, it should be recognized that, in general, the degree of influence exercised by economic and fiscal teams is greater than that of those involved in making environmental policy. Fourthly, there is the crucial question of the relative weight which the political authorities really attach to fiscal/economic and environmental matters. It is well known that these authorities tend to show little regard for the future by adopting very high implicit rates of exploitation in view of the brevity of their mandates and the demand by voters for immediate results. In such circumstances it should come as no surprise that the political leadership —of federal, provincial and municipal governments— focuses its efforts on achieving concrete short-term results in the economic and fiscal spheres.

Notes

[1] ECLAC, *Elements for an effective environmental policy* (LC/L.581(Sem.56/5)), 24 August 1990.

[2] See ECLAC, *Changing production patterns with social equity, op. cit.*, pp. 56-59 and 149-153.

[3] This has been recognized in the case of agriculture. See ECLAC, *Desarrollo agrícola y participación campesina* (LC/G.1551-P), Santiago, Chile, December 1988. United Nations publication, Sales No. S.89.II.G.11.

[4] See ECLAC, *La región frente a la negociación de la biodiversidad* (LC/L.610), Santiago, Chile, February 1991.

Chapter IV

POPULATION AND NATURAL RESOURCES

The relationship between population dynamics and ecosystems is decisive in achieving sustainable development.

1. Population, the environment and resources

Population is a resource –human capital– and at the same time the subject of development, and hence any topics related to the population should be dealt with from both points of view. This chapter will briefly examine the first of these: population as a resource. It also describes the current availability of other natural resources, including land, water, minerals and marine resources. Chapter V deals with population as the subject of development, and the relationship between poverty and sustainable development.

1.1 *The demographic variable*

Since the middle of this century, the Latin American and Caribbean region has experienced a change in its population and environmental profile. Changes in the composition of the population by age, occupation and residence have been accompanied by the tripling of its size, with the urban population moving from a minority segment to the point where it now constitutes the living and working environment of three out of every four inhabitants of the region. Therefore, although it may be possible to predict future changes in its composition, the speed and scale of these changes will be unlike those achieved in the period now drawing to a close, and the basic acquired characteristics will remain unchanged.

During the five-year period 1960-1965, and as a result of the combined effect of the transition to low mortality rates and the lag in the transition to lower fertility, the majority of countries recorded population growth rates on the order of a cumulative 3% per annum.[1]

As a result of an improvement in living conditions and in some aspects of the human environment (food and nutrition, progress in overcoming endemic diseases, coverage of health services, access to potable water), the region made progress in its transition to low mortality rates, reducing the still high infant mortality rates of the 1960s. Life expectancy at birth is now almost 70 years.[2]

The combined effect of demographic factors, development and the spread of family planning, accelerated the transition towards lower fertility rates from the 1970s onward, with the number of children per woman declining from six or more in the 1960s to slightly over three at the present time. The high rates of fertility at the start of the period and their maintenance in subsequent years led to a population structure that was characterized by a large proportion of youth under 15 years of age (40%) and, subsequently, to a heavy increase in the labour force (4% per annum). The size of the cohorts born in the years when fertility rates were high, in turn, has dampened the effect of the reduction in the number of children on the decline in the rate of population growth.[3]

Population growth was accompanied by changes in the rural- urban profile and in the occupational composition of the population. Ninety-four per cent of the total population increase in Latin America during the period 1960-1990 of 230 million was recorded in urban areas.[4] This increase was caused, often in similar proportions, by the expansion of the resident population and by rural-urban migration. Taken together, the Latin American and Caribbean region emerged in the 1990s with an urban population similar in proportion to that of the developed countries and more than twice that of Asia and Africa: in Asia, the proportion of inhabitants engaged in agriculture doubled, while it tripled in Africa.[5]

The rural population, following an increase of 10 million in the 1960s, remained stable from the mid-1970s onward at some 124 million. The main population pressure on natural resources in agriculture is of urban origin, whose dramatically expanding market favoured mechanization and the introduction of technology in the production of foods and fibres. Widespread mechanization of commercial agriculture and the expansion of large-scale livestock-raising led to an increase of the man/cropland ratio in marginal lands, which, however, continued to be the lowest in the developing world.[6] This pressure by the rural population on the land continued to be excessive in the traditional areas with small-scale farming ("minifundios"), exacerbated in many cases by the combined action of fragmentation by inheritance and the expansion of large export-oriented agroindustrial enterprises and the continuous expansion of livestock-raising activities.

The apparent contradiction between the low man/cropland ratio and the persistence of zones which are particularly exposed to deterioration, such as minifundio areas, is explained by the extreme levels of concentration of land ownership and use.[7] The region has the highest ratio of concentration of land ownership in the developing world and in those countries where the agricultural frontier has expanded over the last three decades, the high levels of concentration may persist or become even higher in the newly cleared areas.

The percentage of the urban population residing in the largest city increased in most of the countries of the region, where 14 cities of over two million inhabitants and two of over 15 million already existed by 1985.[8] The strain on the physical environment involved in sustaining some of these big cities has been growing; some are trapped between mountains, while others are situated on enclosed bays or on the banks of large rivers, all of which has aggravated air pollution, water pollution and the risk of floods. Even in cities located in valleys with abundant water supplies, increasing demand for water has necessitated huge investments in construction works, with severe consequences for the environment, in order to ensure adequate supplies (see box IV-1).

In these cities, the combined effect of a large population, its rapid rate of increase and the introduction of various technologies (such as stationary emission sources, automobiles and buildings that are crowded together), has exceeded the tolerance limit of the physical environment,[9] thereby requiring corrective actions which are very often unaffordable to the country in the short and medium term.

The countries which by 1960 had for all practical purposes begun their transition towards lower mortality rates and had made great strides towards the achievement of low fertility experienced, in later decades, only some of the challenges arising from population growth and urbanization (high rate of dependency of the labour force, explosive increase in urbanization and concentration of the urban population in one large city). This relatively better situation was more pronounced in those countries with agricultural frontiers than in those without, and in those with orderly demographic transitions (Barbados, Chile, Uruguay) than in those which underwent more dramatic changes along the way (Argentina, Cuba, Jamaica). The demographic causal factors behind the problems of environmental deterioration were marginal or local, with economic and technological factors predominating.

On the other hand, for those countries which will experience a demographic transition in the next three or four decades, a trend towards more severe environmental degradation may be expected. These are countries of less relative economic strength and management capacity (public and private) to deal with foreseeable environmental problems and to take the actions required to overcome them. The extreme case is that of countries without agricultural frontiers, which are already facing extensive erosion and loss of their water resources.

1.2 *Urbanization*

Urbanization, its conditions and characteristics, are the physical expression of the development styles adopted by society. Man occupies, exploits and transforms the natural environment, tailoring it to satisfy what he perceives as his needs; the result are human settlements, cities or a built-up environment. The process of urbanization in the region reflects the unsound economic and social development styles being adopted by the countries. Some of the characteristics of the process of urbanization in the region are not intrinsically negative and become so only when they constitute obstacles to the achievement of balanced and sustainable development; such characteristics include the following:

Concentration of the population, production, services and decision-making in a small number of urban centres. In several countries up to 50% of industrial output (and the generation of industrial wastes) is concentrated in the main city.

High growth rates of the urban population, which will convert Latin America into the most urbanized region of the world in the next century.

High deficits in the provision of basic infrastructure and services, particularly in low-income urban sectors and rural areas.

Limited control over disposal of waste from domestic and productive activities and over the use of land resources. Only a small number of cities in the region have waste water treatment systems, and many of them have solid waste disposal systems which cover less than 50% of their waste production.

There are three key elements which determine the environmental sustainability of urbanization: its location and the use of land; the demand for inputs for maintaining residential and productive activities; and the waste discharge into the natural environment from urban activities. In order to guide these processes, there must be direct intervention in i) the form, growth and distribution of settlements, ii) the type and intensity of activities to be undertaken and iii) the way in which such activities are carried out (see box IV-2).

Box IV-2
RATIONALIZATION OF URBAN TRANSPORT IN MEXICO CITY

The global environmental control programme adopted by the Mexican Government for the nation's capital with the financial and technical co-operation of the United States, Japan, Federal Republic of Germany, France and the World Bank has an estimated cost of between US$2.5 and US$3 billion. In order to co-ordinate the efforts to combat the high level of pollution caused by the 2.5 million vehicles and 30 000 industrial enterprises of the Greater Mexico City area, which emit 4.8 million tons of pollutants per year, various interministerial committees were formed to prepare appropriate policies and supervise operations.

The measures which have been designed fall within the following five areas: rationalization of urban transport, production of clean fuels, use by industries and power stations of less polluting fuels, restoration of the vegetation of the Greater Mexico City area, and finally, modernization of industry. Only the first of these areas will be dealt with here.

The first actions taken, in the winter of 1989, concerned public and private transport, since it is estimated that 83% of the pollutants come from vehicles. In order to encourage the population to replace the use of private vehicles with public transport, the authorities decided to rationalize, improve and expand the latter. Thus, for example, the routes followed by 60 000 small private 14-passenger buses which travel between the suburbs and the centre of the city were either eliminated altogether or changed so that these vehicles only transport passengers to the metro stations or the main bus lines, thus reducing their presence in the city-centre area. The authorities are considering increasing the fares of private buses in order to spread the cost of the adjustment and compensate bus drivers for potential economic losses caused by the shorter routes.

At the same time, action was taken to improve the lines served by large buses, through measures such as the scrapping of old diesel engines and the adoption of emissions standards. The fares on these buses were increased by 300% in order to cover the cost of the new engines and expand underground railway construction work. The circulation of the new buses and the work to expand the metro began immediately, so that users would link the fare increase in their minds with improvements in the public transport service.

Other regulations designed to discourage the public from using private vehicles are the prohibition on parking in the city centre and in the main streets of the city, and the prohibition of private car use one day a week, depending on the last number in the license plate. Failure to observe these regulations is punished with heavy fines. A further measure to discourage the use of private transport was the 12.5% increase in the price of gasoline, which also helps to finance the environment programme.

In addition, automobiles must be tested in inspection centres twice a year, and these centres are punished with fines or total closure if cars which passed through them are later found to be polluting the environment in spite of having passed the test. It was also decided that new cars must be provided with catalytic converters, and once the new converters are installed the use of lead-free gasoline will be made compulsory. This latter measure is expected to involve a big adjustment effort, as 95% of the gasoline produced in the country contains lead. The refineries will have to be modified and lead will have to be removed from them and from the distribution system.

Finally, with regard to the replacement of polluting fuels, fuel oil has been replaced with natural gas in 40% of the power stations. As such gas is scarce and costs three times more than fuel oil, the price of electricity for industrial use was considerably increased, thus reflecting the higher cost of this resource.

The implementation of this first set of measures –the reduction of private automobile use, inspection of motors, replacement of bus engines and the use of natural gas instead of fuel oil– made it possible to reduce pollution by 15% in six months.

In order to avoid repeating the failed attempts of the past, the policies adopted should be aimed at overcoming some of the obstacles to the implementation of these activities. In practical terms, proper management of urbanization means that the objectives of national development and its priorities should be translated into specific physical actions. This requires the formulation, on a priority basis, of action strategies in the following areas:

Technological development, for the purpose of bringing the existing links between development, the natural environment and the attributes of settlements down to more operational and qualitative terms, since, for example, it is not always correct to assume that small or medium-sized cities are necessarily forms of settlement that are preferable to large metropolises.

The development of practical instruments and mechanisms for incorporating the criteria of sustainability and development (including changing production patterns and social equity) into the management of settlements.

Enhancing the legal framework and competence of local governments (municipal or regional) to enable them to intervene in aspects of development and environmental sustainability, thereby permitting effective complementation and application of the purely physical interventions which these authorities have traditionally carried out. This requires greater efforts towards the process of decentralization and deconcentration of decision-making, income distribution and investment allocation.

The processes of regionalization and municipalization under way in the region offer considerable opportunities for the development of institutional mechanisms (institutional capital), which allow for the co-ordination and reinforcement of the work of the various agents involved in environment-related activities. Local governments in particular, because of their proximity to the actual problems and because they act more directly under the scrutiny of the community, are institutions that offer greater possibilities for success in co-ordinating the application of environmental policies.

1.3 *Rural population, migration and the agricultural frontier*

Over the last few decades the rural population has had an extremely low overall growth rate, and this trend is expected to continue. While rural areas still have a higher fertility rate than urban ones, the low growth rate is due to the simultaneous occurrence of an equally high mortality rate and continued migration to urban areas, and in particular the selective migration of women of childbearing age. Demographic indicators point to a close link between the population's living standards and environmental quality. This relationship contributes to environmental deterioration by constraining recovery processes, in turn leading to heavy outward migration.

While rural-urban or inter-city migration are the most consequential, migration from one rural area to another has also increased. It has even been noted in some countries that rural-rural migration is as significant as rural-urban migration. Within this type of migratory movement, temporary migration has been acquiring greater significance, for it is associated with increasing opportunities for seasonal work as a result of the more intensive exploitation of land in the more modernized areas.

The colonization of agricultural frontiers is one type of rural-rural migration which, although dating back to the early years of the century, has only in the 1960s begun to be focused on as a means of resolving problems of employment, land access and soil degradation, although it also responded to the growth in demand from the more developed urban markets and to speculative land management. In this context, Bolivia, Brazil, Colombia, Ecuador, Mexico, Panama, Paraguay and Peru are some of the countries which have initiated efforts at colonizing and expanding their agricultural frontiers. This, however, does not seem to have been a solution to problems involving population redistribution, lack of jobs and inequitable access to land, and has had negative ecological impacts, creating serious problems from the point of view of the human environment.

The rural population in frontier areas generally lives under very difficult conditions, with a low standard of living, makeshift dwellings and little access to education and medical care, all of which contribute to a low nutritional level and provide fertile ground for the spread of disease. One problem which has attracted attention, for example, is the resurgence of malaria and its spread into new areas, particularly in the new frontier regions such as the Amazon Basin. Other factors which have contributed to its expansion are –in addition to the resistance of the vectors to traditional control methods– the continued presence of makeshift housing and poor living conditions, lack of environmental sanitation and ignorance of preventive actions.

1.4 *Conclusion*

In brief, following a period of high population growth rates, the region has shown a downturn in these rates. This means, at least, that the pressure on the environment exerted by the mere increment in the number of persons is tending to lessen. The problems which persist, and which are perhaps worsening, are derived rather from the spatial distribution of the population and its dynamics and modalities (urban growth without infrastructure, depredatory expansion of the agricultural frontier), institutional conditions (concentration of land and minifundio-style farming) and production technologies in the countries where the population lives and reproduces.

2. Use of the region's natural resources

A presentation follows of the situation and prospects for the exploitation of the natural resources of Latin America and the Caribbean, with emphasis on those aspects related to sustainability. It should be pointed out, by way of introduction, that over the last two decades substantial changes have occurred in the region in terms of access to and use of resources. These are due both to small-scale activities carried out by many economic agents and to large-scale activities of a few individual agents. Examples of the former are activities engaged in by poorer sectors which result in urban sprawl or destruction of forests by slash-and-burn agriculture;[10] examples of the latter are mining and fishing.

The region has suffered from a significant and irreversible loss of its genetic biodiversity, soil loss due to erosion and the loss of native forests. In economic and social terms, the most serious environmental problems are associated with irrational urban expansion. These are followed by profound damage to coastal areas and some bodies of inland water. Without doubt the most direct harm to the population is caused by the contamination of water. The problems of air pollution, while serious in many cities, are relatively less pervasive despite their association with systems of production which can only be modified and controlled at high cost.

2.1 *Land use*

Land in the region is a resource which, from the point of view of its human exploitation, is continuously increasing. The expansion of the agricultural frontier, the profound changes in land use and the discovery of new mineral and energy deposits occur daily. This, however, takes place erratically because governments are poorly equipped to provide guidelines to users of the resource. This situation is even more complex if account is taken of the fact that more than 50% of the population is poor and to a large extent marginalized from State services and assistance.

Only about 7.5% of the total land surface of the region is arable. Of the rest of the land, 1.5% is used for permanent crops, 28.1% for grazing land, 48.2% for forests and the remaining 14.6% for other purposes (see table IV-1).

On the other hand, agricultural land has serious constraints on its use, so that the percentage of cultivable land is calculated at only between 8% and 16% of the total. Other projections expand the possible cultivation area to as much as 27% and 32%. However, the cost of adding and managing new land is increasing daily. The incorporation of new land in desert areas, for example, costs more than US$20 000 per hectare, as against US$2 000 for the recovery of abandoned terraces in the high Andean regions of Peru and Bolivia. The cost of recovering salinized land is also US$2 000 per hectare. It would be even more profitable to increase productivity per hectare before seeking to extend agricultural frontiers [11] (see box IV-3).

During the period 1970-1987, land devoted to crops and grazing increased by 70 million hectares. This process took place spontaneously and independently, with the exception of a few specific projects. The expansion of pasture land was at the expense of native forests, with the result that almost 72 million hectares of wooded area were lost. In other words, 6.9% of the forested area that existed in 1970 disappeared. In Brazil and Mexico the largest relative number of hectares were destroyed. From the standpoint of surface area, however, the countries most affected by deforestation were Costa Rica, El Salvador, Nicaragua and Saint Lucia.

Much of the increase in land under cultivation (12.5 million hectares) was devoted to modern and high technology crops which have tended to create environmental problems in these areas owing to the indiscriminate use of pesticides, fertilizers and other chemical substances. Although these inputs are used in smaller quantities in the region than in the developed countries, ignorance of how to apply them or the fact that they are toxic substances or products which have been banned outright in the developed countries entails certain problems.

Livestock-raising is one of the activities with the greatest impact on the ecological system, particularly in tropical and hillside areas. Its main characteristics in the region are its low technological level and location in areas that are unsuited for exploitation. In 1989 the region had 317 million head of beef cattle, representing 25% of the world total.[12]

Erosion is a more widespread form of land degradation in the region. In hillside areas, this phenomenon is extremely common and has forced the abandonment of vast areas of land. The

Table IV-1

LATIN AMERICA AND THE CARIBBEAN: LAND USE

(Thousands of hectares)

Use	Estimated area (thousands of hectares)			Percentage breakdown	
	1970	1987	Difference	1970	1987
Cropland	120 258	150 720	30 462	6.0	7.5
Permanent crops	24 750	30 330	5 580	1.2	1.5
Grazing	529 646	563 542	33 896	26.4	28.1
Forests	1 038 975	967 144	-71 831	51.8	48.2
Other	290 960	292 853	1 893	14.5	14.6
Total	*2 004 589*	*2 004 589*	*0*	*100.0*	*100.0*

Source: ECLAC, *Statistical Yearbook for Latin America and the Caribbean* (LC/G.1606-P), 1989, pp. 600-607; United Nations publication, Sales No. E/S.90.II.G.1; and World Resources Institute and International Institute for Environment and Development, in collaboration with the United Nations Environment Programme, *World Resources 1988-89*, New York, Basic Books, Inc., 1988, p. 264.

Note: The information provided in this table refers to 25 countries in Latin America and the Caribbean.

annual rates of erosion –measured in terms of sediment loads– in some parts of El Salvador and the Dominican Republic, for example, fluctuate between 190 and 346 tons per hectare (which means that the land probably will lose all possibility of economic use in less than one decade) while in well-managed zones barely five tons per hectare are lost annually. The State has been unable to put a halt to this situation because of the difficulties encountered in helping poor peasants. Moreover, soil erosion caused by low-income sectors reflects other phenomena such as the lack of job opportunities, *inter alia*.

Other phenomena also lead to soil loss. One of these is the loss of irrigated land located in semi-arid valleys, owing to competition for the use of water; another is soil salinization due to the use of inappropriate irrigation techniques. These processes, usually described as desertification, have been estimated to affect more than 33% of irrigated lands. Desertification alone affects more

than 293 million hectares of productive arid land in Mexico and South America.[13]

If agricultural expansion were technically well managed, there is no reason why it should degrade the environment. Over the past 20 years, although public awareness of this problem has increased, the action taken has been inadequate. The State has not done enough to promote private activity and participation, nor has it undertaken large-scale initiatives. It has confined its efforts to the direct execution of a few pilot projects, in many cases thanks to the work of non-governmental organizations or to bilateral contributions, whose effect has been very limited in proportion to the magnitude of the task at hand. Moreover, only rarely has it provided the necessary support to enable users to fully accomplish the environmental management tasks which correspond to them. Little has been done to institutionalize public and private participatory action to resolve these problems. Encouraging progress has been made, however, in some countries such as Brazil, Colombia, Ecuador, Peru and others, where, for example, steps are being taken to set up mechanisms for the management of river basins, the reclamation of agricultural terraces and salinized land and, in general, the promotion of rational natural-resource management activities involving public and private participation.

2.2 *Water resources*

The Latin American and Caribbean region is basically a humid area, although it also has extensive arid zones. Average rainfall in the region is estimated at about 1 500 mm, which is almost 50% higher than the world average. Surface runoff of rainwater amounts to some 370 000 m^3 per year, representing 31% of the freshwater reserves reaching the oceans.[14] Nonetheless, the region suffers from serious water-supply problems due to the distribution pattern of the population and to the fact that extensive agricultural zones are located in semi-arid areas or high mountain regions.

Significant progress has been made over the last 20 years in the provision of drinking water and sanitation services. In 1971 only 78% of the urban population and 24% of the rural population had access to drinking-water systems. Sanitation and sewerage services served only 38% of the urban population and 2% of the rural population. Seventeen years later, in December 1988, drinking water was available to 88% of the urban population and to 55% of the rural population,[15] while 80% and 32% of the region's population, respectively, had access to sanitation and sewerage services. Despite these advances, however, there are still 89.2 million people who do not have a supply of drinking water and 141.1 million who lack sanitation (excreta disposal) systems.[16]

The treatment of waste water is one of the region's major failings. Only between 5% and 10% of sewerage systems provide for some degree of waste water treatment before returning it to watercourses or the sea.[17] This percentage has not changed since 1960, and some of the systems having the greatest coverage treat the smallest percentage of the water they handle. This has created extremely serious problems of pollution in most receiving water bodies. It has been estimated that in 1980 South America alone dumped a total of 127 m^3/sec of municipal sewage into its rivers, lakes and the sea (a volume representing 4.2% of the world total), as compared to 29 m^3/sec in 1950 (3.9% of the world total) (see box IV-4).

Another issue is the growing dependence of some cities, such as Lima and Mexico City, on very remote sources of water. This engenders an unwelcome degree of vulnerability as well as having an adverse impact on the source areas.

Irrigation systems have a long tradition in Latin America and the Caribbean, and the region will no doubt carry on this tradition due to their value as an input for modern agricultural production. Irrigation expanded significantly between 1970 and 1987, with its coverage rising from 10 173 000 to 15 231 000 hectares. These figures, however, represent only 1.5% and 2%, respectively, of the total cultivated area in the region.[18] The countries which have made the greatest contribution to this expansion are Brazil and Mexico.

The high cost of building new dams and the difficulty of obtaining fresh loans are two of the reasons why the expansion of the area under irrigation has slowed during the past decade. In addition, the region has had to undertake large investments of other types in order to consolidate projects which are already under way. Some of the main problems associated with irrigation systems are salinization, the swamping of land, water pollution from pesticides and the destruction of wildlife habitats. Near the coasts, wastes carried by drainage water affect water quality in coastal lagoons and the breeding grounds of certain species.

Water management is also an important consideration in unirrigated zones. Such areas represent 98% of the cultivated land and are home to most of the poor rural population. It is important to recognize that the necessary attention has not been devoted to water use in rainfed zones. While irrigation is a very important means of increasing productivity, a wide range of activities can be undertaken to improve the productivity of the land in those areas where

Box IV-4
WASTE WATER DISPOSAL ALTERNATIVES

In 1985, only 41% of the urban population of Latin America had access to sewage systems, and over 90% of all waste water was discharged directly into other water without any kind of treatment. Furthermore, a decade of crisis and recession has reduced the amount of resources which the region can allocate to sewage and water treatment systems. In these circumstances, it is important to draw attention to a number of efforts being made to apply low cost technologies to cope with some of the problems related to the discharge of waste water.

Thus, in Cochabamba, Bolivia, a city with 240 000 inhabitants, an innovative integral sewerage project has been put into operation. New design criteria were applied in order to reduce diameters, gradients and deposits, with the result that costs were also lowered. Additional savings were also made by constructing modular pumping stations. For the future, thought is being given to increasing these savings even further by collecting waste water in stabilization wells, treating it and then using it for irrigation.

In Brazil a similar but simplified drainage system is being used and also a new type of latrine, which works with a smaller volume of water (4 to 5 litres each time instead of the traditional 15 litres).

There are other low cost projects which, although still at the assessment stage, provide useful lessons. For example, in some of the outlying districts of Guayaquil, where the construction of a sewerage system presents serious technical and economic obstacles, ventilated latrines have been built under the self-help system. These latrines operate with a very small amount of water (3 litres). These latrines are now being constructed in Brazil, Colombia and Peru and may become part of the normal sewerage system.

In north-eastern Brazil prefabricated latrines have been installed in rows and can be emptied by trucks using a suction device. In one such project, the user can amortize the cost of a latrine (about US$60) in five years, paying the water and sewerage company for cleaning and maintenance. It is also possible for one third of the payment to be made through contributions in the form of labour.

Even with a sewage system, however, the discharge of waste water may present problems. In

this respect it is worth noting that satisfactory results in the treatment of waste water have been achieved by using waste stabilization wells, which are particularly appropriate in the tropics. They are usually economical and make it possible gradually to obtain water of practically any quality if a number of them are provided, thereby increasing the number of times the water undergoes the stabilization process. These wells have been used extensively in Cuba, Peru and Mexico. The largest series of wells in Latin America, which is located in Mexicali, covers an area of 180 hectares and makes it possible to treat a flow of 1.2 cubic metres of waste water per second.

In view of the inadequate waste disposal systems of the large number of cities of Latin America and the Caribbean which are located in coastal areas, it is common practice for waste water to be emptied into the sea without any treatment. Not only does this have adverse effects on human health and on the ecology, it also causes economic loss by reducing the number of tourists.

Using sewage systems which lead into the sea so that waste water can be discharged some distance from the shore along with limited treatment of waste products able to float, may be more efficient than traditional methods which include secondary treatment for water and the discharge of the waste extracted from it close to the shore. When waste is discharged some distance off shore, it may be dissolved at a ratio of 100 to 1 in a few minutes, thereby reducing the nutrient organic concentrations typical of waste water to levels at which they have no adverse ecological effects. In addition, killing bacteria in a hostile marine environment may reduce the concentration of pathogens to levels equal to or even lower than those achieved through the use of chlorine in secondary emissions.

Systems of this type may be found in Brazil, Mexico, Puerto Rico and Venezuela. The Ipanema system in Rio de Janeiro can process a flow of waste water of six cubic metres per second. Its length is 4 325 metres, its diameter is 2.4 metres, and it has a diffuser 400 metres long which discharges the contents at a depth of 28 metres. Continuous water quality control in the area has shown that a notable improvement has been achieved since the system was put into operation in 1975.

Source: Carl R. Bartone, "Water quality and urbanization in Latin America", *Water International*, No. 15, 1990.

rainfall is and will continue to be the only source of water. Integrated management of farming, forestry and livestock-raising activities, soil development and the selection of suitable seeds are some of the options in such zones. The percentage of budgetary resources allocated for such efforts, which involve, for example, the management of river basins, the control of soil erosion, and research on the adaptation of crops to rainfed areas, is equivalent to no more than 10% of the resources allocated to irrigation and drainage works in the region.[19]

The use of water for *industrial and mining* activities is another important issue in Latin America and the Caribbean because of the major implications such uses have in terms of the catchment and pollution of watercourses. In most countries of the region, water used by these sectors is discharged directly into watercourses without having undergone any form of treatment whatsoever. The total return flow from the industrial and power sectors in 1980 has been calculated at 254 m^3/sec, which is equivalent to 1.3% of the world total. Data for 1950 indicate that at that time only 70 m^3/sec were discharged.[20] The severest impact of the use of water for mining activities is felt in semi-arid zones owing to the very limited volumes of receiving water available in relation to the volumes of discharged toxic wastes.

Although **hydropower generation** does not involve the consumption of water, it does cause some degree of environmental deterioration. Dams regulate the natural flow of rivers and their ecosystems. While there was a decline in the number of dams constructed from 1980 onward in comparison to the preceding decade, the water storage capacity of the new dams increased considerably. Brazil and Argentina, for example, have 62% and 19%, respectively, of the total storage capacity of all the dams and reservoirs built in the region between 1970 and 1984.[21] The environmental impact of large-scale water works is currently one of the most controversial environmental issues, and a great deal of research remains to be done in this area.

The generation of hydroelectricity is a key factor in promoting development and in providing cities with a clean energy supply. The amount of power supplied by hydroelectric plants increased considerably between 1970 and 1987, and the percentage of total energy consumption covered by hydroelectricity climbed from 53.9% in 1970 to 60.3% in 1987, while the use of electricity generated by thermoelectric power plants declined from 46.1% to 37.3% during the same period.

The region's potential hydropower output, estimated at 805 792 mW, represents 35% of the world total. Today, it uses only 9.6% of the world total. This fact, together with the rise in petroleum prices, might be expected to lead to an upward trend in hydropower generation. However, the growth rate of installed capacity averaged 6.5% per annum between 1980 and 1987,[22] a figure considerably lower than the 10.2% average rate recorded during the latter years of the 1970s. The reasons for this decline are the high cost of these works and the economic recession experienced by the countries of the region. The environmental impact of such works should be evaluated in relation to the benefits they bring, such as electrification in urban and industrial areas. One of the environmental benefits derived from the construction of dams has been the greater attention devoted to the management of watersheds in order to control erosion.

2.3 *Mineral resources*

The known mineral **reserves** of Latin America and the Caribbean are located in an area amounting to less than 10% of the potential mineral-bearing territory,[23] whereas in other regions of the world most of the territory which might contain mineral deposits has already been explored and prospected. Even so, the region's known reserves of the principal non-ferrous metals and of iron ore represent a significant percentage of world reserves.

On the other hand, the rates of exploitation of known reserves are higher in Latin America and the Caribbean than in the rest of the world. In view of the long lead time involved in mining projects, resources need to be channelled into identifying new deposits, particularly of tin, gold, silver, bismuth, cobalt, chromium, manganese, mercury and lead. Nevertheless, according to the listing of new investment projects for the period

1988-1995, the region will continue to concentrate 75% of its resources in only three product lines: bauxite/aluminium, copper and iron/steel.[24] This allocation of investment resources indicates that the mining sector is becoming highly specialized. At the present time, mineral exports are concentrated in just eight metal products: bauxite, copper, tin, iron, nickel, silver, lead and zinc.

Most of the output is exported as raw materials, which means that the region provides a very small share of world production of metals, semi-finished and intermediate mineral-based products. Indeed, in 1986 consumption or industrial use in the region outstripped its production levels in the cases of antimony, bismuth, cadmium, chromium, lithium, manganese, mercury, molybdenum, gold, selenium, tungsten, uranium and vanadium.

Making greater and better use of the region's mineral resources requires greater knowledge of its metal resources; the introduction of new technologies to improve its competitiveness while at the same time reducing the pollution generated by its production activities; the development of greater production linkages in the mining, metallurgical and industrial sectors; and an expansion of intraregional trade based on the removal of barriers to trade and the enhancement of the region's international competitiveness.

2.4 Marine resources

As is well known, the marine areas of Latin America and the Caribbean contain a wealth of both living and non-living marine resources, as well as offering opportunities for harnessing water, currents and wind, among other sources, for the purpose of generating power. Fishery resources are the area which has been studied the most extensively so far, and a greater amount of information has been compiled on them than on other marine resources.

The harvesting of the oceans' fishery resources at both the world and regional levels has increased fairly steadily over the past two decades. Indeed, between 1970 and 1988, the nominal world catch rose by 38.3%. Slight declines in global levels were recorded in only

two years during this period, and these were due mainly to a sharp drop in Peru's total catch in the early 1970s. The most recent figures made available by FAO indicate that the world's total nominal catch amounted to 84.6 million metric tons in 1988.

Chile, Peru and, to a lesser extent, Mexico are the principal fishing countries of Latin America, since they are endowed with some of the most productive fishing grounds in the world, mainly thanks to the effects of the Humboldt current. Together, Chile and Peru harvest between approximately 10 and 12 millions tons, which represents about 80% of the regional total. These two countries are also among the six top-ranking fishing nations in the world in terms of the volume of their catches and are the main suppliers of fish meal in the international market.

Chile's and Peru's catches are mainly confined to a limited number of pelagic species (anchovies, sardines, jurel and mackerel) which are harvested by the industrial and semi-industrial fleet and are used almost entirely for the production of fish meal. The unit value of the industrial sector's catch is therefore low in comparison to that of other fisheries which harvest species that bring a better price on the market (salmon, shrimps, tuna, etc.) (see box IV-5).

The non-industrial fishery sector, on the other hand, harvests a relatively small percentage of the total catch and concentrates on more highly-prized species which are sold almost exclusively on the market for fresh fish for direct consumption. The importance of this sector therefore lies in its contribution to employment levels and to the supply of fish products for direct consumption. In addition, because of the type of technology employed, it is more selective and efficient in terms of its use of inputs (petroleum, maintenance of equipment, etc.) and has less of a negative impact on stocks, since it harvests a smaller volume of fish and most of the fish caught are of adequate size. This sector is, however, the most severely affected by the pollution of the sea and the deterioration of coastal areas.

An analysis of the exploitation of fishery resources in the region requires an examination of

Box IV-5
DEREGULATION AND THE FISHERIES ACT IN CHILE

If fishery activity is left entirely to the free play of market forces, without any regulation, there is a risk of causing overfishing and the collapse of the small-scale non-industrial fishery industry, which is an important source of employment in coastal areas. The adoption of purely mercantile criteria in this sector will result in the long run in an allocation of marine resources which is inefficient from the social point of view, inasmuch as it will foster a degree of over-investment which may even endanger the survival of some species.

The limited and uncertain knowledge at our disposal on marine life, the natural fluctuations in the stock of resources –the natural capital–, and the need to conserve this capital are among the reasons why it is essential to regulate fishing by imposing regulations regarding such aspects as the minimum size of the species caught, close seasons, overall limits on catches, forms of fishing, and so forth.

Over the last twenty years, the Chilean fishery sector has registered explosive growth, with catches increasing sixfold between the early 1970s and the late 1980s. It is hard to see, however, how the main factor in the growth of the sector can continue to be increases in the catches, for there are signs of over-exploitation in the main fisheries, namely, coastal pelagic fisheries, demersal fishing for fine species such as hake, and the extraction of shellfish and crustaceans.

Two stages may be distinguished in the development of demersal fishing in southernmost Chile, in line with the degree of opening-up of marine resources to the intervention of the foreign fishing industry. The first stage –one of total openness– runs from 1977 to 1983 and corresponds to the period when industrial fishing was dominated mainly by foreign factory ships. The second stage –one of selective openness– runs from 1984 to the present and coincides with the installation on land of mainly Chilean processing and packing plants.

During the first stage, export markets were opened up in Japan and Spain for frozen products (mainly whole frozen gutted hake and cuskeel), and a fleet of about 11 factory ships was stationed in the area to serve the Japanese, Korean and Spanish trawlers.[*] To begin with, these ships were authorized to operate in the open sea, from approximately the Island of Chiloé down to Cape Horn, under their respective national flags, subject to the payment of fishing licences whose cost was proportional to the size of the catch. After a little while, however, the requirement for payment of a licence was cancelled and the factory ships were assimilated to Chilean enterprises so that they only had to pay tax on their profits. At the same time, by way of conservation measures, maximum catches were fixed and standards were laid down regarding the minimum mesh size of the nets used.

For various reasons, the contribution made by the foreign fishery industry to the development of the area was frankly modest. The enterprises turned in accounting losses or showed barely any profits, so that they paid no taxes. Moreover, their main product (whole frozen fish) formed the raw material for a production chain located and ending in the final market. Thus, the whole preparation process whereby greater added value is given to the raw material took place outside Chile and brought it no benefits. Moreover, the direct employment generated by the factory ships was of little significance (a total of 735 persons), while as the investments were not domiciled in the country they had practically no impact on the economy of the area other than that due to the demand for fuel, shipyard and port services, and other inputs.

The second stage began when restrictions were placed on the entry of factory ships and encouragement was given to the installation of processing plants on land and the entry of other types of ships (refrigerated ships to serve the trawlers and factory ships to serve bottom-line fishing boats) to supply the plants with their raw material. These measures created a new situation, replacing the old policy with one that was fairer to Chilean investors. This new situation enabled the latter to give a fresh boost to the fishery industry, which now extended its activities even to the upper waters of the fiords and channels of the Aysén region.

During this stage, fishery technology became more diversified, especially through the entry of the new ships, and there was a significant expansion in small-scale non-industrial fishing, which became the main supplier of hake for the processing plants, for which it now provides as much as 75% of that input.

Even leaving aside the taxes they pay, the processing plants have made a considerable contribution to the development of the region. Since they submit the raw material to a higher degree of processing, they generate products of higher added value (fish fillets, for example). Furthermore, they provide direct employment for at least 4 000 persons and their demand for raw material maintains the activities of some 15 000 small-scale fishermen. This has been accompanied by the establishment of human communities in previously uninhabited areas and has strengthened economic activity in the region.

The new Fisheries Act, put before Parliament in 1990, provides for two different systems: one permitting free access, and the other permitting restricted access in cases where it has been established that a resource is already being fully exploited. The Act reserves the right of the authorities to impose restrictions on the size of catches and on fishing methods, as well as to impose periodic close seasons in certain cases. In general, it eliminates controls over the level of activity in industrial fishing, but it established at the same time, in cases where a resource is already being fully exploited, a system of transferable individual permits which give the right to a certain proportion of the total annual catch fixed by the authorities during periods when access is restricted. Of these permits, 75% are granted on the basis of the catches made in the years before the state of full exploitation was decreed, while the remaining 25% are sold by public tender.

The inclusion of these individual permits in the Act has given rise to some controversy among specialists. Those in favour of them hold that they represent a system of regulation which prevents over-investment and limits the current administrative discretionality. It is also maintained that control over the size of individual catches will promote the use of more efficient technologies and permit better control of the size of the global catch.

Those who are against these permits adduce both legal and economic reasons for their attitude. Thus, they claim that the granting of exclusive fishing rights is unconstitutional, while from the economic point of view they say that these permits will favour the creation of monopoly rents which will adversely affect the social allocation of resources.

The Fisheries Act reserves a coastal fringe five nautical miles wide for the activities of small-scale non-industrial fishermen, and all vessels over 18 metres long are banned from fishing in this area. However, it is easy to see that this rule does not exclude from the small-scale fishery area vessels which, although not exceeding 18 metres in length, are so extensively endowed with advanced technological features that they do not fit into the category of "small-scale non-industrial vessel".

Source: Guillermo Geisse G., "Problemas y posibilidades de transformación productiva con conservación ambiental en cuatro sectores de actividad de la economía chilena", Santiago, Chile, December 1990, *mimeo* (document prepared for the ECLAC Division of Environment and Human Settlements), and Instituto Latinoamericano de Doctrinas y Estudios Sociales (ILADES), *Trabajo de asesoría económica al Congreso Nacional*, TASC, No. 1, Santiago, Chile, March 1990.

* Whereas in the late 1970s the new international marine legislation restricted the operation of factory ships off the coasts of most countries, in contrast Chile authorized this kind of ship to exploit high-value demersal fish in its Patagonian region.

different species and technologies as well as of regions or countries. FAO estimates indicate that catches in the most productive area in the region (area 87, which includes Chile and Peru), are higher than the maximum sustainable yield according to estimates of the biomass of pelagic species. Current levels of exploitation in that area range between 104% and 288% of the maximum sustainable yields, which clearly shows that a problem of overfishing exists. In point of fact, Peru suffered a collapse of its fishing industry in the early 1970s precisely as a result of overfishing, together with environmental changes produced by the El Niño current.

The non-industrial sector also shows signs of overfishing various species, although on a smaller scale. Some of the clearest cases are the harvesting of "locos" (a variety of abalone) in Chile and of shrimp larvae in Ecuador and Peru, and the overfishing of many coastal species in

which a decline has been seen in the historic levels of catch per unit of effort.

Not enough is yet known about the behaviour (reproduction, migration, etc.) of many marine species, and many important questions therefore remain to be answered as regards the most appropriate levels of catch, closed seasons, the areas where fishing should be permitted and other aspects of their exploitation. In view of this lack of knowledge, it seems preferable to emphasize the conservation of these resources rather than their untrammelled exploitation. This requires international co-operation, and here again an important field is being opened up for negotiation and collaboration.

At the semi-industrial level, areas which have seen increasing development over the past decade include activities involving the cultivation of marine products, such as the planting and harvesting of algae, the cultivation of shrimp, and the use of salmon-cage or ocean ranching production methods. These product lines (algae and salmon in Chile and shrimp in Belize, Colombia, Ecuador, Honduras, Mexico and Panama) are becoming quite important because of their high profitability and the large foreign exchange earnings they bring, despite the ecological and environmental problems associated with this activity.

3. Management of natural resources

The orientation of the use of their resources will constitute a major challenge for the countries of the region in the forthcoming decade. In order to meet this challenge it is imperative that they gear their management systems to the realities of the areas within their territories. The predominant tendency will be to harmonize traditional management systems, which are designed to direct development within certain political/administrative limits, with the other types of systems that are needed to manage components of the natural environment, such as ecosystems, river basins, coastal areas, lakes and oceans, and others. The sectoralized approach which took little account of environmental realities will give way to an integrated approach in which environmental and user needs are taken into consideration in the decision-making process.

There will also be a tendency to intensify the research effort already being made in some areas and to step up pilot projects in these fields. In addition to research on various technical aspects,

economic analyses of the projects will be carried out, and a particular effort will be made to encourage the population to take an interest in these projects. These elements will lay the foundations for initiatives involving everything from managing the exploitation of the marine biomass right up to the reinforcement of legislation for the protection of native forests. This approach will also provide a sound basis for decision-making in respect of investments to provide protection against extreme natural phenomena.

The organized participation of the private sector will be crucial to this process, and in order to make such participation possible, it will be necessary to decentralize government action and strengthen public and private management capabilities. The continuity of State action is as important as its quality. Hence, the management of natural resources exclusively on the basis of investment projects will fail if such projects do not have the necessary institutional backstopping. This subject will be discussed further in chapter VII.

Ultimately, the purpose of natural resource management is to serve the population, which is the subject of development. Yet so far, despite the progress made in recent decades –with the exception of the 1980s, when the region took a step backwards– we have not succeeded in using the available resources to wipe out poverty. The existence of reciprocal effects between poverty and the environment creates a vicious circle which must be broken. This problem will be addressed in the following chapter.

Notes

[1] Latin American Demographic Centre (CELADE), *Latin America: Population Projections, 1950-2025* (LC/DEM/G.82), Demographic Bulletin series, No. 45, year 23, Santiago, Chile, January 1990.

[2] *Ibid.*

[3] See CELADE, *op. cit.*, and Regional Employment Programme for Latin America and the Caribbean (PREALC), *Empleo y equidad: desafío de los 90*, Documento de trabajo series, No. 354, Santiago, Chile, January 1990.

[4] CELADE, *op. cit.*

[5] United Nations, Department of International Economic and Social Affairs, *Prospects of World Urbanization, 1988* (ST/ESA/SER.A/112), Population Studies series, No. 112, New York, 1989. United Nations publication, Sales No. E.89.XIII.8.

[6] Inter-American Institute for Co-operation and Agriculture (IICA), *América Latina y el Caribe. Pobreza rural persistente*, Documentos de Programas series, No. 17, January 1990.

[7] See Food and Agriculture Organization of the United Nations (FAO), "Rural Poverty", *Potentials for Agricultural and Rural Development in Latin America and the Caribbean* (LARC 88/3), annex II, Rome, 1988.

[8] CELADE, "La población urbana y rural y sus condiciones de vida", January 1990, report prepared by the Pan American Health Organization (PAHO), and United Nations, Department of International Economic and Social Affairs, *op. cit.*

[9] It can be indirectly deduced that this limit has been passed when, for example, concentrations of pollutants in the air or water exceed certain standards, or when the average speed of motor vehicle traffic falls below a given threshold, occasioning traffic jams.

[10] FAO, *op. cit.*, annex IV.

[11] With respect to Andean systems, see ECLAC/UNEP, *Sobrevivencia campesina en ecosistemas de altura* (E/CEPAL/G.1267), 2 vols., Santiago, Chile, December 1983. United Nations publication, Sales No. S.83.II.G.31 (vols. I and II).

[12] FAO, *FAO Production Yearbook. 1989*, vol. 43, FAO Statistics Series, No. 94, Rome, 1990.

[13] World Resources Institute/International Institute for Environment and Development/UNEP, *World Resources 1988-1989*, New York, Basic Books Inc., 1989.

[14] ECLAC, *The Water Resources of Latin America and the Caribbean and their Utilization. A Report on Progress in the Application of the Mar del Plata Action Plan* (LC/G.1358), Estudios e informes de la CEPAL series, No. 53, Santiago, Chile, October 1985. United Nations publication, Sales No. E.85.II.G.16.

[15] Pan American Health Organization (PAHO), *International Drinking Water Supply and Sanitation Decade. Regional Progress Report*, Environmental Series, No. 6, Washington, D.C., 1987.

[16] PAHO, *The Situation of Drinking Water Supply and Sanitation in the American Region at the End of the Decade 1981-1990, and Prospects for the Future*, 2 vols., Washington, D.C., 1990.

[17] *Ibid.*

[18] ECLAC, *Statistical Yearbook for Latin America and the Caribbean. 1989 Edition* (LC/G.1606-P), Santiago, Chile, February 1990. United Nations publication, Sales No. E/S.90.II.G.1.

[19] ECLAC, *The Water Resources of Latin America and the Caribbean: Planning, Hazards and Pollution* (LC/G.1559-P), Estudios e informes de la CEPAL series, No. 77, Santiago, Chile, July 1990. United Nations publication, Sales No. E.90.II.G.8.

[20] *Ibid.*, note 4, p. 59.

[21] International Commission on Large Dams (ICOLD), *World Register of Dams*, Paris, 1984.

[22] United Nations, *Energy Statistics Yearbook 1987*, New York, 1989. United Nations publication, Sales No. E/F.89.XVII.10.

[23] Federal Institute for Geosciences and Natural Resources, "Regional Distribution of Mining Production and Reserves of Mineral Commodities in the World", Hannover, January 1982, *mimeo*.

[24] *Engineering and Mining Journal*, London, January 1988, and ECLAC, *Minería año 2000. América Latina: proyectos mineros y su financiamiento* (LC/R.807), Santiago, Chile, October 1989.

Chapter V

POVERTY AND SUSTAINABLE DEVELOPMENT

Difficulty in accumulating capital, in all its forms, is one characteristic of poverty. Experience shows, however, that there are important alternatives to the accumulation of natural capital for the low-income strata.

1. Level of poverty

Towards the end of the 1980s there were close to 183 million poor people in Latin America –71 million more than in 1970 and 47 million more than in 1980. Of the total number of poor people at the end of the decade, about 88 million were indigent.[1] The increase in the number of poor people during the past decade was almost entirely concentrated in urban areas, although the share of the poor population made up of indigents showed a greater increase in the rural area. In any case, whereas in 1970 only 37% of the poor resided in towns, towards the end of the 1980s, over half of them could be classified as urban poor (see box V-1).

Attention should be drawn, first of all, to the variety of situations to be found in the region. According to an ECLAC document,[2] Argentina and Uruguay, on the one hand, have the lowest percentages of poverty, which affected fewer than one out of every six households in both 1980 and 1986. At the other extreme, Guatemala and Peru showed the highest proportions of poverty at the country level. In Guatemala poverty characterizes two thirds of the households, and in Peru about half of them. Between these two extremes there were two groups of countries in which poverty affected between one fifth and two fifths of the total number of households. The first group, with lower levels of poverty, is made up of Costa Rica, Venezuela and Mexico, whereas Panama, Colombia and Brazil are found in the second group.

The share of indigent households also varied widely from country to country, ranging from levels in the vicinity of 5% in Argentina and Uruguay to over 20% of the households in Peru and even over 30% in Guatemala. The remaining countries fell between these two extremes as in the case of levels of poverty.

A comparison between levels of poverty in 1970 and 1989 makes it possible to view the spread of poverty in terms of variations in levels of income and changes in its distribution. Thus, the two countries with the highest indexes of growth in that period (Brazil and Colombia) are those which exhibited the greatest declines in the level of poverty. In addition, the period 1970-1986 in Brazil and Colombia was not so markedly recessive as in the remainder of the countries. The decline in poverty in Mexico (somewhat less notable) might be explained not only by the increase in its income during the period but also by the fact that it was distributed in such a way that households in the lowest income groups had a larger share in it.

The case of Argentina, where the proportion of the population living in a state of poverty rose by

Box V-1
POVERTY IN LATIN AMERICA: SPREAD AND COVERAGE

The economic crisis that affected the Latin American countries in the 1980s not only brought to light the structural inadequacies of the region's development but also created obstacles to social mobility and cohesiveness. The spread of poverty is one of the primary manifestations of these obstacles.

According to ECLAC estimates, 37% of Latin American households were living in poverty and 17% in indigence by the end of the 1980s. As calculated by the same source, these percentages reached 31% and 12%, respectively, in the urban areas and 54% and 31% in the rural areas. The figures, compared to those of 1970, show both a sharp increase in urban poverty (from 26% to 31%) and a significant drop in rural poverty (from 62% to 54%). Changes in the same direction, but of lesser magnitude, appear to have occurred for indigent households.

Poverty in Latin America today is mainly an urban phenomenon resulting from the burgeoning of its main cities (in the last 20 years, the urban portion of the region's total population rose from 58% to 69%) and the fact that the upward trend in poverty indexes has been concentrated in these areas, especially during the crisis period. Thus, while in 1970 only 37% of the poor resided in urban areas, the proportion had risen to over half (57%) by the end of the 1980s. On the other hand, the extremely poor or indigent today, as in 1970, continue primarily to reside in rural areas, despite the rise (from 31% to 45%) in the urban proportion of the indigent population.

LATIN AMERICA: POVERTY TRENDS AND COVERAGE

(Percentage of the population and millions of persons)

	1960	1970	1980	1986	1989
Poverty (%)	51.0	40.0	41.0	43.0	44.0
(persons)	110	113	136	170	183
Indigence (%)	26.0	19.0	19.0	21.0	21.0
(persons)	56	54	62	81	88

Source: ECLAC, *Magnitud de la pobreza en América Latina en los años ochenta* (LC/G.1653-P), Santiago, Chile, March 1991; and ECLAC/UNDP, *¿Se puede superar la pobreza? Realidad y perspectivas en América Latina* (E/CEPAL/G.1139), Santiago, Chile, December 1980.

LATIN AMERICA: EXTENT OF POVERTY IN 1989

(Projection based on 1986 figures)

	Households				Population			
	Poverty		Indigence		Poverty		Indigence	
	Thousands	%	Thousands	%	Thousands	%	Thousands	%
Total	34 600	37	15 800	17	183 200	44	87 700	21
Urban	20 300	31	7 600	12	103 700	36	39 400	14
Rural	14 300	54	8 200	31	79 500	61	48 300	37

Source: ECLAC, *Magnitud de la pobreza en América Latina en los años ochenta* (LC/G.1653-P), Santiago, Chile, March 1991.

five percentage points between 1970 and 1986, may be explained both by the marked reduction in income and by a deterioration in its distribution. In Costa Rica, Peru and Venezuela, where increases in poverty occurred which fluctuated between one and two percentage points, the national levels of per capita income achieved in 1986 were similar to those of 1970. Costa Rica and Venezuela experienced significant rises in income in the 1970s but recorded bigger declines during the 1980s, which were presumably accompanied by greater concentration.

The behaviour described is also related to the growth of urban and rural population. For Latin America as a whole it is estimated that during the 1970s the percentage of poor households fell from 40% to 35%, while that of indigent households dropped from 19% to 15%. Between 1980 and 1986, on the other hand, the trend seems to have reversed itself, since the figures for both poverty and indigence rose by two percentage points each. The growth of the share of the urban population in nearly all the countries of the region and the fact that the international economic crisis caused relatively greater damage to urban households would explain why between 1970 and 1986 the urban poor as a proportion of the total population rose by four percentage points (from 26% to 30%), whereas in the high-growth years of the 1970s, it fell by only one point. In rural areas, on the other hand, there seems to have been a sizeable reduction in the percentage of poor households during the 1970s (from 62% to 54%), a figure which did not show much variation between 1980 and 1986 although the share of poor people in a state of indigence rose.

In speaking of poverty, the fact that economic and social development has many dimensions must be taken into account. These will determine the differences between the type of poverty which characterizes the Latin American and Caribbean region and that found in the other regions of the world.

2. Population, poverty and the environment

It cannot be shown that a high growth rate of population resulting from a high fertility rate must necessarily be associated with a lower level of development and hence with the existence of poverty. However, the figures available show that there is an association between a country's position in the demographic transition and the degree of poverty it experiences. In addition, existing estimates on fertility showed that, as a general rule, in poor populations fertility rates are two or three times as high as in medium- and high-income sectors. In rural areas, some sectors still show an average of close to eight children per women.

Such high fertility rates in combination with a declining mortality rate owing to primary health care policies produce high natural growth rates. This creates demographic pressure from a basically young population, most of it rooted in poor families, and generates a demand for substantial mother/child health care (including proper environmental health measures) and a marked demand for new employment. In rural areas, however, natural growth may be relatively low owing to high mortality rates accompanied by the emigration of a large number of women of childbearing age.

Because of the patterns of demographic growth in some parts of the region (where there has been a marked increase in urban growth) and the rise in urban poverty, the majority of poor people now live in urban areas; nevertheless, the majority of the rural population is still poor. Owing first to the effects of the crisis of the past decade and second to its own growth dynamics, the poor segments of the population have grown at a higher rate than other sectors.

In the case of both urban and rural areas, impoverishment has close links with the environment. In this connection, mention should be made of the fact that poverty and environmental degradation often occur in the same geographical locations and of the impact of environmental deterioration on the living and working conditions of poor people, who may either overcome or aggravate it. These are essential issues on the environmental agenda of the Latin American and the Caribbean region and can be used for purposes of comparison with other developing regions.

The links between poverty and the environment cannot be viewed as resulting solely from demographic processes taken in isolation but must be considered in connection with many other phenomena of a social, political and economic nature. Poverty in the region is concentrated in a few sectors of the population and in certain rural and urban zones. In addition, in the majority of the countries it occurs in the context of a relatively low ratio between population and natural resources and in national economies which in their majority (some exceptions to this will be discussed below) have the capacity to solve the problems related to poverty in reasonable periods of time (10-15 years).

Long-term studies carried out over a period of 20 years or more show that the gap between the poor and the rest of the population –the poverty gap– has been steadily decreasing. This gap is measured in terms of available income and coverage by or access to basic goods and services (potable water, sanitation, housing, primary health care and basic education). The tendency for the gap to narrow was interrupted in the past decade, particularly with regard to income. The relationship between poverty and the environment needs to be examined in the light of assessments made in respect of a period of intense population pressure (in respect of the total population, including both the dependent and the active population) in countries comprising three fourths of the population of the region.

The relationship between poverty and the environment has been very different in rural as compared to urban areas in forms of dynamics and characteristics. In rural areas, neither the proportion nor the absolute number of traditional smallholders or small producers on the agricultural frontier has varied in 30 years.[3] This has been true in spite of the fact that both the total and the active population have been stable since the 1970s and some efforts have been made to improve land distribution and to increase production and, in some cases, wage employment. Although some of these variables have not changed much and others have shown some slight improvement, the available information indicates that the rate of soil erosion in areas characterized by smallholdings has remained the same or even increased owing to mechanization.

As for migrant farming, which is reported to have increased in the past decade, it provides a means of expanding large-scale livestock-raising at the cost of deforestation and the use of land, which grows poorer and poorer as its natural fertility decreases. The impact of commercial farming on the management of natural, economic and financial resources in rural areas has made it virtually impossible for peasant production to continue in its present state of marginality without eroding the available natural capital.

Commercial farming is an aspect of the rural environment which, in addition to contributing to exports, is increasingly responsible for supplying the expanding urban population, the majority of which falls into the low-income group. With ample land available to them and supported by loans, a road and commercial infrastructure and the State, entrepreneurs have developed a model based on mechanization and the use of chemical agents not always complemented by additional fertilization. The result has been an increase in production, a smaller increase in productivity and a rise in the number of working days. This combination of factors has robbed the soil of its fertility and has required a continued expansion of the agricultural frontier. The deterioration of natural capital has frequently made the production of basic agricultural products, whose prices are compatible with the income earned by the urban poor, more profitable in economic terms, thereby establishing an undesirable link between poverty and the environment.

It is well known that in the urban environment the various social sectors make different contributions to pollution (production of wastes, carbon monoxide, etc.) and use resources (water, land, recreational areas) differently. Frequently the poor pay more for water, both per unit consumed and as a share of their income, when they lack indoor plumbing (or even when they have it), and also for renting urban space.

Although it is frequently heard that urban environmental deterioration affects all urban inhabitants regardless of the level of their income, there is evidence to the contrary. Urban sites at high risk from floods or landslides, close to outlets of toxic gas or traversed by polluted waterways are occupied by the poorest residents; and it becomes more feasible to mitigate the negative impact of pollution and deterioration as people's income levels rise (see box V-2). On the other hand, remedial activities are financed by taxing the general public with the result that the degree of progressivity of financing corresponds to that of the general tax system. The situation is still more inequitable when the population of an entire country pays to improve the environment of its big cities.

The demand for water by residents increases faster than the population. Urban residents put pressure on the water sources so that sources which are increasingly distant from the towns they serve are used, causing greater damage to the environment because of the growing need to organize the distribution of water and extend it to that part of the population which lacks it. The urban poor play a notable role in this demand for water since basic services (water and sewage) are generally accorded priority in all the countries of the region.

The foregoing analysis makes it possible to weigh and measure the contribution made by the poor to environmental deterioration and the relationship of environmental deterioration with poverty. In Latin America and the Caribbean, most of the blame for soil erosion and for indiscriminate slash-and-burn agriculture cannot be laid on the poor, who use less than 5% of the land and forest resources. As for erosion in areas where smallholdings are located, it contributes to

---

Box V-2
FLOODS IN METROPOLITAN BUENOS AIRES IN 1985

The link between poverty and the environment is not a direct result of demographic processes but includes the impact of other social, economic and political phenomena. Thus, for example, urban poverty shows a pattern of spatial concentration that tends to coincide with the most vulnerable areas in terms of environmental hazards or risks of natural disasters.

Metropolitan Buenos Aires occupies an area of approximately 7 000 square kilometres. This territory contains a population of close to 8 500 000 people –the equivalent of 50% of the national urban population and 37% of the total population of the country.

On 31 May and 1 June 1985, 308 millimetres of water fell on Buenos Aires. This caused a flood which made it necessary to evacuate 100 000 people, damaged 2 500 dwellings and 14 000 motor vehicles and left 100 000 dwellings without electricity, telephone service and running water. Public and private firms suffered millions of dollars in losses. The number of victims was tragic.

Low-lying areas in the Belgrano, Núñez, Palermo and Villa Crespo districts, areas in the vicinity of the Riachuelo and lower Flores rivers and urban development sites at Lugano became real traps. The drainage projects completed in them in 1939 had been allowed to exceed their safety margins with no new works being carried out in spite of the rapid urban growth which had taken place in those areas since 1939. This has made Buenos Aires a highly vulnerable city.

All strata of the population are not of course in an equally vulnerable position. One illustration may be found in the greater degree of vulnerability to flooding of a temporary or self-help dwelling by comparison with a dwelling built of solid material. In view of the fact that much of the flood damage is found in parts of the city in which poverty predominates, it is clear that this problem of vulnerability is a socioeconomic and political problem more than a problem of geography.

Consideration must also be given to the enormous shortcomings of the State apparatus in coping with these phenomena as shown both by the failure to take preventive action and by the difficulty experienced in co-ordinating measures designed to deal with the effects of the floods once they had occurred. Community participation organized through the municipalities can play an eminent role in compensating for the inadequacies of the State apparatus, particularly in efforts aimed at achieving results in the relatively short term. For this it is necessary to develop mechanisms which make it possible to institutionalize such participation so that it operates with ease, flexibility and adaptability.

SOME COST ESTIMATES IN RESPECT OF THE FLOOD

	Thousands of dollars
Damage to telephone services	2 675
Damage to electric power supply	4 500
Civil defense expenses	1 275
Damage to dwellings	165 000
Costs relating to loss of working days	24 300
Vehicular damage	1 050
Damage to municipalities	625
Decrease in value added	4 375
Loss of income (transport)	20 400
Damage to movable goods	9 375
Expenditure on public health	12 500
Estimated total	246 075

Source: L.A. Costa and D.N. Albini, "Las inundaciones en el área metropolitana de Buenos Aires", *Medio Ambiente y Urbanización*, No. 23, July 1988.

poverty now and prolongs it into the future generations of small farmers (see box V-3).

The cost of water is also directly responsible for the growth of poverty in cities, and its incidence is greater than it was 30 years ago. Poor rural families, especially the women and children in them, also spend more time and energy fetching water and wood now than they did then, and the difficulty of access to water and firewood contributes more to rural poverty today than it once did.

Conditions of poverty are partially responsible for the continued practice of migrant farming, which has resulted in deforestation and the expansion of the agricultural frontier. In addition, migrant farming facilitates the expansion of extensive agriculture, the concentration of ownership, and speculation in land recently opened up for cultivation; in other words it sets up obstacles to sustainable agriculture and to the elimination of rural poverty in those areas.

3. Indigenous peoples, poverty and the environment

A special section of this paper must be devoted to indigenous peoples, since they constitute a highly vulnerable sector of the population. In view of the demographic, cultural and environmental diversity of this sector, special attention should be focused on at least three groups of people:

Ethnic groups which make up a large percentage of the total population of a country. It might be said that the indigenous culture of countries with such large ethnic groups is associated with the national culture, as is the case with countries such as Bolivia, Guatemala or Peru, where the indigenous sector of the population inhabits much of the territory, both rural and urban.

Comparatively large indigenous populations which inhabit reserves or reservations, in certain specific areas of countries. The Mapuche reservations in

THE VICIOUS CIRCLE OF PEASANT POVERTY IN THE PERUVIAN HIGHLANDS

The peasant communities of the Peruvian highlands, which have the highest poverty levels in the country, live from the exploitation of fragile ecosystems, with little energy and limited availability of resources per unit of land.

The Inca empire, which also covered these territories, developed around the intensive use of high-altitude areas, especially those located at more than 2 000 metres. Taking advantage of the sinuous geography of peaks and valleys required the large-scale construction of terraces and hydraulic irrigation systems. According to the most accepted figure, there were between 350 000 and 400 000 hectares of terraces in the highlands when the Spaniards arrived. More than 60% of these were abandoned due to the demographic collapse of the indigenous population during the colonial period and the destruction of the slopes caused by grazing livestock of European origin.

Agricultural practices introduced by the Spaniards, although less intensive than the preceding ones, significantly accelerated the processes of erosion. Subsequent demographic recovery, owing in part to significant progress in the health field, has brought about greater pressure on the land, thus intensifying the vicious circle of erosion and poverty. Peruvian peasants have tried to survive, through either occasionally working for pay or overexploiting the soil. The highland peasants' marginal ties to the market economy, together with their limited access to new technology and the fragility and low productivity of the ecosystems in which they have settled, have progressively shrunk their resources, just at a time when the population increase makes these resources more necessary.

The vicious circle of poverty and resource deterioration can only be broken through a revaluation of ecosystemic capital based on soil reclamation, mainly by redesigning the terraces and building irrigation works. By virtue of these changes and the incorporation of new genetic technologies and biological and water management techniques it will be possible to improve land productivity and profitability, and augment the food supply.

Aware of this possible solution for the drama of peasant survival, various governmental and non-governmental organizations in Peru have been encouraging, with the help of international agencies, rural development programmes primarily aimed at terrace recovery in the highland areas. Various programmes have already been launched, the biggest of these resulted in the rehabilitation of 1 200 hectares in three years. Although these efforts have greatly benefitted the communities where they have been applied, the total magnitude is far from significant from the national or local standpoint.

Evaluations of terrace conditions indicate that a large part of those that had been partly destroyed could be reincorporated into agricultural production. A study has been made of the possibility of rehabilitating 80 000 hectares over a period of 10 years, at an average cost of US$1 900 per hectare. The study estimates an internal rate of return of 10%, without considering the possible positive external effects, and indicates that this rehabilitation could mean a substantial increase, of approximately 7%, in the country's irrigated land.

In this way, the descending spiral of poverty and the deterioration of resources could be reversed and the quality of life of the highland peasant communities markedly improved.

Source: Nicolo Gligo, "La complejidad campesina en ecosistemas andinos de altura: Bases para políticas de desarrollo", *Sobrevivencia campesina en ecosistemas de altura* (E/ECLAC/G.1267), vol. I, Santiago, Chile, 1983. United Nations publication, Sales No. S.83.II.G.31, vol. I; and Efraín González de Olarte, *Estudio de factibilidad de un proyecto nacional de desarrollo en áreas de recuperación de andenes en el Perú* (LC/R.747), Santiago, Chile, ECLAC, 1989.

Chile provide an example of such populations.

The "forest aborigines", who constitute a tribal culture of limited size and are in danger of extinction as their habitat is destroyed and they are exposed to deadly diseases.

The following considerations apply mostly to the first two categories, although many of the points raised also pertain to the third category.

Special treatment should be given to the formulation of social policies relating to the indigenous population of countries for various reasons of a socioeconomic, demographic and cultural nature and because of considerations based on human rights. From the demographic point of view, it is estimated that the region's indigenous population includes close to 50 million persons. This is in fact an underestimation of the total indigenous population, since the criterion used to define the term "indigenous population" is based on cultural considerations, such as the language spoken. This criterion does not take into account the fact that because of the expansion of primary education and other reasons of a "practical" nature (incorporation of the sector into the market), many indigenous people frequently now use the national language. It is estimated that many young people maintain the cultural traditions of their people although they may not use their mother tongue. Available estimates indicate that indigenous people make up close to 10% of the total population of the region; however, in some countries this figure is well above 50%. In many of those countries, especially in the Andean subregion, it is impossible to imagine rural development policies which do not centre around the indigenous population, which makes up about 80% of their rural population.

In the majority of cases, indigenous people live in much worse conditions of poverty than the rest of society, and their settlements are located in highly degraded areas. Recent studies show that, although there is great diversity in this connection, this segment of the population is subject to an extremely high infant mortality rate, which in some cases exceeds 150 for every thousand live births; in addition, the illiteracy rates for it are higher than those for the other population segments. For example, the 1976 census for Bolivia shows that about 98% of the monolingual indigenous inhabitants were illiterate, and their fertility rates were high. As though this were not enough, the environment in which they live is frequently characterized by unhealthful environmental conditions in that potable water and an adequate system of human waste disposal are not available to them.

In this stratum of the population, most sectors are not integrated into the rest of society in that their patterns of socialization do not conform to those adhered to elsewhere; and they lack formal education facilities, the natural resources and organizational capabilities needed to make their demands known. They are living in a form of poverty which tends to recur generation after generation. Another factor which distinguishes indigenous communities is the culture to which they belong. It sets up barriers which make it more difficult for them to take part in the benefits of development and frequently gives rise to ethnic discrimination.

The great majority of these peoples have a very special relationship with the land, which makes them potential allies in all efforts to protect the environment. Indigenous peoples, most of whom inhabit rural areas or territorial reserves, must subsist on what they can produce there. This is even more true of those who live in forests. The preservation of their very identity depends on their ties to the earth. When indigenous people participate in activities which are detrimental to the environment, such as the plundering of forests in new agricultural frontier areas, this is generally due to their having been expelled from their native soil, which forces them to join groups engaged in the process of land settlement.

Some consensus now exists as to what criteria should be taken into account in formulating development policies geared to the needs of indigenous populations. A basic criterion is that of promoting the enrichment of their culture and the strengthening of their identity. The organizational structures of indigenous communities may help enormously to promote sustainable development programmes since they can mobilize the mystique and solidarity which an indigenous population feels for its institutions and leaders. It is through these organizations that technological progress can be made both in restoring the quality of the earth and in looking for new ways of making use of biological diversity, combining traditional know-how with contemporary scientific progress. It would therefore seem advisable to provide communities with the financial and technical resources they need to increase their production capacity (crop-raising, cottage industries and trade). This would increase their employment opportunities and keep them from falling apart as a people.

With regard to the spoken language, the most practical solution –bilingualism– is already being applied out of necessity. Now explicit government policies are needed so that from childhood on a country's indigenous population may learn both its mother tongue and the national language, which would enable it to preserve its traditions and while at the same time becoming part of the development movement. In short, what is needed is to combine the natural relationship of these peoples to their environment –their ties to the earth, which are an essential part of their culture– with modern technologies which do not violate their lifestyle.

4. Poverty and capital formation

Much poverty is the result of difficulties in accumulating capital. The poor are characterized by a low saving rate and level of investment and by being at a net disadvantage in their capacity to accumulate physical and financial capital. Nevertheless their position with regard to other forms of capital may have some positive aspects.

For this reason, if the poor sectors of society are to accede in a balanced manner to the various kinds of capital which contribute to development, at least two aspects of the problem must be taken into account: i) the nature of the various kinds of capital and their relationship with poor people and ii) the relative advantages of forming those kinds of capital.

As regards natural capital, it should be noted that poor people live in areas where natural resources are scarce and the environment has greatly deteriorated. As stated above, this deterioration is the result of the displacement of their activities to areas where natural capital is not very highly regarded (having minimum available and obtainable rent) or where other forms of capital are virtually absent. This displacement leads to a vicious circle of poverty ("destroy and survive"). The lower incomes are, the more short-term oriented consumer choices will become because of immediate need. Thus peasants, who often live at subsistence level on low-yield land, will continue to use that land regardless of the degree to which it has deteriorated. It would be hard to expect land

(defined by peasants as a consumer good) to become a capital good. Overexploitation of that land will, however, lower its productivity, causing poverty to increase.

The depredation of natural capital also affects patterns of consumption and the net availability of alternative resources. For example, a low-income family meets its energy needs by using firewood, coal or agricultural waste. This puts pressure on woodlands with well-known ecological consequences (changes in climate, erosion, sedimentation). When agricultural waste is burned –instead of being used to protect and improve the structure of cultivable soil–, an additional drop in productivity occurs as a direct consequence of the loss of the organic material from the soil which plays an important and beneficial role in moisture retention and ventilation, *inter alia*. This drop in productivity is reflected in a steady decline in incomes and well-being, and poverty increases.

In urban areas the process of marginalization is similar. Poor people living outside the prevailing economic system experience serious difficulties in gaining access to the net benefits yielded by either formal producer or consumer markets and in gaining access to the income generated by public investment in infrastructure. In addition they live in urban areas where the available resources (water, land) are very limited. The low value placed on these resources is related directly to their quality and to the quality of the environment in general (air, drinking water and sanitation services, housing).

As for financial capital, the comparative advantages of the poor with respect to its formation are minimal. The poor sectors of most economies of the region are unlikely to gain access to capital markets or opportunities for sustained formation. It is also obvious that financial institutions (formal or informal) are much more highly developed in urban areas than in the rural sector. The capacity to form capital in some rural areas is increasing thanks to the development of informal financial institutions. This does not mean that access to these financial markets or the use of available capital do not come at a high cost, which in some cases may be classified as usurious. In both rural and urban financial arrangements, the lack of collateral guarantees (such as ownership of real estate) or inadequacies in institutional machinery (such as provisions for payment in kind or credit facilities), has limited the ability of poor people to form financial capital.

As for physical capital, the ability to accumulate it also depends on where poor families live. In urban areas, the rates of accumulation of physical capital are minimal, and can be changed only by factors outside the economic and social sphere of the poor sector. This results in intervention by the government, which provides public services related to housing, drinking water, sanitation, the paving of roads, etc. When no physical capital is accumulated, a significant number of poor people are left in inhuman living conditions, which will grow worse as competition for land, an extremely scarce resource in large urban concentrations, increases. In rural areas, the formation of physical capital is important for a different reason: it determines the degree of access to development, including access to electrification, road construction, irrigation works, hospitals, marketing centres and other facilities.

The indivisibility of physical capital is central to the process of accumulation. Hospital, road and, up to a certain point, housing, water and sanitation are indivisible in terms of the per capita consumption of the poor. Thus, there are no incentives for them to invest their meagre savings. One way of remedying this problem has been to increase the efficiency of community organizations, which are essential to the accumulation of physical capital, such as rural roads, drinking water supplies and irrigation infrastructure, and to the provision of proper management in order to avoid depredation. The community, as a unit of account in the formation and use of physical capital, is more than the sum of its parts. This fact, which seems so obvious, is essential to an understanding of the potential benefits of other forms of capital.

Institutional and cultural capital (the rules and regulations governing decision-making systems) are very important for the total eradication of poverty. Poor families posses a significant amount of institutional and cultural heritage or capital. In spite of this, most development programmes ignore the existence of these kinds of capital or substitute other kinds of capital for them. Failure to recognize the existence and value of the institutional capital in the hands of the poor is the main cause of the failure of many development programmes. This kind of capital is replaced in two different ways. First of all, it is replaced through systems of education which are out of touch with reality and with the cultural and institutional heritage of poor people. The second way is through the creation of development organizations as substitutes for those which already exist.

The following features characterize the institutional capital of poor people, to which due consideration should be given:

It is not without value: on the contrary, it has a tremendous amount of economic as well as social and environmental significance.

Most of the institutions involved are situated outside of the formal market structure.

Its regulatory structure is fairly complex and reflects the characteristics of a society on which different social systems (indigenous, colonial, post colonial, peasant, etc.) have been superimposed.

Many of the traditional systems of production used by indigenous groups are not sustainable in terms of the management of some natural resources.

The considerations presented above lead to a number of conclusions. First, poverty is a complex problem, whose solution does not consist merely in increasing peoples capacity to sell their labour on existing markets. This solution, in which poverty is viewed as a "non-qualified" input, is not only erroneous but is also counterproductive. Improving the abilities associated with the sale of the services of workers is only one of the requirements needed to relieve poverty, but taken in isolation, it does not suffice. Secondly, poverty will not be eradicated unless poor people are given a better chance to accumulate capital. Increasing only one or two kinds of capital will not save people from poverty. Consideration must be given to the comparative advantages of poor people in all spheres of accumulation. Finally, neither institutional nor natural capital has so far been used effectively in programmes to combat poverty.

5. The relationship between natural capital formation and poverty

There is some regional evidence that poor people have a tremendous capacity for accumulating natural capital. It has been shown that the return to inputs which have so far been regarded as "unproductive", when placed in the hands of the poor, may be increased by implementing certain programmes in areas where natural resources exist. The once inevitable trade-offs between growth, equity and sustainable development are no longer so. On the contrary, equity programmes aimed at the development or management of natural resources are showing great potential in the countries of the region. Forestry programmes with a "social" dimension, small-scale fish hatchery and fishery projects and the development of small-scale livestock-raising (in areas suitable for grazing) are three ways in which the poor can be helped to accumulate capital.

Forestry programmes have been of help to small farmers and even landless peasants. The success of such programmes has been due to the fact that the trees planted required little space, the species sown normally met their growth targets and, in some cases, little maintenance was required. Moreover, the amount of money or other forms of input required for such projects is also minimal. After a few years, the trees begin to represent an enormously important form of capital in the lives of poor families since they are not only a source of income (sales to sawmills) but also provide shade, food for livestock and a source of supply of firewood, in addition to their other advantages.

Fish hatcheries also provide low-income sectors with a means of accumulating capital. With proper design and technology, in most cases such projects can be implemented on any scale; nor do they compete for arable or any other kind of land. In fact, many of these are carried out on land which can be used in no other way, such as flood plains or wasteland. In a number of countries of the region, including Panama, fish hatchery programmes have yielded a net profit for poor families and for isolated communities in mountain areas. The productive use of water is a logical and relatively easy step to take by people living in rural areas. In cases where there have been problems in obtaining loans or financing, the fish ponds have been used as collaterals. Just as forestry programmes yield large profits in terms of energy (firewood and coal), fish hatcheries are very profitable in terms of nutrition.

Small-scale livestock-raising, in either open or closed areas, has yielded significant benefits for thousands of families in the region in terms of income, nutrition (milk) and environment (protection of grasslands). In these programmes, positive results may be observed in the areas of growth, equity and sustainable environmental development. In some cases, the animals raised are also used for transport, farm work and other pursuits typical of a farm region. Milk production helps to improve nutrition while increasing the short-term availability of cash.

6. Technology and poverty

All the ways in which the poor can accumulate capital depend on the availability of technology. Technologies involving the intensive use of physical capital require advance capital formation to an extent which is beyond the possibilities of the poorest people. On the other hand, the application of technologies which facilitate the accumulation of capital through the use of labour can initiate a process capable of breaking the poverty cycle.

In addition, the increased application of advanced technologies which enable human, physical and natural resources to be used to enhance sustainability makes it easier to raise the real incomes of all the members of the community. In this way, technological development makes a decisive contribution to sustainable development. This subject will be considered in the following chapter.

Notes

[1] ECLAC, *Magnitud de la pobreza en América Latina en los años ochenta* (LC/G.1653-P), Santiago, Chile, March 1991.

[2] *Ibid.*, annex 2.

[3] PREALC, *Empleo y equidad: desafío de los 90*, Documento de Trabajo series, No. 354, Santiago, Chile, October 1990.

Chapter VI

TECHNICAL PROGRESS, COMPETITIVENESS AND SUSTAINABLE DEVELOPMENT *

The incorporation and dissemination of technical progress helps to harmonize the objectives of international competitiveness with those of sustainable development. In Latin America and the Caribbean sustainable development has a bearing not only on the quality of life but also, and very much more so, on the standard of living of the population.

1. Introduction

International competitiveness based increasingly on the incorporation and dissemination of technical progress in a context in which great economic and political value is attached to environmentally sustainable development in many parts of the world will probably be one of the hallmarks of the 1990s. The close links between these factors, which have only recently begun to be perceived, are explored in this chapter.

In this connection, it is necessary to:

Examine the nature of the growing international competition and technical progress and their effects on sustainable development in Latin America and the Caribbean.

Consider the situation of the region in the international context in the light of its own particular natural resources and their development and the kind of entrepreneurial leadership which now exists.

Assess the relationship between international competition, technical progress and sustainable development on the basis of the link which exists between energy and changing production patterns. This link is the mainstay of that relationship, and by studying it it will be possible to compare the situation in Latin America and the Caribbean with that in the other regions of the world.

Describe trends in the market for "environment-related" technical goods and services, assessing the impact of sustainable development on the industrial sector, i.e., the way in which industry and environment interact.

2. The convergence of international competitiveness, technical progress and sustainable development

International markets are now clearly in the process of globalization and regionalization. This process has been set into motion by a notable decrease in communications and transport costs, by the ability of some nations to incorporate

* For a more detailed study of these topics, see ECLAC, *Tecnología, competitividad y sustentabilidad* (LC/L.608), January 1991. (Document prepared by the ECLAC/UNIDO Industry and Technology Division.)

technological progress and to disseminate it through their system of production, by entrepreneurship and by the incorporation of additional countries, particularly countries in South-East Asia, into the international market.

Globalization and regionalization depend on the ability to compete in international markets, an ability which is increasingly based on the capabilities of individual entrepreneurs and countries to incorporate technical progress and disseminate it through the system of production of goods and services. This is known as genuine or structural competitiveness.[1] One of its most salient characteristics is an increase in the amount of resources devoted to research and development both in the industrialized countries and in the newly industrialized countries which are now being successfully brought into the process of the globalization of markets.

In spite of this, however, it has proved impossible to exceed the growth rate of productivity recorded in the 1950s and 1960s. One possible explanation is that the emerging technological paradigm requires that enterprises, institutions and policy be so thoroughly overhauled that the effects of the new pattern will be felt only to the extent that these changes actually occur.

These new approaches to organization are aimed at enhancing flexibility in the production process and at cutting the costs of production, both of which are reflected in the quality of the goods produced –the factor on which today's competitiveness is based. The concepts of just-in-time inventory, zero defect and total quality control relate to this phenomenon; in order to use these techniques, closer links must be formed among suppliers, producers and users, something which has been made possible thanks to the rapid progress being made in the field of information technology.

In addition, the design, production, distribution and marketing processes make it possible to shorten the time required to respond to new market demands and provide the incentive for a rapid increase in the formation of alliances among enterprises of different countries and sectors.

The growing importance of design accompanied by automatization in production, distribution and marketing is rapidly eroding the comparative advantage of cheap labour. Competitiveness today is based on other factors, including the quality of the goods and services produced, the rapidity and reliability of their delivery and the capacity to diversify them as required by consumers in the industrialized countries.

The comparative advantage based on the availability of natural resources is also experiencing erosion. The effort to save energy in the industrialized countries since 1973 affects product design, manufacturing processes, transport systems and the nature of household appliances. This is the most visible effect of the phenomenon, which has many other aspects. It is in fact technological development and international competitiveness which make it possible first to develop synthetic products and introduce new materials and, secondly, to enhance efficiency in the use and saving of raw materials.

Environmental concerns play no small role in the above-mentioned trends. Sustainable development has in fact become a universally recognized value. The imperative of environmental sustainability has given rise to additional costs and also to a tremendous effort in the realm of technological innovation aimed precisely at counteracting negative effects on the environment and at increasing the ability to compete. In future the links between technical progress in the realm of protecting the environment on the one hand and international competitiveness on the other will be increasingly close.

3. Consequences for Latin America and the Caribbean

The comparative advantages of the past, which were responsible for a tremendous boom in exports, will be challenged in the next few years if certain developments occur (a decline of demand, the emergence of new competitors, the need for environmental-protection regulations or an increase in remunerations and in the tax burden). In particular, the traditional growth strategy based on intensive use of natural resources (a strategy which was stressed in the 1980s because of the need to service the external debt) has been subject to increasing criticism since, although it does make it possible to increase the short-term growth rate, various environmental costs may be felt with even greater force in the medium term, as has, in fact, been the experience of the region in recent years (see box VI-1).

Box VI-1
PROJECTS IN PEMEX'S ECOLOGICAL PACKAGE

Petróleos Mexicanos (PEMEX) has identified eight investment projects as being strategic priority projects, whose specific purpose is to supply fuels of internationally recognized ecological quality at a cost of US$1 034 000 000; these are products aimed at reducing pollution caused by the combustion of gasoline, diesel fuel and fuel oil and at cutting down on emissions of sulfur from the Eighteenth of March Refinery. The main areas of action in PEMEX's ecological package include:

1) Gasoline. PEMEX has set itself the goal of raising the octane content of the gasolines it produces without using tetraethyl lead and adding oxygenated components to them in order to ensure fuller and more efficient combustion. To this end, the enterprise has plans to reconvert its naphtha reformers, replacing the process of semiregeneration with one of continuous regeneration in seven of its leading refineries; it also plans to install three pentane and hexane isomerizing plants and six plants producing oxygenated compounds (TAME, MTBE and methanol). The cost implications of the projects relating to gasoline production are US$413.4 million –the highest in the "package".

2) Diesel fuel. This project envisages the installation of four plants for the hydrodesulfurization of diesel oil to obtain a fuel of internationally recognized ecological standard, by reducing its sulfur content from its present range of 2% to a range of 0.10%. The project will cost US$200 million.

3) Fuel oil. Here too a product of internationally recognized ecological quality is being sought, by reducing its present sulfur content of 4% to 0.8%. This project involves the construction of a large number of plants for such processes as the hydrotreatment of waste, the generation of hydrogen, fractionation, polymerization, gas sweetening and sulfur recovery. The cost implications of the investments involved amount to US$402.9 million.

4) Sulfur recovery. This project will be carried out in the Eighteenth of March Refinery, the only PEMEX operation in the Metropolitan Area of Mexico City and calls for both the modernization of the present recovery unit and the installation of a second unit of the same type in order to give the process greater reliability. This component of the ecological package, in combination with the installation of facilities for the recovery and control of hydrocarbon vapors in supply and distribution depots, calls for a total investment of US$17.7 million.

It should be stressed that the projects in the "package", which represent a total investment of US$1 034 000 000, imply a large demand for capital goods, especially in connection with traditional products of boilermaking, equipment for heat exchange (interchangers, reboilers, coolers, heaters, condensers), pumps and compressors, reactors and distillation towers, regenerators and turbo-machinery. This demand is expected to have a positive impact on the national capital goods industry, engineering firms and employment in manufacturing.

The co-ordination of and follow-up on the action needed to give shape to the projects in the package (in a period of between 18 and 48 months) is in the hands of the unit responsible for the executive co-ordination of the ecological package; this unit is under the management of a group of associates consisting of members of the Office of the Deputy Director of Petrochemicals and of the Office of the Deputy Director of Industrial Transformation (both of which are on the second level in the company hierarchy). The task of executive co-ordination of the ecological package (third level in the hierarchy) is divided into two sections, one dealing with sulfur reduction projects and the other with gasoline improvement projects.

In general, these projects are not aimed so much at raising production capacity as at producing fuels of the same quality of fuel as those now produced, but with ecological components of the highest international standard. In spite of this, and also of the fact that it will no longer be possible to make the maximum income from domestic sales of fuels and the production of tetraethyl lead will be reduced considerably, it is estimated that the rates of return of all the projects will be positive, although the level of those rates would seem to indicate that the projects might not be embarked upon on the basis of commercial considerations alone. Thus, PEMEX is making a substantial effort which indicates its commitment to cleaning up the environment of Mexico City.

Moreover, although there is no consensus on the future scenario concerning the transfer of technology to the developing countries, there are indications of growing technological protectionism on the part of the industrialized countries.

These two developments –the erosion of the traditional competitive advantages on the one hand and the emergence of technological protectionism on the other taken in combination with a third factor of growing importance– "environmental protection" –provide the sustainable development strategy of the countries of the region with a difficult task. This situation will represent a threat to the markets for export which have already been conquered and even to potential markets unless a way can be found to move ahead fast enough in the technological field.

It is within this framework that Latin America and the Caribbean have adopted the goal of enhancing their competitiveness and raising the standard of living of their population –a goal which favours the incorporation and dissemination of technical progress in all activities relating to the production of goods and services.

Within a context of greater technological protectionism and increased demand for technology, the main ways of acquiring access to new techniques will undoubtedly be by importing equipment and signing of agreements between enterprises, which will involve some traditional or new form of direct investment. Alliances between national and international enterprises will become increasingly important as channels for the transfer of technology.

4. Technology, competitiveness and natural resources: relative position of Latin America and the Caribbean

4.1 International insertion and natural resources

As in the rest of the world, the economic concepts which prevailed in the region were based on the assumption that natural resources would be forever available and that the environment as a whole was all but infinite. Natural resources were regarded as a frontier to be conquered, and the insertion of the region in the international economy was based on that idea, which is directly reflected in the type of entrepreneurial leadership which characterizes the region.

In Latin America and the Caribbean, most of this entrepreneurial leadership is located in the realm of natural resources, processed or raw. As table VI-1 shows, in countries such as Argentina, Chile and Venezuela 75% or more of the 10 largest enterprises, whose sales represent close to 30% of GDP of those countries, are found in natural-resource-based sectors. In Brazil and Mexico, the two largest countries in the region, the sales of the 10 biggest enterprises amount to the equivalent of 15% of GDP, and close to 60% of those sales are concentrated in sectors associated with natural resources.

The basic difference between Latin America and certain OECD countries which are heavily endowed with natural resources is that, in those countries, industrialization is to a large extent supported by the processing of these resources. This is reflected in the capacity of such countries to develop technologies conducive to the integral use of their natural resources. This characteristic of industrialization directly favours the capacity of those countries not only to provide impetus for a new economic perspective in which technical progress, natural resources and environment are taken into account but also, and even more important, to embark on a broad spectrum of technological innovations.

During the 1980s, some of the leading enterprises in Latin America and the Caribbean learned this lesson and began to develop broad-based programmes in the field of environmental sustainability.

4.2 Competitiveness and natural resources in the OECD market

In addition to being the largest and fastest growing market in the world today, the market made up of the member countries of OECD also has the strictest environmental standards, and compliance with them may soon become a prerequisite for entry into the market.

Over the past decade the structure of imports of the OECD countries has been changed significantly. Natural resources, fuels and manufactures based on natural resources are showing a tendency to lose their share in the market, while manufactures not based on natural resources are showing a marked increase.

Care should be taken, however, not to underestimate the importance attributed by the OECD countries to their own domestic markets and available natural resources in defining their productive and technological paradigms in a way that is compatible with their own particular preferences and environmental needs. One important consequence of this may be the already perceptible emergence of protectionist barriers raised on the assumption that other countries have failed to comply with environmental standards relating to products, manufacturing processes and raw materials. These barriers may seriously affect some products in which natural resources play an important role. Since exports based on natural resources account for a large share in Latin America and the Caribbean, this may turn out to be a decisive issue.

It may be assumed that some of the region's exports to developed countries will remain exempt from environmental requirements, particularly in the case of exports which do not compete with domestic products (and are therefore subjected to less protectionist pressure) or exports to low-income consumers (who are not so willing to absorb cost increases stemming from environmental protection).

The important thing is that the environmental dimension has become a significant variable in any strategy relating to exports to industrial countries, in the first place because the need for environmental protection has now become a requirement which affects a large and potentially larger share of the demand of those countries and, in the second place, because environmental

Table VI-1

LATIN AMERICA: PERCENTAGE DISTRIBUTION OF THE SALES OF THE 10 LEADING ENTERPRISES IN SELECTED COUNTRIES, 1989

	Latin America	Argentina	Brazil	Mexico	Chile	Colombia	Peru	Venezuela
Total	100	100	100	100	100	100	100	100
Natural resources (not including petroleum)	13.0	5.4	13.0	...	59.6	...	44.8	14.3
Petroleum	65.9	57.9	39.3	56.3	24.8	50.8	36.5	71.5
Manufactures								
- Based on natural resources	4.9	12.4	14.6	3.5	11.9	21.2	5.1	4.5
- Not based on natural resources	11.3	5.4	18.5	26.5	...	6.0	...	1.6
- (Automotive industry)	4.4	5.4	7.2	26.5	...	6.0	...	...
- (Capital goods)	...	...	113	...	...	...	...	...
Other sectors	4.9	19.2	14.6	13.7	3.7	22.0	13.6	8.1
Sales of 10 largest enterprises/GDP	10.7	31.4	14.6	14.7	38.2	14.9	20.9	29.5

Source: Joint ECLAC/UNIDO Industry and Technology Division, on the basis of data obtained from *América Economía*, No. 44, October 1990. The figures relating to GDP were taken from World Bank, *Development Indicators*, vol. IX, No. 37, 26 September 1990.

requirements differ enormously from country to country and are frequently changed; so it is becoming necessary to keep an eye on them in order to ensure permanent access to the OECD market; and finally because the growing value which society attaches to environmental requirements, even when the importing country does not explicitly insist on them, means that they can be turned into an instrument for differentiating between products, which is a particularly useful device in markets with relatively steady demand.

It is also true that the requirements imposed by developed countries do not eliminate the environmental problem caused by externalities linked to the production process (e.g., air or water pollution at the production site). Some transnational corporations have moved to developing countries in order to avoid the costs relating to environmental regulations in developed countries although the goods they produce may be in compliance with environmental requirements of the importing countries. When this happens, the developed countries are "exporting their environment" with diverse consequences. However, although the production processes used by firms which have relocated may not meet the requirements of their home country, they sometimes damage the environment less than the processes used by national enterprises. In such cases, the net result of the relocation may even be positive for the environment of the recipient country. It is still necessary, however, to monitor these relocation processes very closely.

5. Technology, competitiveness and environmental sustainability: The energy system

Perhaps the clearest indication of the links between technological change, competitiveness and sustainability is provided by the changes experienced by the energy/production system. The technological pattern which has been emerging since the 1970s includes –among other factors which make it different from the pattern which preceded it– high-cost energy and requirements relating to environmental sustainability. In order to adapt to the new conditions, it was necessary to introduce technical changes in the energy/production system with a view to meeting the new, stricter requirements in the areas of international competitiveness and environmental sustainability. The industrialized countries led the way in this effort to overhaul production patterns, while in the Latin American and Caribbean region inertia against it was again manifested at the level of production and technology. The region cannot postpone the task of catching up in those areas in the 1990s.

5.1 *The energy crisis and changing production patterns*

In recent decades the world energy system has been profoundly affected by the oil shocks of 1973 and 1979 (the effects of the crisis in the Gulf are still not known) and the slowdown in the growth of the world economy.

Up until the first oil crisis, an increase in the consumption of energy was regarded as an essential requirement for economic growth, and it was felt that the use of energy produced on a large scale would increase as economies became more sophisticated.

The slowdown in energy consumption as the OECD countries' pattern of production changes is the result, first of all, of an attempt to make their economies less vulnerable. Secondly, it is caused by the need to cope with more intense competition in the realm of international trade and finally it comes in response to a wish to increase environmental sustainability. In order to meet that goal, the OECD countries introduced energy-efficient technologies, diversified their sources of energy supply and made their energy system more flexible.

Thus, since the 1970s, energy intensity (the ratio between the final consumption of energy and GDP) has been experiencing a significant decline in the industrialized countries not only because of the introduction of technological changes but also due to the moderate growth rates of energy-intensive industries (steel, heavy industry in the chemical sector, non-ferrous metallurgy,

Table VI-2

SELECTED OECD COUNTRIES AND LATIN AMERICA: ENERGY-INTENSITY TRENDS

Indicators	Years	Countries				
		United States	Japan	France	Fed.Rep. of Germany	Latin America
Energy intensity	1970	142	151	137	125	102
in terms of GDP	1973	156	163	138	124	100
(1985=100)	1981	121	112	105	103	97
	1986	97	99	98	103	98
	1987	96	97	98	99	100
Energy intensity in	1970	168	193	210	157	84
terms of industrial	1973	168	190	165	147	77
production	1981	133	119	115	112	89
(1985=100)	1986	94	93	95	95	94
	1987	96	91	93	92	101

Source: Joint ECLAC/UNIDO Industry and Technology Division. Data for Latin America was compiled on the basis of information obtained from OLADE.

cement, etc.) in contrast with the dramatic expansion of technology-intensive industries.

Although the methodology of separating the impact of energy saving technologies from the impact of structural change is difficult, it is estimated that technological innovation accounts for between 66% and 75% of the drop in energy intensity. Table VI-2 summarizes the overall energy-intensity trends in some OECD countries and in Latin America.

These figures reflect the results of policies implemented by OECD countries to promote the efficient use of energy and natural resources. The energy-intensity indexes for Latin America show no change whatsoever at the level of the economy as a whole but do denote an increase in the energy intensity of industry.

5.2 Energy and its effects on the environment

Medium- and long-term environmental problems of universal concern include several which are directly related to energy use. Some of these have an impact at national or international level, as is the case of the greenhouse effect, the destruction of the ozone layer, deforestation and desertification, acid rain and the disposal of nuclear waste.

In addition to the problems just mentioned, there are others of a more local but equally important nature, including population migration; flooding of croplands and climatic changes caused by large hydroelectric power plants; the exploitation of mineral deposits in a way which causes soil deterioration, water pollution and hydrogeological alterations; and nuclear accidents, pipeline explosions and oil spills at sea (see box VI-2).

Supplying energy to areas where it is in short supply or of unsatisfactory quality makes it possible to make progress in such areas as the creation of new productive activities, the improvement of the productivity of existing activities and the introduction of changes in the structure of employment and the distribution of income. Properly conceived hydroelectric power projects make it possible to recover deteriorated

Box VI-2
THE ENVIRONMENTAL ACTIVITIES OF PETROLEOS DE VENEZUELA, S.A.

As has happened in the case of other oil companies, environmental concerns have only recently begun to be taken into account in conducting the routine activities of Petróleos de Venezuela, S.A. (PDVSA). Environmental activities have, however, become increasingly important as is shown, for example, by the creation of an office for environmental management in the parent company and in each of its subsidiaries, a committee on environmental affairs which operates between subsidiaries to co-ordinate their activities and, finally, an ecological and environmental research office within the Venezuelan Technological Institute of Petroleum (INTEVEP), the PDVSA subsidiary for research and development. PDVSA plans to invest close to US$142 million in environmental affairs in 1991.

PDVSA activities in connection with the environment are centred around two major concerns –first, production processes and their impact on the environment and second, products and their conformity to the prevailing standards and specifications in domestic and external markets.

Oversight and improvement of production processes

The company's early environmental efforts with regard to its production processes related to the growing awareness in Venezuela of the danger of exhausting its petroleum resources. As soon as this danger began to be felt, programmes designed to save oil resources at national level and to conduct an intensive search for additional energy sources or energy alternatives began to be devised. In this connection, mention should be made of the efforts to explore the Orinoco bituminous belt and the attempts to replace oil by gas in domestic consumption. The considerable energy resources discovered in the Orinoco region were responsible for increasing PDVSA's concern for the environment, since the deposits found contained primarily extra-heavy crudes with a high percentage sulfur (2%-4%), nickel and vanadium and therefore could not be refined in conventional plants and increase the danger to the environment.

More recently, the bulk of the company's efforts were directed towards minimizing the environmental impact of its production processes, with special emphasis placed on the adoption of preventive measures. These efforts took the form of environmental impact assessments and periodic inspections aimed at minimizing the impact of the petroleum sector on the environment. The first environmental impact assessment concerned was carried out in 1979 for the purpose of analysing the possible effects of developing the petroleum resources in the Orinoco area, a region which at that time, in spite of the fact that its remote geographical location made access to it difficult, was already regarded as Venezuela's main source of energy for the near future. Environmental impact assessments similar to the one referred to have become common since then, and the company has made them requisite to any new or expanded project. Since 1979 PDVSA has conducted 30 studies of this kind.

In 1986 the company strengthened its preventive maintenance programmes by introducing routine environmental inspections for the purpose of ensuring compliance with periodically updated standards of security, in the hope of reducing the risk of accidents. The main objective is to prevent spills of toxic products by carrying out regular technical inspections, installing protection systems and replacing and repairing equipment in time. A special effort has been made to limit the danger of spills caused by corrosion by implementing a programme for the specific purpose of cleaning and replacing used tanks in the national system for hydrocarbon distribution and storage.

Another form of preventive action concerns the introduction of new, demonstrably cleaner, technologies in the production processes. One of the most promising programmes in this respect is that for the incorporation in petrochemical plants of new technologies which will make it possible to eliminate the use of mercury in the production of sodium hydroxide. New processing techniques have been introduced in the leading refineries with a view to reducing harmful atmospheric emissions. This includes, in particular, the installation of gas desulfurizing plants in all refineries. The contribution made by INTEVEP to the design of these new technologies has been significant, particularly in the creation of new catalyzers for the demetalization of crudes and the reduction of the levels of nickel and vanadium in the corresponding waste.

river basins, to divert water resources for use as drinking water and/or the irrigation of croplands and to reduce desertification and erosion.

Unless the proper precautions are taken, however, the construction of hydroelectric dams will affect both the biophysical and the social environment involved; the use of energy in urban transport or of fossil fuels in industry will cause pollution whose intensity will depend on the technology used, the quality of the fuels consumed and the degree of maintenance of the equipment; defects in the thermal quality of dwellings and in cooking and heating appliances will seriously affect the quality of life and the health of large sectors of the population (see box VI-3). As for transport, inefficient or poorly designed transport systems will pollute the environment, especially in metropolitan areas.

Box VI-3
ENVIRONMENTAL IMPACT OF DIFFERENT ENERGY SOURCES

Although this schematic presentation has certain limitations as to the scope and relative importance of the environmental impact had by various energy sources, it nevertheless provides an overall view of the close links which exist between energy and the environment and draws attention to the different effects of the various sources at different stages in their exploitation, from extraction of the energy resource to disposal of the waste produced.

Brief comments are made below concerning the more far-reaching of those effects. The first sector considered is the coal industry, since coal seems to be the energy source which has the most adverse impact on the environment.

– Resource extraction

The exploitation of opencast coal mines alters the topography of their sites and deteriorates the land under exploitation.

Underground mines weaken the surface ground, causing problems in connection with roads, bridges and other structures built above the mines.

Mining generates waste, which must be deposited on nearby land so that it cannot be used for farming.

– Resource processing

The pulverization of coal generates a large number of particles, which increases the danger of fires and explosions. The gasification of coal pollutes waste water through the condensation of the tars produced.

Electric power generation

The combustion of coal produces flying particles and acid rain and contributes more than the burning of any other fuel to worsening the greenhouse effect.

– Waste disposal

The ashes produced by the combustion of coal become flying particles. Coal ash must be deposited on extensive sites, and this may limit the possibility of putting them to agricultural use.

As for petroleum, its most adverse impact relates to acid rain, which results from electric power generation. However, recent accidents during transportation, loading and unloading make it recommendable to place greater stress on the adverse effects which petroleum may have.

As for nuclear energy, it seems to be among those energy sources which cause least damage to the environment. The as yet unresolved problems of radioactive waste, accidents in nuclear power plants and the possible proliferation of nuclear weapons cannot, however, be ignored.

As for the generation of solar electric power, it must be noted that when this is done on a large scale, vast tracts of land are required for the installation of the necessary photovoltaic cells or solar collectors. This limits the possibility of using such land for farming.

As for ethanol and methanol, the following effects may be noted:

– Raw material extraction

Because the raw material needed to produce these alcohols is obtained from crops planted specifically for that purpose, the problems typical of any monoculture arise. The possibility of obtaining high yields from these crops depends on the use of fertilizers, weed killers and fungicides, normally composed of chemicals, with the consequent environmental effects.

– Raw material processing

Accidental methanol leaks may damage the sight or respiratory systems of refinery workers.

Finally, it should be noted that reference is made here only to the generation of electricity, with no mention made of the part played by its use, which contributes significantly to environmental deterioration. By the same token, it should also be noted that the possible adverse effects of large hydroelectric power stations have not been touched upon.

The industrialized world has led the way in the search for solutions to these problems; some of the solutions found are short-term solutions, while others apply to the longer term. Short-term solutions include: i) restricting emissions of CO_2, SO_2, and NO_x, ii) stressing the development of equipment designed to control "down-stream" emissions and iii) promoting the use of nuclear energy on grounds that it does not emit the kind of toxic oxides or gases which produce the greenhouse effect. Of the longer-term solutions, mention may be made of: i) international agreements on reduction of emissions; ii) the financing of research on as yet insufficiently defined problems, such as those related to the greenhouse effect; iii) the establishment of standards and regulations on levels of emissions and efficiency of equipment; iv) the development of sources which cause less pollution; and v) the initiation of energy conservation programmes.

In the context of Latin America, consideration should be given to those options which best respond to regional requirements, with thought being given to the availability of natural, technical and financial resources and to the need to achieve a sustainable form of development.

It is therefore of vital importance to make an effort to increase, on a permanent basis, the efficiency of energy use, for reasons both of international competitiveness and of sustainable development. Atmospheric pollution (sulphur and nitrogen oxides and carbon dioxide) varies almost proportionately with the energy intensity of any given activity. For each petroleum equivalent ton of fuel (PET) 2.4 to 4.5 tons of carbon dioxide (CO_2) are emitted. It takes one hectare of woodland to absorb the CO_2 produced by burning one ton of coal.

International experience shows that a powerful tool for obtaining lasting results from energy conservation and environmental protection programmes is the establishment of standards and regulations for users and suppliers (manufacturers of equipment, housing designers and builders, boilers and kiln operators, etc.).[2]

5.3 Energy and sustainable development in Latin America and the Caribbean

During the 1970s and part of the 1980s, Latin America and the Caribbean carried out large-scale projects in the energy sector, particularly with regard to the generation of electricity. The sector absorbed a high percentage –in some cases, over 50%– of the public investment of the countries of the region. According to the same source, the external debt of the sector amounts to close to US$80 billion, 60% of which corresponds to the electricity subsector.[3]

Since the growth forecast for the coming years will call for annual investments of between US$15 billion and US$20 billion, a difficult future for the region may be predicted. These difficulties are compounded by widespread financial deterioration of service enterprises owing to the recessive economic climate and the gap between public service rates and real costs, high losses of electricity, mismanagement and, in some cases, weaknesses in infrastructure and maintenance programmes.

In addition it must be noted that the alternatives consistent with sustainability are not always in accordance with the priorities of development financing agencies. Thus, between 1972 and 1990, more than 90% of energy financing from multilateral and bilateral development agencies was earmarked for large-scale projects, whereas only 1% was allocated to energy conservation projects.

Consequently, from the energy perspective, sustainable development calls for the adoption of the following measures in Latin America and the Caribbean:

i) formulation of an energy planning strategy from the standpoint of end use;

ii) implementation of a resolute, enterprising energy conservation policy;

iii) provision of energy to low-income sectors;

iv) adoption of energy options which minimize negative environmental impacts by maximizing the use of the least polluting renewable energy sources and fossil fuels;

v) in countries which must develop their energy sources on the basis of local resources whose exploitation damages the environment, such as coal and biomass, incorporation of technologies which keep their impact down to a minimum;

vi) solving of the problem of financing the sector;

vii) improvement of the management of service enterprises;

viii) strengthening of regional energy institutions; and

ix) laying of the foundations for the development of extensive regional and international co-operation in the sector.

As these measures suggest, an energy sector with enough sustainability to meet the development requirements of Latin America and the Caribbean can be achieved only by significantly reducing that sector's external vulnerability, considerably increasing the efficiency of energy production and use, helping to eliminate environmental degradation and minimizing any adverse environmental impact which might be caused by the region's energy system.

In view of the responsibility the industrialized countries bear for the deterioration of the environment down through history and the fact that it is impossible for the developing countries to tackle the energy and environmental problem in isolation, the industrialized countries should assume a large share of this task.

The countries of the region in conjunction with more highly developed countries and with support from international financial agencies should establish machinery for transferring their positive experiences in these fields, providing the technology, capital and manpower needed to ensure the massive dissemination of technologies which promote efficient use of energy and the application of renewable energies. The establishment of information centres on appropriate technologies for this purpose would be a highly positive step in this direction.[4]

International co-operation designed to meet these objectives will contribute more effectively to world environmental sustainability than the enforcement of carbonic acid gas quotas and/or restrictions on the exploitation of resources. It is also better than policies designed to promote intensive exploitation of natural resources in order to meet external debt commitments in the short term.

6. Industrialization, enterprises and environmental sustainability

6.1 Industrialization and sustainable development

In the developed countries it has become generally accepted that industrialization is an important factor in environmental deterioration. In Latin America and the Caribbean, with the usual differences from country to country and with omissions and variations, industrialization followed the same lines as in the developed countries. During the next decade it is expected to provide the key to changing production patterns, primarily because it is responsible for the incorporation and dissemination of technical progress but also because, in the new circumstances of the decade, it will be necessary for industrialization to go beyond the narrow sectoral margins within which it has been confined and form links with areas concerned with the exploitation of primary commodities and with services in order to integrate the production system and promote the gradual homogenization of the levels of productivity within it. Breaking away from sectoral boundaries is one of the keys to changing production patterns and to the new phase of industrialization.[5] In terms of environmental awareness, the region lags behind the developed countries. If it wishes to raise the standard of living of its population, however, it is vital for it to continue to promote industrialization in accordance with the new guidelines set, incorporating the experience of the industrialized countries in their efforts to co-ordinate growth, competitiveness and environmental sustainability.

In Latin America it may be observed that the sectors with the greatest environmental impact in the 1980s (consisting primarily in capital- and natural-resource-intensive industries which produce intermediate products, such as the petrochemical, paper and cellulose, metallurgy and iron and steel industries, petroleum refineries and tanneries) have increased their share in regional production, world production and exports to the OECD countries. During the same period, the share of these commodities in production in the developed countries decreased. If this trend continues without incorporating the technology needed to reduce or eliminate the adverse impact of these activities on the environment, localized situations of severe environmental deterioration similar to those found in developed countries may occur in the region.

In the developed countries it may be noted that, in the few cases for which systematic data exist,[6] technology designed to correct end-of-the-line environmental damage still predominates. The so-called "clean technologies" (for which no strict definition exists), which are based on innovations in equipment or processes designed to deal with environmental damage before the end of the production process, attract about 20% of the total environmental investment (as opposed to 80% for end-of-the-line technology). This percentage is considerably higher in certain sectors such as those engaged in the production of paper and paper products, chemicals, petroleum and transport equipment. The adoption of "clean technologies" would help to save on energy and raw materials, reduce waste, improve the quality of the goods produced, raise productivity and shorten the idle time and reduce the health hazards of workers. For all these reasons, it may be seen that the time it takes to recover investment is short. Nevertheless, the rate of dissemination of "clean technologies" is low even in the developed countries, which is usually attributed to problems of access to technological information and financing and to the peculiarities of the prevailing environmental regulations. They will probably begin to be used more widely in the next few years, however.

In the case of Latin America and the Caribbean, whose industry is in the process of change owing to the opening up of the economy, it is essential to design and implement a strategy aimed at the widespread introduction of "clean technologies" while profiting from the experience acquired in their countries of origin with regard to overcoming the obstacles to their dissemination. Special attention should be drawn to the importance of transferring these technologies from large enterprises to medium-sized and small firms for which market incentives may not be enough. We should not underestimate the magnitude of the efforts related to technological adaptation and innovation required before technologies already invented and available in industrialized countries can be used effectively.

The design of the strategy mentioned above calls for much research into the environmental effort now under way in areas relating to production in Latin America and the Caribbean, at the level of sectors, enterprises and legislation and with regard to the kind of incentives and resources which might be used to bring about behaviour in line with the objective sought on the part of the various protagonists (large public enterprises, national and foreign; small and medium-sized undertakings; regulatory agencies; engineering firms; lending institutions; training centres; institutions providing technological support and the mass communications media). The composite findings obtained, supplemented by information concerning institutions and enterprises in the developed countries which would be willing to co-operate could lead to realistic and effective programmes whose support and strength would come from resources available both in the region and in the developed countries (see chapter X).

6.2 *The organization of production and sustainable development: Trends*

At first, measures aimed at environmental conservation consisted of end-of-the-line treatment of industrial emissions and in sending waste products to landfills. Enterprises encountered few restrictions on the disposal of the waste they produced, but with the passage of time, serious problems arose as to its elimination.

In densely populated regions, the volume of solid waste of industrial and domestic origin has risen concomitantly with the growth of population and consumption, the result being a space problem in connection with the final destination of the waste produced. In addition, it has been shown that rubbish dumps constitute an additional source of pollution since they affect groundwater, soil and air quality in their vicinity and hence the welfare of the people (usually poor people) who live nearby.

In addition, some industrial waste is toxic and must be treated or put into special containers prior to its final disposal; and the cost of such end-of-the-line treatment has risen considerably.

The most common way of dealing with these problems is by means of technological innovation. Production processes are modified in order to reduce the production of waste as much as possible and also to change its composition, making it a less potent source of pollution. This is the "clean technologies" approach. Some of the more traditional forms it takes include making use of certain waste products which have completed their life cycle, the recirculation of by-products and waste water within industrial plants and the recycling of durable containers and recovery of used paper.

A growing number of industrial enterprises, particularly large enterprises, have set up units at various organizational levels which are responsible for dealing with environmental questions. Enterprises are also beginning to incorporate the environmental component systematically into their strategies and operational procedures. In addition, they try to shape the attitudes of their staff through technical training programmes. In some cases, the concern of enterprises for the environment even extends into the local community in their vicinity, for the prevention of any kind of hazard, including health hazards. When this happens, enterprises act as centres in which people learn how to meet the environmental challenges of the coming decades.

An appropriate technological solution to some pollution problems has not yet been found, for reasons of cost or effectiveness or for other reasons. The determination shown by the authorities of some countries to deal with these problems has, however, done much to stimulate a high degree of development and technological innovation. In this connection, small- and medium-sized firms are playing a leading role in the development of new environmental technologies and in their commercial application.

6.3 The market for goods and services for environmental protection

Within the scenario described above, a new "environment-related" goods and services market is springing up. Most of the products available in it are not new; it consists rather of certain goods and services which have been regrouped to meet stricter legal requirements and a growing demand based on environmental conservation objectives. This market also offers enterprises and entrepreneurs opportunities to diversify and to set up new lines of business. The goods and services used to protect the environment make up a vast range of products as diverse as attempts made by enterprises to solve their pollution problems.

Much of the growth of the demand for goods and services to protect the environment has been spurred by the application of environmental legislation in the form of programmes, regulations and standards. The promulgation of each special law or regulation gives rise to a new wave of demand for certain goods and services of this type, which later stabilizes. Although waves of demand for industrial goods and services may overlap in time, they are not synchronized. Consequently, the aggregate demand for environment-related goods and services also shows rather wide annual fluctuations.

Industrial statistics and censuses only partially cover the costs of purchasing these products because enterprises find it difficult to separate these categories, which frequently include other items. It can, however, be noted that according to figures provided by the Environmental Protection Agency (EPA) of the United States of America, in 1985 the total cost of environmental protection as a share of GDP were as follows: United States, 1.7%; Federal Republic of Germany, 1.5%; Netherlands, 1.3%; United Kingdom, 1.3%; France, 0.9% and Norway, 0.8%. The trends and projections established for the United States of America and Western Europe show an increase in the share of the cost of environmental protection in GDP.

A very good indication of the boom in this market is the number of international fairs specializing in environment-related products. In this connection mention can be made of the International Trade Fair for Waste Disposal (IFAT), held at Munich, Germany, every three years; the International Trade Fair and Congress for Engineering in Environmental Protection (ENVITEC) in Düsseldorf, Germany, which is also held at intervals of several years, and the Environmental Tech Expo (ETE), to be held at Chicago in April 1991. The German fairs, which have been operating for a number of years, both attract a growing number of exhibitors and visitors. The Environmental Tech Expo in Chicago will be the first fair held in the United States of America in which the whole range of environmental technologies are exhibited. A number of exhibits specializing in various environmental topics are also held in the United States.

The market for goods and services to protect the environment does not set up high barriers against the entry of new competitors. This is illustrated by the fact that in the Federal Republic of Germany, this segment of the market included close to a thousand suppliers at the beginning of the 1980s, and their number has now grown to over four thousand.

A large number of the enterprises specializing in the supply of environment-related goods and services are small- and medium-sized undertakings since environmental protection projects usually call for specific solutions, which gives small- and medium-sized suppliers certain advantages due to their flexibility and capacity for innovation. Recently, however, this market has experienced some penetration by large enterprises, whose strategies consist in the diversification of their production programme, the creation of subsidiaries, the acquisition of specialized firms and the formation of joint ventures.

Suppliers who are able to provide integral solutions along with their production technologies and have not specialized in only one environmental area have the competitive advantages in this market. In addition, large enterprises have a greater financial capacity than small firms. In some cases, small enterprises have reacted by seeking forms of co-operation in the task of adapting to changing market conditions.

6.4 *The market for goods and services for environmental protection in Latin America and the Caribbean*

The demand for goods and services used for environmental protection in Latin America and the Caribbean is not the same as in the developed countries. The countries of Latin America and the Caribbean are more concerned about sustainable development than about environmental protection as such.

Insufficient attention was paid to infrastructure projects relating to environmental protection and basic sanitation during the past decade because of economic stagnation. Since, in addition, the debt crisis made it necessary to gain foreign exchange, export efforts were usually concentrated on sectors associated with the exploitation of natural resources. This combination of circumstances put heavier pressure on the environment.

In order to learn about the activities and programmes carried out by large Latin American enterprises to promote conservation of the environment and sustainable development, a questionnaire was sent to a number of such enterprises in October and November 1990. Its findings revealed, *inter alia*, what investment efforts the enterprises were engaged in in various fields. The sample was made up of industrial firms in Brazil, Chile, Mexico and Venezuela which exploit or process natural resources and are engaged in activities relating to petroleum, mining, metallurgy, iron and steel, cement, cellulose and paper, foodstuffs, electric power generation and, in one case, tourism. The enterprises in respect of which information was obtained are identified in table VI-3.

The replies to the questionnaire and other information collected indicate, in general terms, that all expanded and newly built (in the past five to 10 years) industrial plants as well as all plants projected for the immediate future are provided with environmental protection facilities and

Table VI-3

LATIN AMERICA: GENERAL DATA ON SELECTED LARGE LATIN AMERICAN ENTERPRISES, 1989

Country	Enterprise	Ranking[a]	Sales (millions of dollars)	Employees (number)	Sector	Ownership[b]
Brazil						
	PETROBRAS & DISTRIBUIDORA	3	11 571.0	60 126	Petroleum	S
	CIA. VALLE DO RIO DOCE	34	2 072.2	23 415	Mining	S
	NESTLE Brasil	43	1 766.8	10 338	Foodstuffs	F
	ELECTROSUL	166	565.4	4 439	Electricity	S
	ARACRUZ CELULOSE	268	356.7	4 750	Cellulose/paper	P
	PARACATU		106.5	550	Mining	F
Chile						
	CODELCO	8	4 029.9	27 303	Mining	S
	ENAMI	116	742.4	2 986	Mining	S
	CIA. PAPELES Y CARTONES (CMPC)	232	420.7	36 762	Cellulose/paper	P
	CIA. DISPUTADA DE LAS CONDES	310	310.8	1 500	Mining	F
	NESTLE CHILE		350.0	3 500	Foodstuffs	F
	EPERVA		44.0	700	Fisheries	P
Mexico						
	PEMEX	1	15 073.9	...	Petroleum	S
	NESTLE MEXICO	132	670.6	5 800	Foodstuffs	F
	CEMENTOS TOLTECA (PLANTA ATONILCA)	180.0		710	Cement	P
	SIDEK DIVISION SIDERURGICA				Iron and steel	P
	SIDEK DIVISION TURISTICA		250.0	5 000	Tourism	P
Venezuela						
	PDVSA	2	12 483.7	45 069	Petroleum	S
	CVG	23	2492.8	35 539	Mining	S

Source: Joint ECLAC/UNIDO Industry and Technology Division, on the basis of information taken from *América Economía*, No. 44, October 1990, and information supplied by enterprises.

[a] Construed on the basis of information concerning the annual sales of the 500 largest enterprises in Latin America as of 31 December 1989.

[b] S: State   P: Private (local)   F: Foreign private.

incorporate "clean" technologies in accordance with modern technical standards. In cases where it was possible to compare the investment in environmental protection with total investment in the projects concerned, the figures obtained show that new Latin American plants meet international standards. These data support the estimates made concerning the potential demand for goods and services used in environmental protection in Latin America and the Caribbean, at least in so far as the production sector's component of that demand is concerned. In estimating that demand, it must be borne in mind that investment in environmental protection is heavier in industrial activities related to the exploitation and processing of natural resources.

The present investment in goods and services relating to environmental protection in Latin America, estimated on the basis of information provided by manufacturers of equipment and the leading user firms in selected countries of the region (Brazil, Mexico, Chile and Venezuela) amounts to close to US$2 billion.

In view of the prospects that Latin America will recover its growth in the 1990s, which would be accompanied by a rise in the investment coefficient, and in consideration of the need to progress gradually towards sustainable development, it may be concluded that the regional demand for "environment-related equipment" will expand at an estimated rate of not less than 10% a year on average in the coming decade –a rate which is comparable to that recorded in the developed countries in the 1980s.

As for the findings of the survey on supply conducted in some countries of the region, they indicate that in those countries which are most advanced in terms of industry, local supply can meet much of the market demand, both qualitatively and quantitatively. There are two exceptions to this general rule –one in the category corresponding to measuring instruments and automatic equipment, which are to a large extent imported. The other exception relates to the mechanical, electric and electronic components of equipment. Local supply of such components has not kept pace with the finished products, sometimes because of the limited size of the local market or because of existing relations with specialized suppliers abroad.

6.5 *Entrepreneurial strategies for sustainable development*

By comparing the findings of the questionnaire designed for a number of large Latin American enterprises with the criteria used by the United Nations in respect of sustainable development [7] some idea can be formed of the progress shown by Latin American management in this respect.

The subjects covered by the questionnaire included technological research and development and investment programmes related to protection of the environment and their impact on production costs and on competitiveness, measures adopted with regard to organization, and, finally, the purposes for which these various programmes and measures were established.

An analysis of the data obtained shows that in spite of the difficulties they experienced during the 1980s, large Latin American enterprises have established effective policies in the realm of environmental protection. It may also be seen that the majority of the enterprises surveyed are determined to expand these policies with a view to the gradual incorporation of concepts of sustainable development (see box VI-4).

The data obtained also show that in addition to the progress they experienced in the field of environmental protection, the companies surveyed also encountered some difficulties in various areas. In the area of research and development, the effort made by enterprises to develop new processes and products would seem to be insufficient. The oil companies constitute an exception to this observation, particularly with regard to the development of new refining processes for the manufacture of ultra-refined benzines, clean fuels and additives. An important incentive in this case is the prospect of being able to place these products on export markets.

A number of limiting factors may also be observed in connection with investment in environmental protection. Old factories do not always have the facilities they need to protect the environment to the degree required. Some public

Box VI-4
CORPORACION VENEZOLANA DE GUAYANA AND
ENVIRONMENTAL PROTECTION

The Venezuelan Corporation for the Guayana Region (CVG) was established for the purpose of encouraging and co-ordinating the economic and social development of the Guayana region, integrating it with the country as a whole, in accordance with the general orientation of the National Plan. In order to achieve this objective, the CVG gave priority to industrial development in the region, creating and promoting a series of basic industries that are at present operating under its control.

CVG is made up of the following firms:

CVG Ferrominera del Orinoco C.A., iron ore processor;

CVG Venezolana de Ferrosilicio C.A. (FESILVEN), ferrosilicon producer;

Interamericana de Aluminio C.A. (INTERALUMINA), Aluminios del Caroní S.A. (ALCASA) and Industria Venezolana de Aluminio C.A. (VENALUM), producers of aluminium;

CVG Compañía General de Minería de Venezuela, engaged in the exploitation of gold-bearing deposits, and

Electrificación del Caroní (EDELCA).

The corporation also has investments in another group of firms that are related to mining and metallurgical activities and are established both within the country and abroad.

In subsidiary firms of CVG, and likewise in some of the enterprises associated with it, environmental control units have been organized. The units of the first group together are composed of 48 persons (nine technicians and 39 professionals), whereas those of the second group work with a total of 25 persons, mainly technicians and manual workers, under the direction of a professional. In brief, 73 persons (including 40 professionals and 18 technicians) are involved in environmental control work.

These operative units have an environmental pollution control laboratory and equipment valued at US$1 million.

The different industries affiliated with CVG are using similar methods for measuring the impact of their activities on the air, water and soils. In addition, they are organizing environmental education campaigns within and outside the industrial plants and are carrying out programmes in the area of industrial hygiene (evaluation of the level of noise, gases, dust, heat, illumination, radioactivity, basic hygiene and ergonomics).

The firms associated with CVG are also carrying out programmes designed to control specific environmental problems they are facing, primarily those related to air and water pollution and the handling of solid waste.

In the industrial zone of Matanzas, sizeable investments have been made in equipment for controlling environmental contamination. The following figures give an idea of the magnitude of these efforts:

— Investment in equipment for air pollution control: US$32 million.

— Investment in equipment for water pollution control: US$1 million.

— Annual cost of operation and maintenance of pollution control equipment: US$2 million.

At the regional level various initiatives have been undertaken for confronting environmental problems. The following may be mentioned as examples:

— The National Experimental University of the Guayana Region, in co-ordination with the main CVG firms, plans to offer post-graduate studies in environmental sciences.

— In conjunction with the Ministry of the Environment and Renewable Natural Resources (MARNR), CVG has been making plans for the installation of an early warning network for air and water quality in industrial areas.

— The main CVG firms, MARNR and other official and private institutions have held four regional seminars on environmental conservation.

— In order to comply with existing legal regulations, CVG has also been working on a project designed for short-term actions on problems related to the management and elimination of toxic and dangerous waste.

In 1990, the corporation created a new department, the Office of the Vice-President of Environment, Science and Technology, whose purpose is to enforce, on behalf of MARNR, national land management policies and to defend, improve and conserve the environment in the Guayana developing region. It is also responsible for encouraging, systematizing, harmonizing and consolidating the scientific and technological work of the corporation and its firms.

enterprises in countries with financial difficulties are periodically subjected to cutbacks in their investment budgets. Works for the protection of the environment, in particular, are frequently the objects of decisions to postpone or suspend their projects. Finally, it seems that insufficient attention is still being paid to changing production processes as an alternative to end-of-the-line treatment of emissions and waste.

In the area of organizational measures, it may be observed that enterprises are still making little use of environmental auditing from outside. At the same time, access by public and private entities to environmental information available in the enterprises is still limited in some respects. Enterprises still seem unclear as to their assessment of the impact of environmental protection measures on production costs and competitiveness. They only note that measures adopted to protect the environment have in general had a positive effect on their public image. As for the reasons why enterprises have established environmental protection programmes, the replies sometimes reflect a defensive attitude. To some extent, enterprises still wait for governmental intervention or local community action before adopting corrective measures in respect of environmental problems. The nature and effectiveness of these actions depends on the existing decision-making (institutional capital) systems and community participation in such decision-making, a subject to be dealt with in the following chapter (chapter VII).

A set of proposals for solving the problems noted in this chapter may be found in chapter X.

Notes

[1] See ECLAC, *Changing Production Patterns with Social Equity, op. cit.*

[2] Thus, for example, the response of the Government of the United States of America to the oil crisis consists of four policies aimed at: diversification of energy sources, promotion of oil exploration in its own territory, establishment of oil reserves in case of another crisis and energy conservation. Of the four, the one which lasted the longest and had the strongest economic impact was the last one named. In France, on the other hand, a number of regulations and ceilings have been in effect since 1974 with regard both to the thermal characteristics of buildings and dwellings on the one hand and energy consumption by vehicles and the operation of industrial equipment, on the other.

[3] OLADE, *La deuda externa del sector energético de América Latina y el Caribe*, Quito, 1988.

[4] See International Environmental Technology Transfer Advisory Board (IETTA), *Draft Final Report*, Washington, D.C., 10 December 1990.

[5] See ECLAC, *Changing production patterns with social equity, op. cit.*

[6] See UNIDO, *Industry and Development: Global Report 1990/91*, chapter III, 1990.

[7] United Nations, Economic and Social Council, "Transnational corporations and issues relating to the environment: Report of the Secretary-General" (E/C.10/1990/10), 28 March 1990.

Chapter VII

INSTITUTIONS AND SUSTAINABLE DEVELOPMENT

As the production base of the economy changes, institutional factors will be what determines the degree of equity and sustainability of development. Thus, in order to achieve environmentally sustainable development, the institutional framework will have to be adjusted.

1. The nature of institutional capital

Institutional capital is playing an increasingly crucial role in determining the sustainability of development. The term encompasses all those norms and relationships (i.e., decision-making systems) which make it possible to expedite and consolidate changes in production patterns while promoting greater social equity. In building a link between institutional and natural capital, consideration should be given to the following elements: the system of incentives, the organization of development, the management of the economy, the role of the State and of the private sector, and community participation.

The system of incentives includes instruments which have an effect in the market as well as those whose influence is felt outside the market. The characteristics of economic and social incentives were discussed in chapter III, which focused on market-based policies such as taxes, subsidies and prices. In the section on environmental policy, examples were given of extra-market incentives, such as property rights, production quotas and legislation. The present chapter will deal with the subject of environmental legislation, and reference will be made to some of the features unique to incentives which operate outside the market setting.

The organization of development influences the level of sustainability from two different angles: the capacity for policy-making and the capacity for policy implementation. An essential point which should be stressed at the very outset is that the spatial distribution of resources does not conform to geopolitical boundaries, and a special organizational scheme is therefore required in order to address resource-related issues. A case in point is that of river basins, whose management requires the involvement of a number of different public and private organizations. During the 1960s, and even earlier in some isolated cases, government agencies for the management of river basins began to be created in response to the demand that their development be carried out on an organized basis. The existence of these agencies has permitted co-ordinated action to be taken by the various ministries concerned (e.g., of public works, agriculture, etc.).

One of the challenges which the region has before it is to expand the traditional spheres of action of development-related institutions, since a sectoral division of economic activity is a very ill-suited structure for dealing with ecosystems. The persistence of outmoded organizations militates against the preservation of a nation's heritage and greatly reduces the economic efficiency of physical and financial capital.

The region does not yet have the unified approach and organizational stability needed for the execution of regional development projects or programmes. Indeed, the usual procedure is quite the reverse: hierarchical levels and structures are created outside the framework of existing mechanisms which tend to disappear soon after the flow of financing has ended. This course of action reveals a faulty understanding of the nature of institutions, and because of this misconception the tendency is to make the mistake of creating new organizations rather than strengthening existing national structures (particularly at the local level).

These new organizations disrupt the existing usage pattern of different forms of capital, thereby creating an unstable situation. If the mix of different forms of capital entailed by the new organization differs substantially from the pre-existing mix, then the new organization will survive only as long as the supply of resources used to create it remains available. If a country's capital portfolio is compared with the capital portfolio of these new organizations, it will be seen that these artificial structures function only if, for example, their supplies of human capital (consultants) and financial capital (loans) are permanently available. If either one of these forms of capital is alien to a country's overall economic projects, these organizations will disappear.

The improper *management* of economic and social activity –at the level of the economy as a whole, a sector or a specific natural resource– has begun to wreak havoc in some areas of the region.

The management of environmental problems is particularly complex when it calls for a joint effort on the part of a number of different institutions which are not accustomed to working within an interdisciplinary or inter-agency setting. For example, river basin management requires the efforts, on a co-ordinated and flexible basis, of various organizations in order to execute projects dealing with infrastructure works, farming, animal husbandry, vegetation and forests, waste management and pollution control, water and land management; and the control of silting. Each of these activities is usually carried out by a different organization.

The many different uses made of natural resources give rise to a variety of interactions within a single area whose boundaries are not clearly defined, and which cannot be drawn so as to conform to geopolitical boundaries. Therefore, in order to deal with such issues a special type of organization is needed, as in the above-mentioned case of river basins.

Many of the forms of interaction which, in theory, would appear to be conflictive are not necessarily so in practice. When such incompatibilities do arise, however, they are often the result of faulty planning or shortcomings as regards the formulation of criteria of sustainability.

The main types of incompatibility or potential conflicts which arise in connection with resource use include competition for space as such and the environmental degradation that results when adjacent activities have a detrimental effect on one another.

Interference between activities located in the same area may also spread to others, thereby giving rise to instances in which ecosystems come under the attack of distant activities as well. In addition, the interaction among different uses may change, since the use made of resources may vary over time. Yet another factor is that the use being made of a resource at the present time (or the degradation or destruction of a resource as a consequence of the use made of another) may preclude possible future uses. This complex sequence demands the establishment of institutional arrangements capable of coping with these variables.

Cases in which intra-governmental responsibilities pertaining to natural resource management and environmental protection are inadequately defined have arisen time and time again in the region. Jurisdictions almost invariably overlap, since most government units are organized on a functional/sectoral basis and horizontal inter-agency links are a rarity.

When an effort is made to plan and manage the development of natural resources in a way which will be conducive to sustainability, the various ecosystems should be regarded as a complex but integral whole while bearing in mind their limitations and those of their spatial context (see box VII-1).

Box VII-1
THE ENVIRONMENTAL SANITATION TECHNOLOGIES COMPANY (CETESB)

The Environmental Sanitation Technologies Company (CETESB) is a mixed public-private enterprise carrying out functions delegated by the government of the state of São Paulo for pollution control and environmental conservation. The government of the state of São Paulo owns 99.8% of the shares; the management and the members of the Board of Directors own the rest. The Company operates independently in all legal and financial matters and, as regards its substantive operations, is linked to the Department of the Environment of the state of São Paulo. It is empowered to grant environmental licenses for urban development, industrial projects and automobile engines. It is also responsible for monitoring environmental pollution in the area of Cubatão, where its performance has been recognized as successful.

CETESB can be regarded as an *avant garde* organization in the environmental field, not only in the state of São Paulo but in the entire country, since it provides technical co-operation and assistance to various national institutions, including the Brazilian Environment Institute (IBAMA).

Following a recent reorganization exercise, the research work of CETESB has now been decentralized and is conducted in units scattered among various sectors. Although CETESB has fewer resources than in the past, it has continued to perform a variety of tasks, mainly in the fields referred to below.

In the field of water quality, CETESB carried out an important study for the development of large deep-water deposits discovered eight years earlier during oil prospecting in the western part of the state of São Paulo. These waters have a very high level of fluorine and were treated through an activated alumina process. The study was conducted in association with Aluminio Nordeste S.A. (an ALCOA subsidiary), which also financed the construction of the pilot plant. The process has been duly registered and is now being incorporated into equipment manufactured in the United States.

With regard to reforestation, CETESB research made it possible to introduce a new technique for producing seeds compacted in pellets, the use of which resulted in a considerable rise in the yield from the area sown from aircraft and helicopters, which finally reached an average of two trees per square metre.

With regard to liquid effluents, most of the studies were aimed at finding ways of adapting exogenous techniques to conditions in Brazil. The technological advances made in this regard were applied to the production of sugar and alcohol, cellulose and paper, citric fruit juices, instant coffee, chocolates, and other products.

The main instruments and processes developed in this field included the anaerobic filter, the upflow anaerobic digestor, and a system used in Metropolitan São Paulo in which the activated sludge process was adopted in order to obtain optional parameters and remove certain nutrients, such as nitrogen and phosphorous.

In connection with solid effluvia, CETESB research resulted in some entirely new methods, including the following:

- Successful use of a by-product of the production of sugar cane alcohol as a fertilizer.

- Dissemination of a process which makes it possible to treat residue from petroleum refining by applying a special technique known as "land-farming".

- Special processes for eliminating sludge emanating from galvanoplastics industries, for adjusting the pH balance in certain chemical and metallurgical processes, and for doing away with toxic heavy metals and hospital waste.

- Treatment of urban and industrial waste through a procedure, selected from among various alternatives, in which upflow aerobic digestors are used in combination with activated sludge.

In the agroindustrial sector, a method of selective collection and recycling, which was awarded a prize by the Government of Japan, was designed and put into practice. Important advances were also achieved in the cultivation of earthworms for the production of humus and of algae for feeding microcrustaceans and ornamental fish.

In another kind of initiative, CETESB worked with the National Industrial Property Institute (INPI) in putting together a full inventory of technological inventions related to the environment. The company also publishes a periodic report which lists all new patents and requests for patents relating to environmental sanitation registered throughout the world.

The Cubatão project

A noteworthy project which CETESB has been implementing for a number of years is aimed at restoring the environment of the industrial zone of the Municipality of Cubatão. This operation, which receives financing from the World Bank, and is an example of a successful exercise and also provides a good illustration of how costly it can be not to undertake timely, preventive action in the planning and installation phases of the construction of an industrial complex in which pollution is a risk.

The Cubatão industrial park, which covers 100 square kilometres, is located in a region where unfavourable climatic conditions, from an environmental standpoint, prevail. The park was located in this Municipality largely because a Petróleo Brasileiro (PETROBRAS) refinery was already operating in the same area. In 1985 that area generated 3% of Brazil's gross domestic product while at the same time releasing nearly 1 000 tons of pollutants daily, 25% of them in their solid state.

In 1984, a five-year programme for controlling environmental pollution went into effect under CETESB management. The programme's resources, provided by the World Bank, were received by the government of São Paulo, and transferred through the pollution control programme (PROCOP) to the industries located in the industrial park. For their part, those industries have together contributed close to US$400 million to the execution of the project.

The success of the project is evident. Since 1986 no emergency situation due to air pollution has arisen in the Municipality, and states of alert declined steadily until 1989, when none were declared.

In complete fulfilment of the targets set, air and water pollution have been reduced by almost 90%, and soil pollution has disappeared altogether. At the same time, 286 sources of pollution, representing 75% of the total number of such sources are under systematic observation.

A hillside stabilization project was also implemented to shore up the slopes at Serra do Mar, which had been badly damaged by erosion resulting from deterioration of the forest cover. By sowing a total of 3 billion seeds, from the air, it was possible to cover 60 square kilometres of slopes with trees.

The United Nations Environment Programme (UNEP) now believes that the Cubatão experience should be repeated in other regions of the world affected by similar problems.

Source: ECLAC, "Tecnología, competitividad y sustentabilidad" (LC/L.608), Santiago, Chile, January 1991. (Document prepared by the Joint ECLAC/UNIDO Industry and Technology Division.)

Institutional mechanisms are unquestionably the primary tool for ensuring the success of the above approach, and the interrelationships which exist in terms of institutional areas of responsibility therefore play a vital role in efficient environmental management. Thus, an effort to seek out co-ordination mechanisms which do not involve the creation of additional institutions or an over-concentration of administrative power and which are flexible, versatile, and do not create bureaucratic stumbling blocks appears to offer a means of ensuring that the State and other organizations will truly place themselves at the service of the quest to change the region's production patterns while promoting social equity and environmental sustainability (see box VII-2).

The roles of the public and private sectors in the accomplishment of development tasks have been the subject of an ongoing debate in the region and have been heavily influenced by the countries' political structures, processes of democratization and prevailing development goals. Regardless of the outcome of this debate, however, it is important to realize that public and environmental policies will not achieve their objectives unless the State undergoes a transformation and the private sector improves its management capacity.

The new approaches called for in order to change the region's production patterns with social equity and environmental sustainability cannot exclude either the public or the private sector.[1] The active participation of the private sector is a crucial factor in controlling and managing the environment. By the same token, strategies for achieving sustainable development cannot be implemented by an atrophied public sector. Many externalities which have already been discussed in chapter III attest to the need for an effective and lasting form of State intervention. The countries' institutional structures therefore need to be such as to reinforce their democracies and their political and social coalitions within a context of stability, and a national and regional consensus is essential in order to make this possible.

Organized, timely community participation significantly increases the economic effectiveness of physical and financial capital. In order to achieve an environmentally sustainable form of development, the people and the communities which are the subject of that development must be incorporated into the decision-making process. Furthermore, the various forms of community participation are vital in order to prevent the plunder of natural resources, particularly in cases where public or private property rights are not clearly delineated and rationally exercised.

In the short term, the countries of the region need to lay the institutional foundations for a joint form of management by the private sector, the State and the community. This is where non-governmental organizations (NGOs) have an important role to play, since they enjoy comparative advantages within the sphere of community organization and especially at the level of family-centered programmes. These NGOs, acting on the basis of agreements with the national governments, can make a significant contribution to institutional change.

Finally, reference should be made to the subject of cultural capital or heritage. Culture, as an expression of the lives and activities of the people, is not unrelated to the question of sustainable development strategies. There are many human settlements whose cultural survival hinges upon the management of natural resources. Indeed, some indigenous settlements have been subject to extremely misguided forms of interference, and the absence of suitable protective institutions encourages economic agents to despoil the very resources on which they depend.

2. Organizing for sustainable development

Since the end of the Second World War, the way in which public institutions have evolved has largely been determined by the approaches to development which have prevailed at any given time. Thus, at least four major stages can be identified in this process of organizational change. The first corresponds to the period during which it was thought that physical and financial capital were the scarcest forms of capital and natural capital the most abundant. Consequently, economic growth was equated with construction and infrastructure projects, and the civil services of the region were modified accordingly. This was the period that saw the creation of ministries of public works as well as large State construction and national service enterprises. In addition, as a logical complement of this strategy, financial institutions were founded to promote development.

The second stage is associated with the period during which development was largely viewed in terms of the need to overcome the problem of poverty. The participation of the potential beneficiaries of development was regarded as an integral part of the process of change. During this stage there was a shift in the objectives of a number of ministries and regional and local bodies, as well as various community organizations. The most prominent programmes during this time were those concerned with integrated rural development, public services, food self-sufficiency, and other efforts to alleviate poverty. These forms of organization were

complex and fragile, however, owing to the difficulty of devising effective participatory structures, and this was compounded by the sociopolitical instability of many governments.

This was succeeded by a third stage when macroeconomic management became the chief focus of attention of the development effort. As the region entered into a stage of broad-spectrum economic management involving structural and sectoral adjustment programmes, the institutional apparatus began to undergo sweeping changes: a reduction in the size of the civil service, privatizations and an increase in the relative importance of government units and levels concerned with finances and with monetary and financial policy.

The fourth stage represents a return, although within a new context, to the issues of growth and social equity, but these elements are now combined with considerations of environmental sustainability. This is the stage which is now beginning, and various countries in the region have been entering into this stage since the end of the 1980s. The challenges now being faced by the region call for organizational structures which correspond to the three objectives entailed by this conceptual framework.

The region has a wealth of past experience in this connection which should help to guide future organizational reforms. The first lesson to be drawn from these experiences concerns the need for a sufficient awareness of the importance of carrying out reforms within a framework of stability, participation and progress, overcoming the old "either-or" propositions, such as that which at one time characterized the view taken of private versus State efforts. The nature of the fulcrum for these reforms will depend upon the way in which each country resolves such questions as those of participation, association, concerted action and consensus-building for development.

The second lesson refers to the need to set in motion processes of organizational reform within a reasonable period of time. Hasty action could, as in the past, result in social costs that outweigh the expected benefits. Experience has shown that the most successful organizational reforms have been based on an awareness of the fact that strong, effective organizations cannot be built overnight. Institutional modifications conducive to sustainable development should be a long-term goal. There are no instant recipes or formulas for organizational changes, especially when they involve changing the population's behaviour patterns.

3. Environmental administration and management

Efficient institution-building with a view to the achievement of an environmentally sustainable and socially equitable form of natural resource management entails a process involving the following steps:

Substantially increasing the pool of information needed for decision-making purposes. Today, decisions relating to natural-resource and environmental management are taken on the basis of inaccurate or insufficient information –or, at times, simply no information at all. Information as an input for development will play a pivotal role in determining the extent of the countries' bargaining power. The governments will have need of greater bargaining power as environmental restrictions –and the standards that go along with them– inexorably become an increasingly integral part of the world of international trade and development financing. Furthermore, this pool of information will become a crucial factor in enabling the countries to capitalize upon their comparative advantages *vis-à-vis* the international market.

Upgrading capabilities for assessing and executing regional development programmes. The spatial dimension of resources and of the environment makes it necessary to stress the territorial dimension of development when undertaking the institutional modifications required to improve such capabilities, which will therefore involve a redefinition of units of analysis or of geopolitical and administrative units. This means that the countries will have to increase the responsibilities of environmental and natural-resource development agencies and delegate greater powers to regional development offices and corporations.

Strengthening educational, training and research institutions. The chief aim in this regard is the provision of training for civil servants involved in environmental matters. The research effort, for its part, should become a pivotal element in the accumulation of knowledge, technological change, and the protection of the natural heritage.

4. The international and regional legal framework

An analysis of the international legal framework in respect of environmental issues and an in-depth examination of the regional and subregional situation in this respect have been set forth in other studies recently published by ECLAC.[2] For the sake of brevity, this section will confine itself to the presentation of a synoptic overview of the legal instruments which have been approved or signed, as well as those already in force which govern the relationships between development and environment at the international and regional level.

The United Nations Conference on Environment and Development will be held within the broader context of an ongoing debate in many multilateral forums concerning the restructuring of the legal framework for international economic relations. This framework includes instruments which were formulated quite some time ago but whose tenets nonetheless continue to be of concern to the international community, such as the resolutions issued by the General Assembly at its sixth special session in 1974,[3] as well as more recent ones, such as the Declaration on International Economic Co-operation, in particular the Revitalization of Economic Growth and Development of the Developing Countries, which was adopted in 1990 by the General Assembly at its eighteenth special session,[4] the declaration issued by the World Summit for Children,[5] and the International Development Strategy (IDS) for the Fourth United Nations Development Decade which was adopted by the General Assembly.[6]

All these instruments have a common denominator. They emphasize the need to promote economic and social development through international co-operation; to revitalize the economic growth and progress of the developing countries; to promote international economic co-operation for sustained growth of the world economy; to realize the basic right of all human beings to a life free from hunger, poverty, ignorance, disease and fear; and to work for fruitful results at, among other forums, the United Nations Conference on Environment and Development, to be held in 1992.

4.1 *International instruments*

Some of the instruments cited below are already in force while others have been signed but are not yet in effect; still others have as yet only been approved. It is essential that the countries of Latin America and the Caribbean should analyse the relevance of their full adherence to each of these instruments, since despite the weaknesses from which some of the texts may suffer, they are in general the product of a delicate, negotiated balance whose objectives can be realized only through the active participation of the countries of the region in the mechanisms for which they provide.

The categories into which these instruments are grouped generally correspond to those used in the provisional agenda set forth in the report of the Preparatory Committee for the United Nations Conference on Environment and Development. In each case the most important legislative sources are listed. This presentation has been prepared for the purpose of providing background information for use by the countries in forthcoming negotiations.

a) *Protection of the atmosphere: Climate change, ozone depletion, and transboundary air pollution*

The Vienna Convention for the Protection of the Ozone Layer was adopted on 22 March 1985 and entered into force on 22 September 1988. It establishes the obligation of States to co-operate by means of systematic observations in the assessment of the effects of human activities on the ozone layer; to adopt legislative or administrative measures in that respect; and to harmonize policies to control, limit, reduce or prevent activities under their jurisdiction or control which have adverse effects on the atmosphere.

The Montreal Protocol on Substances that Deplete the Ozone Layer was adopted on 16 September 1987 and entered into force on 1 January 1989. It institutes a freeze on the production of three halons (chemicals required to produce fire extinguishers) and the five most destructive chlorofluorocarbons (CFCs). It was further agreed that the consumption of CFCs would be reduced by 50% by 1998.

The Helsinki Declaration on the Protection of the Ozone Layer, which was adopted in May 1989 at the first meeting of the parties to the Vienna Convention and the Montreal Protocol, calls upon all States to accede to the Vienna Convention and the Montreal Protocol. The signatory countries also agreed to phase out the production and consumption of the CFCs designated as controlled substances in the Montreal Protocol. The targets outlined therein are to be met as soon as possible but in no case later than the year 2000.

At the Meeting of the Parties to the Montreal Protocol on Substances that Deplete the Ozone Layer held towards the end of June 1990 in London, 122 countries pledged to put an end to the use and production of halons and chlorofluorocarbons (CFCs) by the year 2000, as well as setting sequential targets for their reduction: 50% by 1995 and 85% by 1997. As a parallel step, the industrialized countries created a fund of US$160 million to permit third world countries to gain access to substitutes for these propellants.

The United Nations General Assembly recently decided to consolidate the negotiations concerning climate change by establishing an intergovernmental negotiating committee, which is open to all member countries and is supported by UNEP and the World Meteorological Organization (WMO).[7] The committee is to prepare a framework convention, and related instruments, containing appropriate commitments concerning which an agreement may be reached. In drafting the convention, the committee will take into account the proposals made by States participating in the negotiations, the work of the Intergovernmental Panel on Climate Change, and the results of various international meetings on the subject, including the Second World Climate Conference.

It is hoped that the negotiations regarding the framework convention and related instruments will be completed before the United Nations Conference on Environment and Development, to be held in June 1992, so that the convention may be opened for signature by States at that time.

The General Assembly also decided to establish a voluntary fund for the purpose of supporting developing countries, in particular the least developed among them and small island countries, in participating fully and effectively in the negotiations, and has invited Governments, regional economic integration organizations and other interested organizations to contribute generously to this fund.

Finally, as a means of reaffirming its fullest support for the consideration of this issue, the General Assembly also decided to include an item concerning the protection of global climate for present and future generations of humanity on the provisional agenda of its forty-sixth session.

b) *Protection of the oceans and all kinds of seas, including enclosed and semi enclosed seas, and coastal areas; and the protection, rational use and development of their living resources*

The most important international instrument on this subject is the United Nations Convention on the Law of the Sea, which has not yet entered in force. It is considered to be one of the most important achievements of the United Nations since the signing of its Charter. This landmark instrument is the result of almost 10 years of negotiations which led to a balanced text that is an embodiment of international solidarity and of the interdependence of the nations of the world (see box VII-3). The Convention regulates every possible issue relating to the Law of the Sea, creates innovative institutions and sets forth economic and social concepts not usually found in instruments of this type. The Convention is especially meaningful for Latin America and the Caribbean because of the valuable contribution made by the countries of the region both in substantive terms and within the context of the corresponding negotiations. It has been signed by 156 States and has been ratified by 43 States. A total of 60 States must ratify the Convention in order for it to enter into effect.

Box VII-3
MEXICO: FEDERAL SEA ACT

Some of the major problems which hinder efforts to incorporate considerations relating to the oceans and seas into a national development strategy are the myriad areas of expertise involved in the utilization of marine resources, the erratic pattern in which jurisdiction over the relevant areas is distributed among government agencies and the difficulty of setting up appropriate mechanisms for consultation and co-ordination to avoid disputes and redundancies.

The activities of government bodies usually overlap because most State agencies are organized on a functional basis, and horizontal inter-agency links are rare.

Furthermore, since integrated management concepts have not yet come into general use, the various agencies conduct their activities as isolated undertakings, without having a grasp of the overall system of which they form a part.

The effort to avoid such failings often leads to

extreme solutions, such as, for example, the creation of a "super-agency" which takes over complete responsibility for a given sectoral matter and which, in addition to demanding an extremely high level of fiscal expenditure, ultimately leads to more inefficiency and a greater lack of specialization.

Mexico, through its Federal Law of the Sea of 8 January 1986, has been able to avert these problems and to set up a coherent legislative/institutional system without resorting to the enactment of an inordinate number of legal provisions or the creation of new institutions that would place a burden on State finances.

This accomplishment was made possible by the gradual incorporation of the provisions of the United Nations Convention on the Law of the Sea into the country's legal system. Mexico gave material expression to its ratification of these provisions through the promulgation of statutes, many of which now form part of its body of constitutional law, and through a relatively brief law known as the Federal Sea Act.

Mexico has thereby established a genuinely effective statute on the sea by modernizing and streamlining its national laws so as to improve the management of its natural resources without becoming embroiled in an arduous legislative process; it has spontaneously created effective co-ordination mechanisms and has promptly fulfilled its international obligations.

The Federal Sea Act states, for example, that the Federal Government shall apply the law of the sea through the various government units designated as competent national authorities in accordance with the powers granted to each, thereby creating an overall framework for the co-ordination of the relevant activities, whose implementation is entrusted to specific sectoral bodies.

The chapter of this act which concerns the protection and preservation of the marine environment provides that in the exercise of the nation's powers, rights, jurisdictions and prerogatives within the marine areas of Mexico, the nation shall apply the Federal Environmental Protection Act, the General Health Act and related regulations, the Federal Water Act and other statutes and regulations. The result is a comprehensive body of law governing the protection of the marine environment which optimizes the use of existing rules and regulations without resorting to additional legislation or new institutional structures.

Three States in the region have not signed the Convention. The specific obstacles which have prevented these countries from doing so do not detract from the outstanding contributions these same States made both to the shaping of many of the concepts set forth therein and to the negotiation of the instrument itself. The Convention introduces concepts and institutions which reaffirm the right of States to use their natural resources and provides mechanisms for exercising that right. Moreover, it opens up genuine opportunities for the integral development of seas adjacent to the coasts of signatory countries. Thus, the Convention introduces compelling socioeconomic concepts and definitively upholds the concept of integrated resource management as a sine qua non of environmental sustainability. Two related instruments should also be mentioned: i) the conventions concerning the protection of the marine environment adopted within the framework of the International Maritime Organization (IMO), and ii) General Assembly resolution 44/225, which was adopted on 22 December 1989, on large-scale pelagic driftnet fishing and its impacts on the living marine resources of the world's oceans and seas.

c) Protection and management of land resources: Efforts to combat deforestation, soil loss, desertification and drought

Many of the existing instruments in this area relate to matters which fall within the purview of the Food and Agriculture Organization of the United Nations (FAO), UNEP and, to a lesser degree, the United Nations Educational, Scientific and Cultural Organization (UNESCO).

The main such instruments are the Programme of Action on Agrarian Reform and Rural Development, the Plan of Action to Combat Desertification, the Tropical Forestry Action Plan, the World Conservation Strategy, the World Soil Charter, and the UNESCO Programme on Man and the Biosphere.

d) Conservation of biological diversity

The instruments in this field are varied and represent an important basis for consultations since biological diversity is coming to be recognized as one of the chief tools of sustainable development. Although a detailed analysis of these documents would be beyond the scope of the present discussion, some of the main instruments in this area are: the World Charter for Nature; the portions of the World Conservation Strategy which concern the conservation of living resources for sustained development; the Convention on Wetlands of International Importance Especially as Waterfowl Habitat, which was signed at Ramsar in 1971 and the Protocol amending that convention, which was signed in Paris in 1982; the Convention concerning the Protection of the World Cultural and Natural Heritage, which was adopted in 1972 in Paris at the General Conference of UNESCO (see box VII-4); the Convention on International Trade in Endangered Species of Wild Fauna and Flora (CITES) of 1973; the Convention on the Conservation of Migratory Species of Wild Animals, of 1979; and the amended version of the 1946 International Convention for the Regulation of Whaling.

In pursuance of the aim of conserving biological diversity, it will be important for the countries of the region to monitor the activities of

Box VII-4
GUATEMALA: TIKAL NATIONAL PARK

Tikal National Park, which is discussed in *Our Own Agenda*, a document prepared by the Latin American and Caribbean Commission on Development and Environment, serves as another example of how international legal instruments, when suitably incorporated into a country's legal system, can support national efforts to achieve sustainable development.

Our Own Agenda cites Tikal as an example of a successful effort to establish and manage areas subject to special protective measures, a course of action whose ultimate aim is the protection of biodiversity.

Here we will consider the case of Tikal from a legal perspective, supplementing the analysis presented in the above-mentioned document with a review of the international legal instruments signed by Guatemala which directly or indirectly contribute to the preservation and sound management of the cultural and natural heritage of Tikal.

At Guatemala's request, Tikal has been placed on the World Natural and Cultural Heritage List under the terms of the Convention concerning the Protection of the World Cultural and Natural Heritage, which Guatemala signed in 1979. The country's position as a party to this international instrument has clearly been facilitated by the support for the cause of environmental protection which Guatemala had already exhibited in 1955 when it officially designated Tikal as a protected area.

By joining together the concepts of nature and culture, which had previously been regarded as separate or even opposing elements, the Convention permits a sound management of both the archeological heritage, which is the chief concern in this case, and the extremely valuable natural heritage of the area.

One of the main objectives of the Convention is to establish, by means of international contributions, a fund for the protection of the cultural and natural assets that have been placed on the World Heritage List. This fund will, *inter alia*, permit the countries concerned to secure technical assistance, provide them with access to expert assistance in pinpointing or combatting the causes of the degradation of these assets or in formulating protective measures, and contribute to the training of national specialists in conservation techniques.

The States parties undertake to incorporate the protection of these assets into comprehensive planning programmes, to establish facilities for their protection, to conduct scientific and technical studies and to adopt the necessary legal, administrative and financial measures for these purposes.

In addition, Guatemala is party to a wide range of other international instruments relating to the subject of biological diversity which also help to safeguard the heritage of Tikal. One such instrument is the Convention on Nature Protection and Wildlife Preservation in the Western Hemisphere of 12 October 1940, whose signatories pledged to establish national parks and reserves. Another is the Convention on International Trade in Endangered Species of Wild Fauna and Flora (CITES) of 1973, which creates a system of protection based on import and export permits that can also be used to help safeguard the park's natural resources.

The example of Tikal illustrates how a dynamic interaction between international and national legal norms, whereby nations respond in a versatile manner to international mandates, can also be used as an effective tool for furthering the countries' efforts to achieve an environmentally sustainable management of their resources.

the special panel of experts on biodiversity convened by the United Nations Environment Programme, which has begun work on the preparation of a legal instrument on this subject.

e) *Environmentally sound management of wastes, particularly hazardous wastes, and prevention of illegal international traffic in toxic and dangerous products and wastes*

Some of the most noteworthy instruments on these subjects are the following:

General Assembly resolution 1653(XVI), entitled "Declaration on the prohibition of

the use of nuclear and thermo-nuclear weapons" (1961).

Treaty Banning Nuclear Weapons Tests in the Atmosphere, in Outer Space and Under Water (1963).

Treaty on Principles Governing the Activities of States in the Exploration and Use of Outer Space including the Moon and Other Celestial Bodies (1967).

Treaty on the Non-Proliferation of Nuclear Weapons (1968).

Treaty on the Prohibition of the Emplacement of Nuclear Weapons and Other Weapons of Mass Destruction on the

Sea-Bed and the Ocean Floor and in the Subsoil Thereof (1970).

General Assembly resolution 2936(XXVII), entitled "Non-Use of force in international relations and permanent prohibition of the use of nuclear weapons" (1972).

General Assembly resolution 3478(XXX), entitled "Conclusion of a treaty on the complete and general prohibition of nuclear weapon tests" (1975).

Convention on Early Notification of a Nuclear Accident (1986).

Convention on Assistance in the Case of a Nuclear Accident or Radiological Emergency (1986).

Basel Convention on the Control of Transboundary Movements of Hazardous Wastes and their Disposal (1989).

The draft code concerning nuclear wastes approved by the International Atomic Energy Agency (IAEA) expert group, which establishes principles governing the international movement of nuclear wastes. The draft code was submitted to the General Conference of the IAEA in September 1990 in the course of negotiations playing a fundamental role in the effort to expand the coverage of the Basel Convention, which specifically excludes nuclear wastes.

4.2 Regional instruments

Two types of instruments are included in this category: those which refer specifically to natural resources and the environment, and general instruments which offer opportunities for promoting a better management of natural resources and environmental sustainability. Instruments in the first group include the following:

Convention on Nature Protection and Wildlife Preservation in the Western Hemisphere (12 October 1940).

Agreement for the Establishment of a Latin American Forestry Research and Training Institute, under the sponsorship of FAO (18 November 1959).

Treaty for the Prohibition of Nuclear Weapons in Latin America (Treaty of Tlatelolco, 14 February 1967).

Convention for the Conservation and Management of the Vicuña (20 December 1979).

Treaty for Amazonian Co-operation (3 July 1978).

Recommendation concerning the formulation of an American declaration on the environment by the Organization of American States (OAS).

Instruments of a general nature include the following: the agreement concerning the institutional system for the River Plate basin; the Central American Commission on Environment and Development; the Andean Pact; the Caribbean Community (CARICOM); the Acapulco Commitment to Peace, Development and Democracy (29 November 1987) and subsequent declarations of the Group of Rio; and General Assembly resolution 41/11, "Zone of peace and co-operation of the South Atlantic" (27 October 1986).

4.3 Some final observations

Based on the above analysis and presentation, a number of observations may be made concerning two different aspects of the subject. Some of these observations refer exclusively to the question of internal organization or action at the regional or international level, while others specifically concern the strengthening of the region's bargaining power in world forums.

The region is aware of the need for concerted action to cope with many of the environmental conflicts which arise and for the definition of concepts relating to socially equitable and environmentally sustainable forms of integrated management. It is also felt that it will be possible to pinpoint the origin of many of the factors hindering the implementation of a sound form of natural resource management. Furthermore, the international and regional legal system assigns a pivotal role to the State, particularly as regards the task of formulating an environmental policy in keeping with the reorganization of the industrial structure and technological innovation.

Although, generally speaking, the existing conventions and agreements are appropriate in the sense that their provisions represent a suitable response to the situations they are intended to regulate,[8] the fact they are relevant or appropriate does not necessarily mean that they can be implemented or put to use; their actual operability will depend on compliance with them, i.e., on the translation of their provisions into changes in the countries' internal legal systems and, hence, into concrete action on the part of States to fulfil the commitments they have made at the international, regional and subregional levels.

It is important to note that some international treaties, such as the United Nations Convention on the Law of the Sea, which have not yet entered into force have nonetheless had a very strong multiplier effect. Indeed, a multitude of legal provisions have been established at the national level which give expression to the principles contained in the Convention on the Law of the Sea within the internal legal systems of many countries (including some which are not parties to the Convention).

At the national level, the laws of each country need to be analysed in order to determine the extent to which they are conducive to the State's achievement of its objectives. The State should assume a more active role in the following areas:

a) The design of plans and strategies for the management and conservation of the physical environment, and the co-ordination of each of their components with other government policies;

b) The planning and co-ordination of baseline studies and inventories of environmental resources and sources of pollution, and the implementation of natural heritage accounting programmes;

c) The management, restoration and conservation of natural resources at the level of river basins, national parks and other integrated systems;

d) The adjustment of the legal framework for natural resource use and conservation in the light of technological advances and new scientific findings; and

e) The planning and construction of the infrastructure needed to monitor environmental performance, and the pursual of a national effort to internalize the commitments undertaken at the international and regional levels.

At the regional and international levels, steps need to be taken to organize and strengthen the present regulations governing environmental matters. Greater advantage should also be made of existing regional organizations. These topics are discussed further in chapter X.

In considering aspects of the subject relating specifically to the negotiations to be conducted during the preparatory stages and the 1992 conference itself, three points should be borne in mind. Firstly, the international context in which these negotiations on development and environment are to take place must be clearly defined. Clearly, the countries of the region cannot separate their endeavours in this regard from their efforts in such other forums as the General Agreement on Tariffs and Trade (GATT), the United Nations Conference on Trade and Development (UNCTAD) and the United Nations Conference on an International Code of Conduct on the Transfer of Technology. Secondly, past experiences should be exhaustively analysed in order to ensure that the forthcoming negotiations do not give rise to further disappointments. For example, the upcoming negotiations concerning an "Earth charter" call for a re-examination of the process which led up to the formulation of the 1982 World Charter for Nature. Finally, the countries of the region should seek greater co-operation with the countries of Africa and Asia within the framework of commitments made under existing instruments, such as the Basel Convention on the Control of Transboundary Movements of Hazardous Wastes and their Disposal, or the Vienna Convention for the Protection of the Ozone Layer and the corresponding Montreal Protocol.

Notes

[1] See ECLAC, *Changing Production Patterns with Social Equity, op. cit.,* pp. 149-153.

[2] See *La cuestión oceánica en América Latina frente a la Conferencia de las Naciones Unidas sobre el Medio Ambiente y el Desarrollo. Un espacio de análisis para las políticas de la región* (LC/R.911), 3 September 1990, and *Contexto jurídico internacional y regional vinculado al desarrollo, el medio ambiente y los recursos naturales* (LC/R.953), 18 December 1990.

[3] On that occasion the General Assembly adopted the Declaration and Programme of Action on the Establishment of a New International Economic Order (resolutions 3201(5-VI) and 3202 (5-VI)), whose principles were reaffirmed in resolution 3281 (XXIX), which contains the Charter of Economic Rights and Duties of States.

[4] See United Nations, *International Economic Co-operation, in particular the Revitalization of Economic Growth and Development of the Developing Countries* (A/S-18/14), 30 April 1990, especially the annex containing the corresponding declaration.

[5] See United Nations, *World Declaration on the Survival, Protection and Development of Children* and *Plan of Action for Implementing the World Declaration on the Survival, Protection and Development of Children in the 1990s,* New York, 30 September 1990.

[6] See United Nations, *Report of the Ad Hoc Committee of the Whole for the Preparation of the International Development Strategy for the Fourth United Nations Development Decade* (A/45/41), 11 October 1990.

[7] Forty-fifth session, Second Committee, agenda item 81, A/C.2/45/L.93, 11 December 1990.

[8] In respect to the relevance of these instruments, i.e., the extent to which their provisions provide suitable means of responding to social needs and of arriving at solutions for the problems they address, see *Contexto jurídico internacional ...* (LC/R.953), *op. cit.*

Chapter VIII

FINANCING AND SUSTAINABILITY

The achievement of sustainable development hinges upon the net supply of available financing, the formulation of new financial instruments and the materialization of necessary changes in investment practices.

1. Introduction

Financing sustainable development is not easy. Problems arise in three different areas: firstly, in that of the more traditional type of financing aimed at ensuring sufficient levels of investment to permit production capacity to expand at the desired pace; secondly, in the area of the financing required –in terms of amounts and suitable terms and conditions– to rectify past environmental errors; and thirdly, in respect to the appraisal, promotion and financing of new projects and technologies to reconcile the need for growth with the need for sustainability.

The difficulties existing in the first of these areas have already been discussed elsewhere.[1] It has been estimated that in order to raise investment to the equivalent of 22% of the region's gross domestic product (GDP), an additional US$70 billion of financing per year is needed. However, this figure has been calculated on the basis of historical investment/GDP ratios and therefore takes into account neither the need to correct past environmental mistakes nor the need to avoid such errors in the future. If these factors were to be incorporated into the calculations, then the figure would be even higher.

Indeed, according to the figures presented in this study (see chapter VI), it has already been necessary to invest around US$2 billion per annum in the region for goods and equipment designed to prevent or control environmental problems caused by production activities, primarily manufacturing and mining. If a reasonable estimate of other necessary environmental investments or expenditures, based on what occurs in other areas of the world, is added to this sum, then the figure rises steeply. If the need to redress past errors is taken into consideration as well, then it would not be surprising if the amount of financing needed to make the region's development sustainable bordered on US$10 billion per year.

Even this high figure may be a conservative estimate. The developed countries invest between 1% and 2% of their GDP to improve or maintain their quality of life (see chapter VI). The region's environmental needs and the approach it takes to environmental problems are very different, and the low figure of the annual investment range of over US$10 billion to US$20 billion yielded by the calculation of the same percentage of GDP for Latin America is no doubt the upper limit of any reasonable range of environmental investment and expenditure in the region.

2. Financial capital and natural resources

The above estimates provide some idea of how difficult it will be to finance sustainable development unless the countries of the region receive a net transfer of financial resources. If the region is to succeed in changing its production

109

patterns while promoting greater social equity and environmental sustainability, its rates of capital formation will have to be increased significantly and be reflected in progressively higher levels of investment. Hence, financial capital is unquestionably a key link in the chain of development.

However, the problem is not entirely one of quantity. The type of financing is also important. By virtue of the very nature of ecosystems, dealing with them calls for new formulas and instruments. Indeed, a worldwide consensus as to this fact has come into being and has recently been expressed in the creation of bilateral and multilateral investment funds.

Methods of evaluation, incentive systems and financing instruments all need to be carefully reviewed and modified in order to adapt them to the requirements of sustainable development. As we strive to solve certain critical problems in the region, such as the debt issue, we must seek ways of reconciling sustainability with growth.

The development of domestic capital markets and the availability of external financing on favourable terms are crucial elements in all these respects. In poorly developed financial markets, funds are available only for short terms and the investment horizon tends to grow shorter. Natural resources are reproduced over very long periods, however. There are trees, for example, which require over 50 to 100 years to mature. An irrational utilization of such resources will therefore result in their irreversible depletion or destruction. A use rate in excess of the "critical zone" (i.e., the maximum sustainable yield) is enough to start the resource off on a downhill slide from depletion to extinction. The greater the degree of irreversibility, the narrower the margin available for development. Many natural resources are indivisible; if they are divided, they lose important characteristics which are an inherent part of their function. Finally, natural resources are not homogeneous; on the contrary, climatic, economic and social factors make them highly heterogeneous.

These differences do not diminish the high degree of complementarity existing between financial and natural capital. Given the levels of development of the region's economies, the implementation of environmentally sustainable policies is out of the question unless full advantage is taken of domestic and international capital markets. Since these markets serve an integrative purpose at all levels, they provide access to the use of certain types of resources, particularly in those cases in which gaining such access demands large sums of money.

There are, however, certain rigidities which need to be recognized. The presence of such rigidities becomes apparent, for example, when a financial instrument's repayment period is shorter than the timespan required for the natural resource to reproduce itself. In these cases, investments intended to improve the use of these resources are "unprofitable" from the standpoint of those responsible for managing the budget. This situation arises in the case of both national and international financial instruments. At the national level, it is difficult for this type of operation to compete successfully for financing against alternative investments. This is partly because it is the present generation which must make the financial commitment, whereas the resulting benefits can only be looked for over the long term. Another reason is that environmental projects generate a disproportionate demand for current financial resources owing to maintenance and operational requirements as well as those of sustainability.

In view of the above, financial markets need to be strengthened and developed in order to permit the region to attract a larger volume of resources whose payback periods, conditions and interest rates will be better suited to the purposes of natural resource development and preservation. Generally speaking, the purpose of such markets should be to promote and attract long-term savings, and institutional savings may be a good starting point for such an effort.

The search for appropriate means of financing the region's development effort has been going on for quite some time. In the agricultural sector, for example, there are a number of instances in which forms of payment –the kind of financial capital– are defined primarily on the basis of the market for the products in question rather than on the production cycle. In the light of the fact that special financing instruments have come into use for such activities as scientific research and technology transfer, the question arises as to whether there is a justification for the creation of special funds for financing sustainable development.

3. Justification for special financing

As is also true of many other areas of the world, the region not only needs more resources; it also needs special funds that can provide financing on favourable terms. The scope of this statement is not confined to the issue of the external debt burden that is weighing down the countries of the region (see box VIII-1).

Since the relevant externalities stem either from production or from the conditions of financing, sustainable development requires production or financial subsidies within the context of a market-based resource allocation system. This means that distortions transmitted via the financial system have to be avoided and that the way in which financial capital is to be transferred to the sectors entrusted with the development of natural resources has to be clearly defined. Granting such subsidies *via the budget* is the most effective form of accomplishing this. To that end, it is necessary to *justify such subsidies* and to strengthen the State's role in order to obtain them.

At the international level, it is important to *distinguish between the "allocation" and the "incidence" of environmental measures*. Bearing this distinction in mind, a case can be made for a country to reallocate its resources so that other countries receive some benefit. In such instances, the country could be granted special financing which the State could then distribute in the form of subsidies in such a way as to achieve the desired allocation. It would of course be unacceptable for a country which was called upon to transform its activities but which did not receive any of the benefits deriving therefrom to have to bear the entire cost of the actions it took on behalf of other countries at their market value. The situation is much the same when a change occurs in incidence of costs, since those who are affected should receive compensation. It is therefore essential that the State be strengthened so that it can obtain special funds from the countries benefiting from its actions with which to finance subsidies for natural-resource development.

A similar line of reasoning should enable the State to impose taxes to finance investments that favour a more rational use of natural resources. If these investments benefit other agents, the tax burden should fall on those agents. By the same token, this reasoning might also justify taxing agents which allocate their resources in ways that augment other agents' costs.[2]

It is also important to *distinguish between the conditions for gaining access to financial capital markets and access to the exploitation of natural resources*. Given the conditions of poverty and marginality in which large segments of the rural population in Latin America live, it is common for them to have access to natural resources, but not to the formal capital market. The sectors which find themselves in this position operate on the basis of a large financial differential (market rates far above social discount rates) which leads to an irrational use of natural resources. This situation also justifies the levying of taxes and efforts to secure special international funds to subsidize integral programmes of investment in human capital, natural resources and production.

Other situations which generate externalities and which justify taxation or special funds for subsidies include the following: i) those in which the overall discount rates are too high to justify long-term programmes; ii) cases involving the protection of environmental diversity and the conservation and protection of flora and fauna; iii) in situations where the aim is the net protection of the cultural heritage of certain human settlements; iv) when it is a question of meeting institutional requirements, such as a need for more information, scientific research, or monitoring and evaluation; and v) in situations relating to global agreements (such as those relating to the ozone layer, the greenhouse effect, protection of the oceans and biodiversity).

The success of a fund of this type will depend on the *criteria for allocation and return* which are used. Such a fund should be used to provide financing only for programmes which are to be undertaken within the framework of global environmental agreements and national

Box VIII-1
GLOBAL ENVIRONMENT FUND

The Global Environment Fund is a pilot programme through which developing countries may receive donations or concessional loans to help them implement projects that may serve to protect the global environment. Projects in four different areas may be covered by this programme:

a) Protection of the ozone layer. The Fund will assist developing countries to begin developing or using substitutes for chlorofluorocarbons (CFCs).

b) Limitation of the greenhouse effect. With a view to reducing emissions of such gases as carbon dioxide, CFC and methane, the Fund will support the development of new energy sources and the efficient use of existing sources, as well as fostering the use of more appropriate technologies and fuels and reforestation or effective forestry resource management.

c) Protection of biodiversity. The Fund will aid developing countries to preserve specific areas in order to ensure the protection of their ecosystems and their biodiversity.

d) Protection of international water resources. The Fund will collaborate in projects designed to: strengthen planning capabilities to prevent oil spills; reduce the pollution of international water resources; prevent and clean up toxic wastes in rivers which, due to their volume of flow, have a major impact on international water resources; and conserve unique water sources or resources.

In keeping with its experimental nature, the Fund will provide resources, initially in modest amounts, for programmes and projects relating to the global environment whose aim is to seek out ways of strengthening analytical, regulatory and supervisory capabilities at the local level and to evaluate means of sharing existing or new technologies. Owing to the Fund's experimental character, its operating procedures will have to be selective.

The programme calls for broad-based, multilateral financing of the Fund which is to be administered under a tripartite agreement among the World Bank, the United Nations Development Programme (UNDP) and the United Nations Environment Programme (UNEP). It is hoped that initial contributions to the Fund will total approximately US$1.5 billion. Cofinancing agreements may also play a part in the Fund provided that they are of a highly concessional nature.

The Fund will finance the implementation of investment projects which a) would not be justified at the national level if their total cost were to be covered entirely by the executing country, but whose cost could be reduced by means of concessional financing to the point where a reasonable threshold of net benefits would be achieved; or b) would be justified at the national level but would require that added costs be incurred in order to generate additional global benefits. In the latter case, the concessional financing to be provided by the Fund would be directed towards covering only those additional costs which would generate net benefits at the global level. The Fund will not normally finance environmental projects whose costs and benefits make their execution economically viable for an individual country.

In order to be eligible for financing, projects will have to be in keeping with international environmental conventions and with the environmental strategy or programme of the country in question, use available appropriate technologies, generate net benefits and have a high priority from a global standpoint. It is expected that most of the projects selected for such financing will be located in countries whose existing or proposed institutional and policy frameworks are conducive to the achievement of the projects' objectives. The Fund will support programmes whose objectives include the reinforcement of those frameworks. Consideration will be given to projects submitted by governments or by government-sanctioned NGOs, as well as projects under review by the World Bank or, possibly, by other multilateral finance agencies.

UNEP will provide scientific and technological co-operation in connection with the identification and selection of projects. UNDP will co-ordinate the financing of the necessary preinvestment activities, while the World Bank will in most cases serve as the executing agency for these activities, with assistance from UNEP and other specialized agencies.

The terms and conditions pertaining to the use of Fund resources will be established by the Fund's participants, which include both developed and developing countries. The World Bank will convene two meetings of the participants each year, during which the countries will evaluate the fulfilment of these terms and conditions and propose any necessary changes, discuss the general policy framework of the Fund, consider the programmes of work of the three executing agencies (World Bank, UNDP and UNEP), and review the progress made in executing these programmes.

environmental policies or which are concerned with promoting a sound use of natural resources, the transfer and use of appropriate low-cost technologies, or the establishment of monitoring and evaluation units. In its most rudimentary form, such a fund's financial capacity will depend upon the governments' estimation of the opportunity cost of the available funds, the accepted investment criteria, and institutional and political capabilities for reallocating the available financial resources.

4. Conditionality and additionality in external financing

Conditionality and additionality are two highly important aspects of the international debate concerning development finance. The former refers to the conditions attached to the financing of certain activities, while the latter refers to the need for a *net increase* in the funding made available for sustainable development by domestic and international sources of financing.

The countries of the region need to prepare themselves to strengthen the capacity of their financial markets to attract domestic and external savings for use in the development of natural resources. In the case of external savings, the topic of conditionality will certainly be the pivotal issue in the negotiations. The key questions to be addressed will be the following: What conditions are acceptable? Which of these will apply to the granting of the loan? What extent of cross-conditionality can be accepted? How are these conditions to be prevented from acting as a new form of protectionism on the part of developed countries?

In the case of domestic savings, the subject of additionality will surely be a crucial issue in terms of the macroeconomic impact of the measures to be taken. The chief questions will be: What effects will taxation have on net savings? How can the financial system be reformed in order to encourage long-term savings? What role does the development of insurance markets play in promoting long-term saving and investment? Is it possible to reform institutional savings systems in such a way as to channel funds to the preservation of natural resources and investment in such

resources? How viable are these measures in macroeconomic terms?

There are no easy answers to these questions. As regards the attraction of external resources, the answers will depend on what benefits the parties to the negotiations hope to receive. It should be emphasized, however, that some apparent bilateral benefits may prove to be costs for the region as a whole. This is the case, for example, of the conditions relating to the protection of international trade and to the limits placed on the development, transfer and use of technologies. If negotiations on these points go badly, they may prove to be a hindrance to regional integration.

During a period marked by the structural adjustment of their economies, the countries have stood firm in their rejection of the idea of cross-conditionality, which tends to penalize recipient countries. The only viable way of avoiding this is to employ strong, effective mechanisms of co-ordination in the negotiation and administration of external loans. The weaker such mechanisms are, the greater the probability that the countries will find themselves subject to cross-conditionality.

This is a high-priority area for ECLAC. As work proceeds on national and regional sectoral studies that will provide more information and contribute to an increased understanding of environmental matters, the region as a whole, as well as the individual countries, will be in a better position to negotiate their loans. The final chapter of this document sets forth a series of proposals regarding actions, studies and programmes to strengthen the countries' bargaining power in this respect.

Additionality is fundamental to environmentally sustainable development. If the financing of this development entails a mere *redistribution* of existing financial resources, this will have a very adverse effect on the countries of the region, especially the poorest of them. These countries tend to be limited by two economic forces. One is the necessity of capital formation, which makes a progressive form of financing for development programmes and investments imperative; the other is the excessive pressure exerted by poverty on natural resources and the environment (see chapter V).

113

5. New instruments: debt-for-nature swaps

One of the financial instruments which has been used in the region is the "debt-for-nature swap". The large external debt accumulated by Latin America during the 1970s had, by 1982, reached a level of US$330 billion, three fourths of which was accounted for by loans from private banks. In the ensuing years this debt continued to grow, although more slowly, and by 1990 had reached US$420 billion, 55% of which is owed to private banks.[3] Most of the remainder represents obligations in respect of bilateral and multilateral agencies.

The debt crisis has prompted the international financial community to accept the fact that a portion of this debt is unpayable. Soon after the outbreak of the debt crisis, a small secondary market emerged on which creditor banks could trade their debt paper at discounts of up to 20%. As the payments problem worsened, the volume of transactions in this market increased, as did the discounts. The total value of secondary-market transactions was estimated to have reached US$65 billion by 1990, while the average discount on Latin American debt paper was around 70% in 1989-1990[4] (see table VIII-1).

The continuation of the debt crisis and the growth of the secondary market led to the creation of debt conversion programmes (commonly known as "swaps") whose object was to take advantage of these discounts to redeem the debt paper circulating on that market. These programmes, most of which involved the conversion of debt owed to overseas banks into productive investments, came into more general use in 1985-1986.

As time passed people realized that this mechanism could be used to finance environmental conservation programmes, and debt-for-nature swaps gained in importance as world concern about environmental protection grew.

Table VIII-1

LATIN AMERICA AND THE CARIBBEAN: VALUE OF EXTERNAL DEBT PAPER IN THE SECONDARY MARKET

(Percentage of fare value)

	1986			1987			1988			1989			1990		
	Jan.	June	Dec.	Jan.	June	Dec.	Jan.	June	Dec.	Jan.	June	Dec.	Jan.	June	Nov.
Argentina	62	65	66	64	52	35	32	25	21	20	13	13	12	13	17
Bolivia	...	6	7	8	9	11	11	11	10	10	11	11	11	...	...
Brazil	75	74	74	72	62	46	46	51	41	37	31	22	25	24	26
Colombia	82	81	86	86	85	65	65	65	57	56	57	64	60	64	65
Costa Rica	...	48	35	35	36	15	15	11	12	13	14	17	18	...	...
Chile	65	67	67	68	70	61	61	60	56	60	61	59	62	65	73
Ecuador	68	64	65	65	50	37	35	27	13	13	12	14	14	16	20
Guatemala	...	52	60	61	67	77	57	...	...	...	...	...	...	...	...
Honduras	...	40	40	40	39	22	22	22	22	22	17	20	21	...	...
Jamaica	...	45	45	45	38	33	33	38	40	40	41	40	40	44	...
Mexico	69	59	56	57	57	51	50	51	43	40	40	36	37	45	43
Nicaragua	...	4	4	4	5	4	4	2	2	2	1	1	1	...	...
Panama	...	69	68	68	67	39	39	24	21	19	10	12	19	12	12
Peru	25	20	18	18	14	7	7	6	5	5	3	6	6	4	4
Dominican Republic	...	45	45	45	45	23	23	20	22	22	22	13	13	17	...
Uruguay	...	63	66	68	74	60	59	60	60	60	57	50	50	49	55
Venezuela	80	76	74	75	71	58	55	55	41	38	37	34	35	46	49
Average [a]	...	64.9	64.2	63.7	58.5	46.5	45.1	45.4	37.7	35.2	31.9	28.0	29.5	33.3	34.7

Source: United Nations, Department of International Economic and Social Affairs (DIESA), on the basis of bid prices compiled by Salomon Brothers, High Yield Department.

[a] Weighted by the amount of bank debt.

5.1 *Experiences in Latin America*

The concept of swaps is a simple one, but in practice they are quite difficult to organize. The main stages entailed in carrying out these transactions are as follows:

A non-governmental organization (NGO) involved in the field of nature conservation or the government of an industrialized country buys a promissory note representing a portion of the external debt of one of the countries in the region at a high discount in the secondary market;

The foreign buyer hands over the promissory note to the government of the debtor country in exchange for a financial instrument denominated in the local currency (cash or bonds). This exchange may or may not give the government in question the benefit of part of the discount obtained by the buyer on the secondary market;

The local-currency-denominated financial instrument is assigned to the financing of a conservation project previously selected by agreement between the debtor government and the NGO or foreign government. Such projects are usually managed by local conservation groups in co-operation with the country's governmental authorities.

By the end of 1990 a total of nine debt-for-nature swaps had been carried out in four countries of the region (see table VIII-2). The face value of the debt redeemed by these means amounted to US$90.5 million, but the corresponding debt paper had cost the foreign buyers US$14 million; in other words, they bought the debt on the secondary market at an average discount of 85%. For their part, the governments of the region had paid the equivalent of US$53 million in local currency in this buy-back operation, which means they received an average discount of 41%, or slightly less than one-half the discount obtained by the foreign buyers [5] (see boxes VIII-2, VIII-3 and VIII-4).

In addition, another six swaps of this type were conducted in five developing countries outside of Latin America and the Caribbean. In these cases the buyers received an average discount of 62% on the debt they purchased, but the governments concerned apparently failed to obtain any of the

secondary-market discount when the debt paper was converted into local currency.[6]

Generally speaking, the environmental protection projects in the region which have been financed by these swaps have had quite similar characteristics. They tend to deal with the protection of areas that are well known for their great wealth of biological diversity, including endangered species; with regions inhabited by indigenous communities; or with the establishment and reinforcement of educational, training and research programmes in the field of ecological conservation. The zones protected by these agreements remain under the country's jurisdiction and are areas in which there is little or no development.

A large portion of the studies done on this subject have concluded that debt-for-nature swaps benefit all parties concerned. They contend that the commercial banks may succeed in divesting themselves of a problematic component of their loan portfolios by selling the debt in the secondary market; conservation groups may be able to multiply the impact of their expenditure because the dollar equivalent of the local-currency instruments they receive in exchange for the debt paper is greater than the amount they initially invested to repurchase the debt in the secondary market; and for debtor countries, the swap serves the dual purpose of reducing their external debt –principal and annual interest payments– and buttressing their policies for the protection of the nation's environmental heritage.

The first debt-equity swaps were justified in the same way. However, as time has passed the experts have begun to evaluate them more critically and to point out their potential disadvantages for debtor countries. Since debt-for-nature swaps are essentially a variation on the same theme, the evaluation of this technique can be expected to arrive at similar conclusions in time.

5.2 *Swaps: alternative opportunity costs*

It is important to analyse the costs involved in debt-for-nature swaps. First of all, various economic studies have shown that partial,

Table VIII-2
LATIN AMERICA AND OTHER DEVELOPING REGIONS:
DEBT-FOR-NATURE SWAPS
(Thousands of dollars)

			External debt redeemed by foreign buyer			Conversion of note into local currency	
	Year	Buyer	Face value	Cost F/C [a]	Discount [b]	Cost L/C [c]	Discount [d]
Latin America							
Bolivia	1987	CI	650	100	85%	100[e]	85%
Ecuador	1987	WWF	1 000	354	65%	1 000	-
Costa Rica	1988	NPF	5 400	918	83%	4 050	25%
Costa Rica	1988	Holland	33 000	5 000	85%	9 900	70%
Costa Rica	1989	TNC	5 600	784	86%	1 680	70%
Costa Rica	1989	Sweden	24 500	3 500	86%	17 100	30%
Ecuador	1989	WWF/TNC/MBG	9 000	1 108.8	88%	9 000	-
Dominican Republic	1990	PRCT/TNC	582	116.4	80%	582	-
Costa Rica	1990	S/WWF/TNC	10 753.6	1 953.5	82%	9 602.9	11%
Total			**90 485.6**	**13 834.7**	**85%**	**53 014.9**	**41%**
Other developing countries							
Philippines	1989	WWF	390	200	49%	390	-
Madagascar	1989	WWF	2 111.1	950	55%	2 111.1	-
Zambia	1989	WWF	2 270	454	80%	2 270	-
Poland	1990	WWF	50	11.5	77%	50	-
Philippines	1990	WWF	900	438.8	51%	900	-
Madagascar	1990	WWF	919.4	445.9	51%	919.4	-
Total			**6 640.5**	**2 500.2**	**62%**	**6 640.5**	

Source: Calculated on the basis of *LDC Debt Report*, 15 October 1990.

TNC : The Nature Conservancy
WWF : World Wildlife Fund
PRCT : Puerto Rico Conservation Trust, Puerto Rico
MBG : Missouri Botanical Garden, United States
NPF : National Parks Foundation, Costa Rica
CI : Conservation International, United States
S : Sweden
F/C : Foreign currency
L/C : Local currency

[a] Outlay required to purchase debt at face value in secondary market.

[b] (Cost F/C face value - 1).

[c] Dollar equivalent of local currency amount exchanged for external debt note. Local currency is transferred in the form of bonds or cash.

[d] (Cost L/C face value - 1).

[e] An additional US$150 000 were mobilized for the USAID project.

DEBT-FOR-NATURE SWAPS: THE CASE OF BOLIVIA

On 13 July 1987 Bolivia signed the first agreement providing for external debt reduction in exchange for a government commitment to protect the natural resources located in one zone of the country. The agreement was drawn up between the Government of Bolivia and Conservation International, a private environmental organization in the United States, and included the following commitments:

a) Conservation International was to purchase US$650 000 of Bolivia's external debt and turn the corresponding debt paper over to the Government, as well as furnishing technical and administrative co-operation for the implementation of an environmental management programme in the designated area of the region of Beni, in the Amazon basin.

b) In exchange, the Government of Bolivia was to ensure the maximum possible degree of legal protection for the 135 000-hectare Beni Biological Station and create three protected zones in adjacent areas: the Yacuma regional park, covering 130 000 hectares; a protected area administered by the Beni Development Corporation (CORDOBENI); and a sustainable area of 670 000 hectares in the Chimanes jungle (forest).

c) The Government of Bolivia was to create a US$250 000 fund to finance the management of the Beni Biological Station, of which US$150 000 in local currency would be provided by the United States Agency for International Development (USAID). The fund was to be administered by the Ministry of Agriculture and Peasant Affairs of Bolivia and a local representative of Conservation International.

Conservation International purchased debt paper having a face value of US$650 000 on the secondary market at an 85% discount, which means that it paid about 15 cents on the dollar for the debt. In addition, it set up an administrative structure for the implementation of conservation plans, conducted studies on the population of the protected area and initiated steps to arrange for special financing from the International Tropical Timber Organization for the purpose of organizing a sustainable forest use programme.

However, a variety of budgetary problems delayed the disbursement of the Government's contribution of US$100 000 for 21 months, occasioning a loss, according to Conservation International estimates, of around US$60 000 in interest. In addition, more than two years after the agreement was signed the legislation concerning the protection of the Beni reserve was still pending, a delay which was due initially to a heated controversy and protracted debate concerning the nature of the agreement, and later to the intricate negotiations held with various indigenous groups in the zone and to the pressure brought to bear by a number of interest groups, including those representing members of the logging industry which have leases in the protected area.

Source: D. Page, "Debt-for-nature swaps. Experience gained, lessons learned", *International Environmental Affairs*, vol. 1, No. 4, 1989.

fragmented debt redemption operations are not necessarily a good deal for a sovereign government. The argument is as follows: when the price of a debt on the secondary market is a reasonably accurate reflection of the chances that the debt will be serviced, then the country participating in the swap ends up paying more than what the debt paper is worth. This is because the bid price is determined by the market, and the market reflects the average value of the total stock of debt (including both its payable and unpayable portions). Thus, the debt paper which is redeemed would have a lower value at the margin than the price paid for it in a buy-back operation on the secondary market. Considered from another angle, the operation is equivalent to granting a subsidy to the banks benefiting from the repurchase transaction. There is also another subsidy, which arises out of the fact that the conditions under which a swap is conducted are usually such that the amount of local currency paid out by the debtor country is a multiple of the price paid for the debt on the secondary market. The reader will recall that, as noted earlier, the countries of the region have exchanged the equivalent of US$53 million in local currency for

Box VIII-3
DEBT-FOR-NATURE SWAPS: THE CASE OF COSTA RICA

In 1987 and 1988 Costa Rica purchased US$69 million of its external debt, representing slightly less than 5% of its total commercial bank debt, for the equivalent of US$33 million in local currency. This sum, supplemented by national counterpart funds, was used to finance the protection and environmental management of national parks, the strengthening of public institutions and non-governmental organizations concerned with environmental matters, and the implementation of reforestation projects and environmental education and research activities.

In August 1987 the Central Bank of Costa Rica approved a plan for swapping US$5.4 million of debt, at a 75% discount, for non-negotiable, local-currency stabilization bonds having a maturity of five years and an average interest rate of 25%. The Banco Cooperativo Costarricense was designated as the trustee, and the use of the resources was to be supervised by a council formed by representatives of the National Park Service (now a non-governmental organization (NGO) but originally created by the Government), the Ministry of Natural Resources, Energy and Mines, and the Fundación Neotrópica (an NGO). The debt paper, whose value fell from 55 to 16 cents on the dollar during 1987, was purchased with about US$900 000 in donations from private organizations in the United States and Europe.

These resources have been used to finance activities and projects selected by the donor agencies from a menu of options presented by the supervisory council. Some of the funds have been used to strengthen the institutional structure of local foundations, as well as for environmental management and education programmes, while a large part of the financing has been employed to purchase land within the areas designated as national parks; the bonds have been used as collateral for loans when cash funds are required for this purpose.

The Governments of Sweden and the Netherlands contributed US$3.5 million and US$5 million, respectively, for the purchase of commercial bank debt. In the former case, debt paper previously bought at a discount through a financial agent in New York was converted by the Central Bank of Costa Rica into local currency at 70% of its value. In the latter case, which was subsequent to the above operation, the Central Bank converted the debt paper at 30% of its value. In the transaction made possible by Sweden's contribution, it was agreed that the bonds, which had a maturity of four years and a 15% rate of interest, would be used to finance a management programme for the Guanacaste National Park and environmental education and research activities. The agreement concerning the resources derived from the operation financed by the Netherlands, which were converted into the same type of bonds as in the first transaction, called for the implementation of a programme providing for the development of tree nurseries as well as loans and technical co-operation for small-scale producers engaging in reforestation activities.

In addition, in November 1988 the Legislative Assembly decided to exempt debt-for-nature swaps from the 8% tax levied by the Central Bank. The resources made available by this measure are to be used to cover extrabudgetary expenses (e.g., firefighting) incurred by the Ministry of Natural Resources, Energy and Mines. The available pool of resources has also been augmented by the frequent contribution of additional counterpart funds, and further inputs of external resources. It was also agreed that an additional US$45 million in debt swaps would be authorized over a three-year period for the purpose of financing natural resource, educational and microenterprise projects.

external debt paper worth US$14 million on the secondary market. This represents a subsidy equivalent to US$39 million, or 44% of the face value of the redeemed debt.[7]

Secondly, debt swaps lead to an expansion of the money supply which may have inflationary effects. There are, however, ways of minimizing the impact of swaps on domestic price levels. For example, many countries have chosen to exchange medium-term bonds for such debts. These bonds spread out the money issue over time

as well as indirectly reducing the subsidy received by the conservation groups taking part in such swaps.

Finally, the conversion of external obligations into local currency increases the effective amount of fiscal expenditure during a time of structural adjustment and severe fiscal constraints, which may well be to a country's disadvantage. Cases of such situations have occurred in countries that are not servicing their external debt punctually.

5.3 *Conversion of bilateral debt*

Thus far, debt-for-nature swaps have involved private bank claims. Nevertheless, it is likely that the conversion of official debt may also serve as a vehicle for financing environmental conservation projects.

One sign of a move in this direction is the proposal concerning external debt contained in the Enterprise for the Americas Initiative which was announced in June 1990 by the Government of the United States. This proposal calls for a reduction of the debt owed by countries of the region to official United States bodies. Under the terms of the bill submitted to Congress by the Administrator, the United States would be willing to: i) reduce the concessional debt, and ii) allow the corresponding interest to be paid in local currency and deposited in trust funds. These funds would then be used to finance national environmental protection projects.

It should be noted that some of the costs associated with the conversion of bank claims do not arise in the conversion of claims held by official bodies. For example, if in order to avail itself of this option, a country must be up to date on its debt service payments to the government in

question, then the conversion of such claims would reduce the country's fiscal expenditure. Furthermore, so long as there is no formula for reducing the value of these obligations other than participation in these environmental programmes, their opportunity cost may be relatively low. Indeed, the fact of the matter is that the only other alternative is to bear the full cost of servicing the debt.

The conversion of debt into environmental protection programmes has both benefits and costs for the treasury of the debtor country, but the costs will be magnified if the country is in the midst of a structural adjustment and suffers from a shortage of fiscal resources. Hence, each transaction should be carefully evaluated in terms of its impact on the population and in the light of possible alternative uses of these scarce resources.

Some of the problems associated with debt-for-nature swaps can be solved if the international agenda in this area is modified. When international conservation groups invest in environmental protection, they naturally prefer those projects which will afford them the highest possible return on their investment. It is therefore not surprising that such groups tend to choose projects having a very high international profile, since these are the ones most closely identified with the groups' interests and are therefore likely to produce the returns and benefits they seek. Developing countries would do well to urge international conservation groups to provide an opportunity for undertaking environmental projects whose benefits will be felt more clearly and immediately by the population of the debtor country. Examples of these types of projects include initiatives to clean up the air, the cities, rivers and the seas. Such an approach is all the more important when the project calls for the use of fiscal resources. In addition, the scope of such projects should not be confined to conservation, but should instead also encompass the restoration or expansion of other forms of natural capital, including reforestation.

6. Nature and styles of future investment

Thus far the discussion has focused on the relationships between financing and environmental sustainability, but the subject of investment practices also needs to be addressed. The region's experiences have demonstrated that *changes in forms of financing engender corresponding changes in investment practices*.

As was noted in chapter III, there is a close relationship between economic policy and the environment, and the secondary and external effects of these policies are so significant that they require special attention. Hence, although the technical design of some investment projects may be sound, the environmental sustainability of these investments may be seriously jeopardized if policies are mutually contradictory. Because of these considerations, a broader definition of such projects is called for.

Consequently, *the traditional style associated with specific-focus projects should be supplemented by sectoral or regional investment programmes*. Such programmes would involve the same aspects as structural adjustment programmes, including such elements as: sectoral or regional policy, management policies and approaches, the development of human capital, institutional management and changes, sectoral or regional investments, services at the sectoral or national level, macroeconomic aspects, the institutional structure of production, roles of economic agents and the State, legislation and formulas for the provision of financing.

There are various examples of these types of programmes in the region. Forestry programmes are one of them. In addition to including elements of specific-focus projects such as those concerned with tree planting, these programmes also involve undertakings at the sectoral or regional level, such as the definition of policies, research, changes in forestry agencies, the training of foresters, national public awareness campaigns, trade and investment policies, or economic incentives for reforestation. These programmes are a more effective means of laying the institutional foundations for the joint participation of the State, the private sector and the community.

7. Financial policy: implementation of a strategy

There are four areas of work involved in the design of financial policies which can contribute to the sustainability of development. The first is *economic policy*, which has an impact on financial resources that can be invested. Within this sphere, financial policies should be such as to promote subsidies for investment in projects directly related to the development and preservation of the environment. If this is done, the interest rate will not be an obstacle to the evaluation of a project on the basis of the social discount rate, as is the case of reforestation projects in Chile. In addition, financing must be provided for the process of internalizing the direct and indirect costs of ecological damage, as well as those associated with the preservation and enhancement of the environment.

The second relates to the promotion of *public and private investment programmes* aimed at preserving the environment. In this case, a distinction must be drawn between the need to reduce the risk deriving from uncertainty as to the profitability of the project (which is not a problem of financing) and the need to cover the risk associated with its financing. Because of the long-term nature of these projects, the latter type is a built-in risk for financial institutions, and its coverage requires the development of means for guaranteeing loans as well as of insurance and risk-sharing mechanisms. These incentives for the financial system should be designed within the framework of a policy directed towards financing sustainable development.

The third area is the creation of *institutions to regulate the ownership of natural resources* in two types of situations. The first is that in which access to a resource is not subject to clear limits (e.g., access to marine resources) and the rate at which individual firms exploit the resource may exceed the optimum social rate of use. The second type of situation is that in which clearly-defined limits have been placed on access to natural resources, but access to the financial resources required for their exploitation is lacking (segmentation of the financial market), and the natural resource is therefore assigned to other, socially inefficient uses. In both cases financial policy should be supplemented by the creation of institutions which delimit the ownership of and access to the various forms of capital in such a way as to reflect the value of the effective scarcity rents of each mineral resource or other stock of natural capital so that the market price of the corresponding flows will be an accurate indication of their opportunity cost. Otherwise there will be a poor intertemporal allocation of resources.

The fourth area is that of the *regulations* governing the incorporation of the costs of ecological damage into the production structures of the economy. Financial policy-makers should look upon the interest rate as a price which influences the selection of technologies for tapping natural resources. Financial institutions should also be subject to regular supervision based on clearly-defined rules and standards for assessing the environmental impacts of their investment projects and lending programmes for commercial and production activities.

8.   An increase in investment capacity

A final consideration is that demands for increased financing for sustainable development cannot be made unless there is an internal capability to design, assess and execute investment programmes. In terms of environmental sustainability, the region's capabilities in this respect are quite limited. The region's civil services have been seriously weakened, and it therefore lacks the elements needed in order to absorb the amount of financing which may eventually become available.

If the effectiveness of the region's institutions in these areas does not improve, the efforts made during this decade to design and implement environmental programmes may end in a resounding failure whose social and political consequences may extend beyond the boundaries of the region and whose global environmental impacts could be serious indeed. Great opportunities for gaining access to financing for environmental initiatives appear to be in the offing during the present decade; there is a great deal of interest in environmental programmes, but it is also true that the region runs the risk of failing to put these resources to good use. The pressure to accept this flow of financing may result in a setback in net terms if the countries accept such financing within a context of severe institutional weakness.

Development finance agencies should therefore consider the possibility of designing special preinvestment programmes in fields relating to sustainable development, as well as special programmes for providing advanced training and facilitating the countries' access to the technologies needed to change the region's production patterns while prompting social equity and environmental sustainability. Such programmes should be an integral part of the countries' short- and long-term strategies. A relative abundance of funding for environmental projects is only *one* of the elements required to solve the region's environmental problems.

Notes

¹ See ECLAC, *Changing Production Patterns with Social Equity, op. cit.*, chapter 1.

² In the international field, a proposal has been made for the establishment of a levy of US$1 per barrel of oil sold, to be earmarked for an internationally managed fund that would be used to finance conservation and environmental clean-up projects.

³ ECLAC, *Preliminary overview of the economy of Latin America and the Caribbean, 1990* (LC/G.1646), Santiago, Chile, 19 December 1990.

⁴ World Bank, *Financial flows to developing countries*, Quarterly Review, Washington, D.C., June 1990.

⁵ Calculated on the basis of data provided in LDC Debt Report, Washington, D.C., October 1990.

⁶ *Ibid.*

⁷ LDC Debt Report, *op. cit.*

Chapter IX

ENVIRONMENTAL SUSTAINABILITY, INTERNATIONAL CO-OPERATION AND THE GLOBAL LIST OF ENVIRONMENTAL PRIORITIES

Global environmental problems are the result of national and local development policies and styles. They can be brought under control only in a context of heightened international co-operation.

1. Environmental sustainability and international co-operation

The United Nations Conference on Environment and Development will be taking place against a background of profound changes in the world. Despite the gravity of recent events in the Gulf, which have introduced disturbing elements at the international level, the rapid détente between the two great powers which have represented the main political and ideological division of the world since the Second World War has been accompanied by a climate of progress towards the free determination of peoples and respect for human rights.

Although the achievements with regard to consolidating the spirit of co-operation in international economic relations and overcoming social problems have not been so marked, there has nevertheless been a certain tendency in recent years to submit economic and social issues of a transnational nature for discussion in multilateral forums, thus complementing a certain propensity on the part of the main developed economies to resort to bilateral arrangements or agreements between a limited number of countries in dealing with such issues.

Examples of this tendency are the multilateral negotiations held within the framework of the General Agreement on Tariffs and Trade (GATT)

with the aim of achieving a new international trade order, and the efforts (so far, rather timid) to reshape the financial and monetary order, at least in part, within the framework of the forums associated with the World Bank and the International Monetary Fund.

The United Nations, for its part, has dealt with the issue of international economic co-operation on a number of occasions during the past year. Among the proposals adopted, mention may be made of the Declaration on International Economic Co-operation, in particular the Revitalization of Economic Growth and Development of the Developing Countries,[1] adopted at the eighteenth special session of the General Assembly, the decisions adopted by the Second United Nations Conference on the Least Developed Countries,[2] the declaration of the World Summit for Children,[3] and the International Development Strategy (IDS) for the Fourth United Nations Development Decade, adopted by the General Assembly.[4] With regard to the present document, mention may also be made of General Assembly resolution 44/228 convening the United Nations Conference on Environment and Development "in the context of strengthened national and international efforts to promote sustainable and environmentally sound development in all countries".[5]

All these documents have various features in common which are worth noting.[6] First of all, they are marked by a greater degree of consensus on various matters than similar efforts made in previous years. In this respect, there seems to have been some softening of the tone of confrontation and denunciation of the past, which had established a clear gap between the positions of the developed and developing countries.

Secondly, there is an acceptance by the developing and developed countries alike that both the domestic efforts of the former and the co-operation of the latter are indispensable elements for closing the gap which separates them.

Thirdly, there is some degree of consensus on the priority issues which should be placed on the agenda for international co-operation to promote development. Thus, for example, the International Development Strategy for the Fourth United Nations Development Decade lays down six objectives that should guide international co-operation in the 1990s, namely:[7]

An increase in the economic growth rate of the developing countries;

A development process which deals with social needs, seeks to achieve a considerable reduction in extreme poverty, promotes the development and use of human resources and knowledge, and is environmentally rational and sustainable;

The improvement of the international monetary, financial and trade systems in such a way as to support the development process;

The establishment of a sound and stable world economy and sound macroeconomic management at the national and international level;

The decisive strengthening of international development co-operation; and

A special effort to deal with the problems of the least developed countries, which are the weakest of all the developing countries.

The countries of Latin America and the Caribbean, for their part, have steadfastly insisted that the net outflow of resources to the industrialized world continues to be one of the main obstacles standing in the way of the renewed growth of many countries of that region, and that a process designed to reverse that situation, including in particular the treatment of the external debt, should be one of the central aims of international co-operation.[8]

Finally, it may be noted that the scope of the decisions in question has so far been rather limited in terms of concrete commitments. Furthermore, they leave the impression that the issue of economic development has still not been given a central place on the list of priorities of the world community, or at least has not been treated with the degree of urgency that the developing countries desire and the circumstances demand.

If humanity were to assign higher priority to the eradication of poverty from the face of the earth, it could achieve that goal, for it now has the technical know-how, the organizational ability and the financial capacity to make considerable progress towards the attainment of this basic objective of the United Nations Charter. However, this calls for a concerted effort and the determined political will of all the parties involved, both with regard to the actions to be taken in each country and as regards the strengthening of international economic co-operation.

There are various reasons for believing that the United Nations Conference on Environment and Development offers, among other aspects, a fresh opportunity to advance towards profounder and more specific action in connection with the agenda of international economic co-operation issues. To begin with, humanity as a whole has gradually become aware of the danger of real ecological disasters. In other words, both individual incidents (the escape of toxic gases in Bhopal, India; oil spills in the ocean and the coastal area of Alaska; the accident at a nuclear power plant at Chernobyl (USSR)) and the danger of irreversible ecological damage that can affect the whole of humanity (climate change, depletion of the ozone layer, loss of biodiversity) now have an immense capacity to mobilize the views of governments and society, especially in the industrialized countries. To this has been added the ecological concern stemming from actions relating to the war in the Gulf. There is also an awareness that these phenomena do not respect frontiers and that multilateral agreements and actions are therefore called for in order to solve a common problem: no less than the survival of our planet.[9]

Secondly, this capacity to mobilize opinion, added to the marked awareness that exists of the need to face a common problem, has the potential for spreading to other areas of human activity. Thus, it is not possible to separate the environmental dimension from that of the economy, since most of the environmental risks are the outcomes of economic and social phenomena: irrational exploitation or unchecked consumption of natural resources, the disposal of the wastes of such exploitation and consumption, population pressures on finite resources and the destruction of the environmental heritage that belongs also to future generations in order to satisfy the demands of the present. These phenomena exist not only in opulent societies with a high degree of development but also, for very different reasons, in societies where situations of extreme poverty still persist and millions of human beings contribute to the plundering of resources because of their imperative need to survive. Consequently, as the Governments recognized when they adopted resolution 44/228,[10] the issue of environmental protection cannot be considered in isolation; it must be placed in a much broader economic, social, political and institutional context.

Thirdly, tackling development and the environment in an integral manner increases the justification for broad agreements between the industrialized and the developing countries with regard to co-operative efforts at the world level. The developing countries can play an important part in helping to relieve some of the great global environmental problems (many of them, it must be admitted, due to the patterns of production and consumption of the industrialized countries).[11] In reality, the developing world as a whole, and Latin America and the Caribbean in particular, will attend the United Nations Conference endowed with considerable assets, in view of their impressive natural resources, their biodiversity and their whole ecological heritage in general, which means that they could contribute to the effort to regulate the world's climate. The

developed countries, for their part, have the financial resources and technology needed to facilitate the use of these assets in favour of environmentally sustainable development. All this could form the basis for a major co-operative effort.

2. Negotiation of global environmental problems

In its resolution 44/228 of 22 December 1989, the United Nations General Assembly listed a number of environmental issues which will also necessarily form an integral part of the debates to be held in the United Nations Conference and all the preparatory activities for it. These issues, which concern in particular the deterioration of ecological systems that go beyond national frontiers, naturally also affect the countries of Latin America and the Caribbean.

The examination and discussion of these types of problems must be based on criteria, fundamental elements and principles aimed at the identification and search for options to strengthen international co-operation. Although these problems have very special characteristics, this does not justify treating them in isolation. In other words, the negotiation of agreements on these issues calls for approaches that take full account of the real economic, political and social conditions of the region.

2.1 *Some criteria for the negotiations*

In order to facilitate the negotiations to be held in connection with the United Nations Conference on Environment and Development, the countries must adopt certain criteria. These are basically of three types: firstly, those concerning resource *allocation* or reallocation; secondly, those involving *resource flows*, such as for example those connected with the compensation that should be given to the victims of environmental degradation caused by others, and also those which refer to the financing of activities aimed at incorporating the environmental dimension into the development process; and thirdly, those connected with the close *association* that exists between the negotiations on debt, financing, trade and the environment.

With regard to the allocation criteria, there are circumstances where improvement of the environment and proper natural resource management call for the reshaping of the very bases of development, including new investment practices and reallocation of production inputs. This is so, for example, when some countries are obliged to reallocate their resources in order to help solve certain environmental problems such as the greenhouse effect or marine pollution.

The criteria on the reallocation of resources by those causing contamination may assume greater importance than the issues of compensation and financing, especially for the developing countries. If the countries of the region ignore the need for the reallocation of resources by the polluters, there is a risk that, within the short term, they will be exposed to still greater pressures to use up their resources, they will suffer a net loss of their comparative advantages and they may be open to an "environmental retaliation" which may take the form of conditionalities of a technical nature. Changes in the styles of consumption and investment of the developed countries fall within this category.

The "environmental retaliation" could operate through the control and management of technological change. If the production technology of the developed countries emphasizes the heavy use of some natural resources such as forests or minerals of which they do not have an abundant supply, or which they have decided to conserve, then the pressure on the countries which do possess those resources could become very intense. The importance of this fact can no longer be overlooked, precisely because Latin America and the Caribbean is a region with an abundance of natural resources. *It is therefore urgently necessary to make an evaluation of the areas where there could be potential pressure on resources.* Such an evaluation should quantify the effects of alternative technological changes and also their impact on the comparative advantages of the region. It would also permit the identification of those activities in developing countries which call for the reallocation of resources. In this respect,

whatever the negotiating criteria adopted, it is essential to take account of *all* the dimensions involved, i.e., "reallocation", "compensation and financing" and "association".

There are various approaches that could be adopted in negotiations: one of them is the principle that *the polluter pays the bill*. Thus, the nation generating most of the pollution affecting, say, the air or water of another country must pay for the damage done.

This principle has various advantages. One of them is that if the measures designed to reduce contamination permit the reallocation of resources in favour of "clean" technologies, this will improve the quality of the environment. On the other hand, it may be that such measures do not provide for the reallocation of resources, in which case the most likely result will be an increase in pollution. Moreover, the limited application of this principle may cause the effects of contaminating policies applied in the past to be overlooked.

The question of compensation, as a negotiating instrument, gives rise to a number of queries which can only be answered after further research: why compensate? how much? for how long? what are the best forms of compensation? Before even trying to suggest how to answer these queries, however, attention must be drawn to certain limiting factors. The most important of these is that the starting points for the parties involved in the negotiations may be very unequal when the existing volume of contamination is very large, the stock of resources is seriously depleted, or the reserves of such resources are very low.

In all these situations, the party seeking compensation is at a marked disadvantage. Where there is accumulated contamination, the compensation should exceed the "pollution flow", since it is also necessary to compensate for the accumulated prior damage done. The difficulties lie in the translation of these phenomena (pollution flows and prior accumulation (or stock)) into monetary values, and in the problems that arise when there is more than one polluting agent. Lack of information (especially on the part of the complainant) is a serious hindrance. When stocks have been depleted, the problem for the party seeking redress is how to calculate what could be considered a "fair" value for the damage done. Such a figure will naturally be higher than the potential market value, since it must include not only the value of the stock but also the opportunity cost of future use. These costs are generally growing and very substantial.

2.2 *Some global environmental issues*

All the items on the agenda of the Conference are of importance to the region. Here, however, we will only refer to a limited number of global environmental problems, viewed from the Latin American and Caribbean standpoint, with the aim of showing how necessary it is to integrate the proposed solutions within the broader context explored in preceding chapters. These problems are the following: the greenhouse effect; the contamination of seas, oceans and coastal areas; loss of biodiversity; and the transport of wastes across national frontiers.

2.2.1 *The greenhouse effect*

It is a well-known fact that the burning of fossil fuels, industrial emissions (CFCs and halons), deforestation, fermentation processes in the course of agricultural activities and the use of fertilizers all contribute to the accumulation of gases in the atmosphere. According to a number of measurements, these phenomena are causing an increase in the mean surface temperature of the earth, and this in turn is changing the world climate and raising the mean level of the oceans.

In 1988, the region contributed some 13% of the total world emissions of carbon dioxide of biotic and industrial origin, and its contribution to the greenhouse effect, at least in this respect, was between 6% and 7%. This is a relatively low but nevertheless significant contribution to the global problem. The countries of the region should therefore join the efforts being made by other nations (especially the developed countries) to mitigate this problem. Consideration should consequently be given to alternative options, such as increasing the use of hydroelectric power in total electricity generation and developing reforestation programmes.

In so far as the countries of the region help to relieve the problem, they will be doing a service to the planet as a whole. Action should be taken to quantify the benefits provided by these efforts, since their implementation will also call for considerable resources, which means that the necessary financing must be made available for the region to be able to make its contribution to global environmental sustainability.

Another aspect which should be taken into consideration in the negotiations on the ozone layer concerns the role played by the dissemination of technology. There is a tendency to move industries with a high pollution potential to developing countries. Many of these industries are subsidiaries of transnational corporations, which set them up in countries with more permissive environmental legislation than their home countries. It has been clearly demonstrated that the most natural-resource intensive and highly polluting industries are growing more rapidly in the developing world. In the negotiations leading up to the United Nations Conference, account must be taken of the possibility that an attempt might be made to use some ecosystems of the region as research spaces for testing new technologies which might represent a high risk for the environment, or for exploring the potential comparative advantages of the local germ plasm or ecosystem. The feasibility of establishing international legal instruments to impose sanctions on such experiments should be studied.

The maintenance or new installation of highly polluting industries represents a threat to the conservation of the environment. This topic must form an integral part of the negotiations on the transfer of technology.

2.2.2 *Protection of seas and oceans*

The magnitude of the problems connected with protection of the seas and oceans is indicated in resolution 1/20, adopted at the first session of the Preparatory Committee for the United Nations Conference on Environment and Development and entitled "Protection of the oceans and all types of seas, including landlocked and semi-landlocked seas, and of coastal areas, as well as the protection, rational use and development of their living resources".

Although the oceans, including coastal seas, are so vast —covering nearly 70% of our planet— they form a complex and vulnerable environment. Many unique species live in the oceans or depend on them for their survival. The oceans are this planet's primary life-support system. They provide most of our oxygen and moisture and condition our weather patterns. For their part, the seas provide food and recreation and form a means of trade. Without healthy oceans, life as we know it today would disappear.

There is substantial evidence that marine and coastal resources are being mismanaged and abused. All too often, the decisions taken in respect of these resources are dictated by narrow, short-term interests. Such decisions are usually taken without having a full scientific knowledge of the potential long-term adverse effects, or without even caring about those effects. In recent years, there has been an alarming increase in the degradation of near-coastal waters, where marine life is most abundant. Even less is known of the deep-sea environment, which is the home of various forms of marine life, but there is increasing evidence that this environment has also suffered damage.

2.2.3 *Biodiversity: a "tradable" good*

The present structure of international trade has a direct impact on the decline in the variety of biological species. This is due to the insufficient incorporation of data on biodiversity (germ plasm) into international trade negotiations. Consequently, in the process of price formation and in determining the terms of trade, biodiversity is normally viewed as being a free good. It should be clearly understood, however, that it must be treated as an integral part of the natural capital of the countries of the region. As long as such diversity is viewed as a mere consumer good, trading activities will rapidly exhaust the reserves of the region in this respect.

As long as this resource is used in a free and easy manner, there will be no incentive in the negotiations to take measures for its conservation. If mechanisms were adopted to raise the value of this resource and provide for recognition of their ownership in international terms, however, this would be an important factor in their conservation. Biodiversity should therefore be defined as a scarce resource and should consequently be assigned a price which reflects its opportunity cost in both spatial and temporal terms. There is an urgent need to incorporate these dimensions of trade not only through the improvement of existing legal instruments such as those implemented by GATT but also through the possible creation of such other instruments as may be deemed necessary.

ECLAC, in conjunction with regional institutions and other United Nations agencies such as FAO and UNEP, could play an important role in the identification and management of biodiversity. The proposal for the establishment of a committee on biodiversity which is put forward in the next chapter is aimed precisely in this direction.

In this field, the region must start practically from zero. The loss of genetic diversity is an issue which concerns the world as a whole, and since our region is perhaps the richest of all in this resource, it is urgently necessary to incorporate this issue in the areas of international co-operation and the international trade negotiations. This has various implications: for example, instruments must be established to rescue and assign their proper value to the knowledge possessed by indigenous peoples (through ethnobiology), as well as to make fair payment to them for this knowledge. This means protecting the intellectual property of the indigenous population, at present arbitrarily appropriated by modern technological methods. Likewise, it is necessary that the instruments regulating the use and exchange of information on biodiversity provide researchers of the countries of origin of the biological specimens collected with access to herbariums and reference collections located in other countries.

It is also important for these researchers to be assured access to advanced training in biotechnology and synthetic chemistry, as well as access to data banks of genetic sequences prepared on the basis of systematic inventories made in areas of high biological diversity. Finally, another fundamental question is that of co-operation and concerted action within the region and between the region and technologically advanced countries with a view to the joint development of technology capable of generating products with high added value –especially non-lumber products from areas of high biological diversity– which ensure the maintenance of such diversity, increased income for the local community and suitable respect for their cultural patterns.

2.2.4 *Transboundary movements of hazardous wastes*

It is estimated that during 1989 some 40 million tons of toxic wastes entered the developing world. According to documents of the United States Environmental Protection Agency (EPA), between 1980 and 1989 the number of notifications by United States companies seeking to export hazardous wastes increased from 12 to 626. A growing proportion of such wastes are being sent to Argentina, Brazil, Mexico and the Caribbean.

It is clear that this question involves elements connected with each of the three central dimensions referred to earlier, i.e., trade, finance and technology. First of all, however, it must be decided once and for all whether or not it is necessary to prohibit trade in this kind of wastes. The 1989 Basel Convention on the Control of Transboundary Movements of Hazardous Wastes and their Disposal provides for the creation of more powerful regional and multilateral instruments than those now in existence. These would totally prohibit the export of wastes from the industrialized nations to the developing countries. Although this issue has not been considered in the international trade negotiations,

it should at least be taken into account in the discussions on financing and technology. At all events, the solution of this problem calls for regional agreements.

Some initiatives which have been suggested in various forums in connection with this issue are:

The establishment of co-operation and co-ordination mechanisms and systems for the exchange and compilation of all data on transboundary movements of wastes, so as to check illegal shipments.

The establishment of mechanisms and systems for the safe repatriation of outdated or banned materials to their countries of origin.

The promotion of regional co-operation with regard to technical assistance and the exchange of information on production methods which generate low levels of wastes, as well as the establishment of regional laboratories to evaluate the hazards caused by such wastes.

There is now an increasing degree of consensus that environmental issues should be dealt with in a manner closely linked with economic and social development. If this consensus is reflected in operational procedures, it will not only facilitate the negotiation of the world's environmental problems but will also –especially in the case of the developing countries– favour the slow but steady consolidation of the bases for sustainable development. The next chapter will deal with this topic.

Notes

[1] See United Nations, *International economic co-operation, in particular the revitalization of economic growth and development of the developing countries* (A/S-18/14), New York, 30 April 1990, especially the annex, which contains the corresponding Declaration.

[2] See *Report of the Second United Nations Conference on the Least Developed Countries* (A/45/695), New York, September 1990.

[3] World Declaration on the Survival, Protection and Development of Children in the 1990s and plan of action for its implementation, United Nations, New York, 30 September 1990.

[4] See *Report of the Special Committee of the Whole to Prepare an International Development Strategy for the Fourth United Nations Development Decade* (A/45/41), New York, 11 October 1990, and especially the text of the International Development Strategy for the Fourth United Nations Development Decade.

[5] General Assembly resolution 44/228, adopted on 22 December 1989, paragraph I (3).

[6] These features are also to be noted in the deliberations of the United Nations Conference on Trade and Development. See, for example, the *Proceedings of the United Nations Conference on Trade and Development: Seventh Session. Report and Annexes* (TD/352/vol.1), New York, 1988. United Nations publication, Sales No. 88.II.D.1.

[7] Report of the Special Committee of the Whole to Prepare an International Development Strategy, *op. cit.*, p. 20.

[8] See for example: ECLAC, *Report of the Sixteenth Session of the Committee of High-Level Government Experts* (CEGAN), held in New York from 22 to 24 May 1989 (LC/G.1569(CEG.16/2)), Santiago, Chile, 28 June 1989, p. 4; ECLAC, Biennial Report (twenty-third session of the Commission) (LC/G.1630-P), Santiago, Chile, June 1990, and especially resolution 507 (XXIII) entitled "Changing production patterns, social equity and the international development strategy", paragraph 10.

[9] In this connection, in resolution 44/228 the Governments declared themselves to be "deeply concerned by the continuing deterioration of the state of the environment and the serious degradation of the global life support systems, as well as by trends that, if allowed to continue, could disrupt the global ecological balance, jeopardize the life-sustaining qualities of the earth and lead to an ecological catastrophe...".

[10] "... environmental protection in developing countries must, in this context, be viewed as an integral part of the development process and cannot be considered in isolation from it ...".

[11] It has been argued on a number of occasions that the industrialized countries have generated an "environmental debt" as a result of the degradation caused by several centuries of development, which has caused not only global environmental deterioration but also specific damage in the developing countries due to the primary sector activities through which the latter entered the international economy. See, for example, UNEP, *Plan de Acción Ambiental para América Latina y el Caribe: una propuesta* (UNEP/LAC-IGWG.VII/4), Mexico City, 29 August 1990, p. 3.

Chapter X

SUMMARY AND PROPOSALS

Successful negotiations require clear objectives; a thorough knowledge of the means available and the relation between those means and the objectives; effective institutions, and strategies in keeping with the real conditions of the region.

1. The United Nations Conference on Environment and Development

The process of changing production patterns which has taken place over the last five decades has been accompanied by adverse effects on the environment in both the developed and developing countries. The increase in production, its forms of concentration and location, and the assumption that environmental damage is a perfectly acceptable cost which does not outweigh the advantages of structural change, have caused the multiplication and intensification of these negative impacts with time. National and regional experience, however, indicates that these disturbances in the environment are nearing intolerable social and economic limits.

When it convened the United Nations Conference on Environment and Development, through its resolution 44/228, the General Assembly expressed the concern of Governments over "the continuing deterioration of the state of the environment and the serious degradation of the global life-support systems, as well as ... trends that, if allowed to continue, could disrupt the global ecological balance". It also noted in the resolution that "the major cause of the continuing deterioration of the global environment is the unsustainable pattern of production and consumption, particularly in industrialized countries".

As changes in production patterns must necessarily continue, however, especially in the developing countries, ways must be sought to ensure that such changes lead to sustainable development. In the resolution in question, the Governments also concurred that "the protection and enhancement of the environment are major issues that affect the well-being of peoples and economic development throughout the world" and decided that the Conference should "elaborate strategies and measures to halt and reverse the effect of environmental degradation in the context of strengthened national and international efforts to promote sustainable and environmentally sound development in all countries".

It is within this general context that the countries of Latin America and the Caribbean must set about the task of defining, from the region's own particular viewpoint, what results it expects from the Conference.

The objectives of the Latin American and Caribbean Governments at this Conference will include both preventing the spread and diversification of existing or foreseeable environmental damage in the region and helping to organize an integrated world society so that

131

differences in the quality of the environment do not represent a new structural obstacle to trade, communications and even relations between countries.

The view of Latin American and Caribbean development offered by the ECLAC secretariat in its proposals for *Changing production patterns with social equity* holds that these changes "must be compatible with conservation of the physical environment". In the earlier chapters of the present document, the many and complex links between development and environment were explored in greater detail. In this respect, it is to be hoped that Latin America and the Caribbean can make a conceptual contribution to the Conference by making clear the full significance of the assertion in resolution 44/228 that "environmental protection in developing countries must ... be viewed as an integral part of the development process and cannot be considered in isolation from it".

The Conference also offers a promising forum for the deployment of major co-operative efforts to resolve common problems in the various spheres of international economic co-operation which are currently being discussed. For example, because of the diversity of their natural capital, Latin America and the Caribbean have considerable assets to offer in helping to mitigate or solve some of the most important global environmental problems, such as climatic change. The developed countries, for their part, possess the financial capital and technology to make it possible for the Latin American and the Caribbean countries to make full use of that natural heritage.

Finally, the countries of the region can reasonably aspire to the attainment of concrete results such as the establishment of standards and regulations on such varied aspects as access to environmentally sound technology; the mobilization of resources for financing sustainable development; training and education to further the protection and improvement of the environment; the protection of natural resources and efforts to maintain biodiversity; a more transparent and open international trade system which avoids discrimination because of, for example, environmental considerations; and the adoption or strengthening of arrangements for the monitoring, appraisal and prevention of threats to the environment. Some basic proposals will be put forward below for seeking agreements that will make it possible to progress towards the establishment of such standards and regulations.

2. Development and environment from the regional perspective

The links between development and the environment are expressed through each of the dimensions that must be taken into account when designing and executing development policies (i.e., the technical, economic, institutional, social and political dimensions). For this reason it is vital to view the sustainability of development within a broad context that goes beyond concern only with natural capital. Thus, achieving sustainable development must necessarily involve *a dynamic equilibrium in the use of all the forms of capital that comprise the development effort*; that is to say, not only human, natural, physical, and financial capital, but also institutional and cultural resources or capital.

Earlier chapters of this document emphasized various systemic aspects, such as economic policy; the creation, transfer and adoption of new technologies; the relation between poverty and the environment; the links between natural resources and the environment; the need to reform institutions; and the terms of financing. These issues, together with those of a global nature, affect all sectors of the population.

It must be stressed that economic policies affect the equilibrium in the use of all forms of capital and therefore cannot be considered as neutral with respect to the sustainability of development. The effects of microeconomic policies are obvious, but those of macroeconomic policies are not so immediately evident, yet they are of great importance since they directly or indirectly affect the total stock and exploitable flows of resources. They also affect the spatial aspects of development, the lead time of investments, time preferences and attitudes towards risks or uncertainties. Structural adjustment programmes have rarely taken account of environmental aspects, and stabilization policies place their stress on the short term.

Although project appraisal methods which take account of their environmental effects are already available, such methods are little used as yet, and furthermore there is a need to incorporate such projects into broader programmes which make it possible to view all their effects. This calls for a higher degree of co-ordination of public policy and better links between macro and microeconomic policies.

Economic policies aimed at sustainable development have as their ultimate objective the improvement of the living standards of the population. People are at once a resource for development and its fundamental concern. Consequently, population-related issues must be analysed from both points of view. As a resource, the population continues to grow rapidly in Latin America, although a process of transition towards lower population growth rates is to be observed. In spite of this process, it is not surprising that problems persist that have more to do with spatial distribution, institutional conditions and production technology than with the growth rate of the population. The process of demographic transition is closely linked with development: if the latter is stimulated, the declines in fertility and mortality rates whose effect is to reduce population growth will occur more quickly. This is why population policy, in its broadest sense, should be an integral part of an environmentally sustainable development policy.

The management, use and distribution of natural resources have not reached an advanced enough stage to permit the eradication of poverty, which is perhaps the most urgent aspect when considering human beings as the main subject of development. Although there is a wide variety of situations from one country to another, altogether poverty affects over 180 million people in the region. The environment and poverty influence each other reciprocally: the poor live in degraded environments and contribute to their further deterioration, while the degraded environment makes it more difficult to eradicate poverty. Although it is difficult for the poor to accumulate capital in its traditional forms, there have been successful examples of accumulation of natural capital as a way of beginning to break the vicious circle of poverty.

Technology can make a decisive contribution to the eradication of poverty. Technologies that facilitate the accumulation of natural capital; "clean" technologies that ease the access of the region's products to international markets; efficient technologies which improve its international competitiveness, and non-polluting technologies that can be used in small-scale activities, especially adapted to medium-sized and small enterprises, which are usually labour intensive, are indispensable in order to improve the living standards of the population of Latin America. The building of consensuses between the governments and private sectors of the countries is particularly important in this respect.

The need for consensus building and community participation at the local and national levels makes it desirable to review the existing institutional framework with a view to adapting it to new and changing requirements. This adaptation refers fundamentally to the process of decision-making, which includes the structures of incentives and disincentives, the organization of development, the management of the economy, the role of the State and of private agents, and community participation. There are no miracle recipes or solutions for this adaptation, and experience shows that the modification of institutions for sustainable development is a lengthy process.

In the international field, progress towards the establishment of appropriate institutions continues, and various relevant conventions and agreements already exist, together with others of a regional nature. Both international and regional instruments bear witness to the growing level of awareness on environmental matters, but there is still a long way to go before achieving a truly effective set of instruments in the field of international co-operation on environmental issues. This could be a further basis for international economic co-operation in the future.

Financing sustainable development presents difficult problems, both as regards the amounts of money involved and the formulas and instruments needed for it. New mechanisms have been created, such as "debt-for-nature swaps", but they

133

have not yet achieved the necessary significance and, in certain circumstances, could even prove to be counterproductive. More financing is required, both domestic and external. In the case of the latter, it is particularly important to take into account its additionality with respect to the currently available resources. It is also necessary for investment projects to be incorporated into broader programmes which take account of all their effects.

3. The commitments needed

The purposes set forth above will be achieved to the extent that society as a whole determines to do so: individuals, communities, nations, regions and the whole international community all have their parts to play in achieving this. Thus, it is essential to develop an awareness in individuals and communities of the need to make development environmentally sustainable, especially with regard to the impacts of various development policies on natural resources and the environment. This process of gradual raising of personal and collective awareness will be expressed through concrete mechanisms of popular participation and consensus. This is where the social institutions, viewed as decision-making systems, assume great importance: it is their task to give concrete expression to the incentive structure, the organizational aspects, the bases for the management of resources, the assignment of roles in the economic and social sphere and the degree of commitment to policies and strategies.

At the *national level*, there are a number of activities which are of priority importance:

Formulating a national policy on education and communication which raises the level of public awareness with regard to problems of environmental sustainability.

Strengthening democratic institutions and machinery for participation, management and regulation. Within this context, the economic institutions are of priority importance, since they represent a synergic source of change in production patterns, equity and sustainability. Special attention should be given to organized community participation in the evaluation and local management of investment projects.

Establishing sound scientific and technological research systems; systems of information, dissemination, monitoring and evaluation at all levels. Because of the complexity of ecological systems, a proper understanding of them is a necessary condition for taking decisions, negotiating and assigning resources. Thus, those who take decisions on environmental issues must have a sound basis for these decisions, i.e., they must have all the necessary information at hand.

Linking the processes of economic and ecological planning. An important tool for this is territorial and environmental administration.

Formulating and executing national, regional and local investment programmes. Environmental sustainability programmes start off at a disadvantage compared with traditional investment programmes (highways, irrigation works, etc.). Measures must be taken to prevent the financial resources available for environmental programmes from being blocked by the lack of suitable institutional capacity.

At the *regional level*, it is essential to link up the national strategies with those at the regional and world levels. Such links are still weak, so it is important to strengthen regional systems or create them where they do not exist. These systems do not call for great institutional infrastructures: the idea is rather to take full advantage and improve the structure of the existing regional bodies. This in turn would strengthen the position of the countries of the region in the negotiations and changes called for by the sustainability of development. The various subregional agreements exemplified by the Central American Commission on Environment and Development, the Special Commission on the Environment of the Amazon Region and the Caribbean Community's Ministerial Conference on the Environment could appraise their potential as regards natural resource management and environmental sustainability, seeking appropriate technical assistance in order to make them more effective in this respect.

At the *international level*, the United Nations Conference on Environment and Development offers not only an opportunity to work out strategies and measures to halt and reverse the effects of environmental degradation at the local, national and world or global levels, but also the chance to progress towards the treatment of the international economic co-operation agenda in greater depth and detail: the issue of protection of the environment cannot be considered in isolation, but must be seen in a broad economic, social, political and institutional context.

4. Criteria and principles

4.1 *On sustainable development*

The focus of any sustainable development strategy must be the people. Natural resources and the environment are merely means which, in conjunction with soundly based democratic and participatory institutions, will help to achieve the objectives of development. There are all too many examples of strategies which have failed because they did not take account of this simple truth. There have been cases where natural or institutional capital were defined as the subjects of a development strategy, instead of the people and communities (the human capital) which not only provide the basis of support for these strategies but are in fact their be-all and end-all. Approaches like this cannot lead to sustainable development.

Other guiding criteria include the following:

There must be explicit recognition of the social, economic and ecological diversity and uniqueness of each country and its regions.

The viability of strategies is determined not only by their inherent nature, but also by the management capacity displayed in their execution.

The effectiveness of management instruments (planning, economic, legal and financial regulations) will depend on how far they are backed up by a suitable management system.

Management systems affect the supply and demand for natural resources and the environment. In order to manage supply, a high degree of technical and cultural knowledge is required, while in the case of demand there must a thorough knowledge of the political and economic aspects involved.

The provision of support and guidance to the formal and informal users of resources facilitates their participation in the formulation and management of environmental strategies and policies.

The State must give support to the lower-income sectors, since in rural areas they occupy spaces which are relatively distant, ecologically fragile, topographically rugged, and of great biogenetic diversity, while in urban areas they occupy high-risk spaces largely devoid of health, education and security services.

Managing natural resources involves a wide range of actions covering large geographical areas. In these actions, high priority should be given to decentralization, with the aim of promoting the activities carried out in support of the State by non-governmental organizations and other institutions and furthering the local management capacity so necessary for giving permanence to the actions in question.

The private and public institutions involved in this process must be linked with each other in a visible and explicit manner, so that the execution of national policies will receive the support of the entire community and there will be no confusion or conflict between the actions of the various agents.

With regard to the latter point, it is necessary to strengthen the social and political institutions, and structures of public participation and consensus-building, which will require, *inter alia*:

Increased knowledge of the existing resources (potential, rates of utilization, levels of investment);

Establishment of monitoring and evaluation capacity which makes it possible to make sound decisions about what policies should be implemented to speed up the attainment of sustainable development;

Definition of programmes to strengthen and develop institutions;

Increased capacity for the execution of development programmes, including their financial and technical assistance dimensions;

Adoption of organizational measures to promote basic and applied research and protection of the natural and cultural heritage;

Strengthening of the basis of political systems within a democratic and participatory context.

The strategies must further integration at both the national and regional levels. There are various dimensions which can be taken into account with regard to relations between countries, including in particular the following:

Definition of environmental standards and regulations concerning regional problems such as health, marine pollution, management of international river basins and the transport and disposal of hazardous wastes;

Establishment of rates of utilization of shared national resources;

Promotion of regional technical co-operation, including the transfer of technology, exchange of information and scientific research, and its co-ordination in the region;

Access to existing experience of economic policies, institutional reforms and public and private investment;

Establishment of an agenda for the formulation of action programmes and aspects that go beyond national frontiers (health, management of river basins, protection of flora and fauna);

Definition of basic measures for the protection of the biodiversity of the region and the preservation of the natural and cultural heritage.

4.2 Sustainable development and the 1992 United Nations Conference

There is an obvious need to formulate a policy for management of natural resources and the environment which incorporates the human –economic, political and social– dimension and also serves an integrative purpose within each sovereign country in matters concerning sustainability. If such a national policy does not exist, management of the economy in general and the bases for bilateral and multilateral negotiation will be seriously weakened.

Among these bases, one of the most important is that *all* governments should play a full part in the preparatory process for the United Nations Conference. This is because at present there are various forums for negotiation engaged in the formulation of international legal instruments which are not of a universal nature; in some cases, participation in these forums has been on the basis of invitation in a personal capacity. It is essential, especially in the stage of formal negotiations, to avoid this replacement of sovereign expressions of will by the personal opinions of experts.

Another concept which should guide the activities of the governments of the region is that of the need to recognize that there is a *congruous link* between liability for creating environmental problems and responsibility for helping to solve them. This link has been expressed in the phrase "the polluter pays".[1]

It should be noted, however, that despite its usefulness as a general guideline, this concept raises some theoretical and methodological difficulties. It could be applied to environmental problems generated in the future, whether they are the responsibility of a country which contributes to global or cross-border environmental problems or whether they are caused by an enterprise which generates pollution affecting the inhabitants of a particular community. However, the concept is more difficult to apply to the total accumulation of environmental problems that have built up over the years.[2]

Finally, it should be explicitly recognized that world or global environmental problems are simply the accumulation of local problems. In this respect, insofar as each country adopts policies aimed at achieving its own sustainable development it will not only be achieving its own objectives but also contributing to the solution of world problems. This is why it has been insistently stressed throughout this document that it is impossible to separate global environmental problems from local and national ones.

5. Some suggestions for formulating a regional position

Local, national and world-wide environmental problems are interdependent and closely linked, although they may call for specific solutions in keeping with the spatial magnitude and the nature of the degradation caused. Moreover, the environmental problems that exist in the developing countries are not due solely to poverty but are due in the main to certain development models which have generally been adopted without the necessary critical appraisal, either by those countries themselves or by the industrial nations. It must also be recognized that the economic development process modifies the environment and interacts with natural capital. The management of the latter is an integral part of the development process itself.

From the preceding chapters, together with the guidelines set forth in the Action Plan for the Environment in Latin America and the Caribbean [3] and in the report prepared by the Latin American and Caribbean Commission on Development and Environment,[4] it is possible to draw some overall guidelines regarding the position of the countries of the region in the preparatory activities for the 1992 United Nations Conference as well as to prepare a Latin American and Caribbean agenda. The cultural, economic and ecological diversity and uniqueness of each of the countries of the region make it advisable to seek such broad guidelines with a view to achieving success in the negotiations, rather than trying to provide specific proposals of general applicability.

This will not try to be an exhaustive list. It merely highlights those issues of special interest for Latin America and the Caribbean which are nevertheless closely linked with the General Assembly's concern over world problems of development and the environment, a matter that was dealt with in chapter IX.

5.1 A regional platform for co-operation in the field of the development and transfer of environmental technology

In the process of changing production patterns on which the region has embarked, there is a danger of the reproduction of localized situations of severe environmental deterioration similar to those registered in developed countries. Such situations may also contribute to the disturbance of world ecological balances in the future.

Technology plays a decisive role in the achievement of environmental sustainability, so that it is necessary to further the adoption of measures that will give access to environmentally sound or safe technologies. At the same time, it will be necessary to strengthen the capacity for scientific research and for the consequent technological development.

In order to secure these objectives it is necessary:

a) To provide support for the strengthening of local, national and regional capacity to develop environmentally sound technologies, which involves:

 – collaboration with local scientific research and development programmes having these aims;[5]

 – measures to enhance the capacity to train professionals and scientists in the appropriate specialties;

 – the installation of laboratories for research and support to programmes for the training of technicians in the use of measurement and analysis equipment;

 – assistance in the establishment of pilot plants and centres for the demonstration of environmentally safe technologies.

b) To promote, in conjunction with suitable local bodies: i) the execution of global and sectoral research projects designed to identify clearly the commercial and institutional obstacles standing in the way of access to environmentally sound technologies and their transfer and ii) the exploration of mechanisms and forms of intellectual property rights which ensure unhindered access to these technologies.

c) To explore ways of mobilizing and applying additional financial resources for the transfer of environmentally sound technologies.

d) To promote the dissemination of information on environmentally safe or sound technologies to small and medium-sized businesses in the developing countries, for which purpose technical assistance should be given for the establishment at the local and international level of mechanisms to enable potential users to gain access to the specialized information centres operating in the developed countries and in international organizations, such as the United Nations Environment Programme and the International Environmental Bureau.

e) To create favourable conditions for the participation of firms from developing countries in industrial fairs specializing in technologies that are environmentally safe and protect the environment, and to promote the holding of such exhibitions in developing countries.

f) To provide support for the formulation of pilot sustainable development projects and programmes in the various fields of production and to assist in the establishment of methods that permit the evaluation of the resulting benefits in situations where effects of a local and world character are involved at the same time.

g) To contribute to the organization of activities which stimulate local demand for environmentally sound technologies, such as, for example, the exchange of experience on trading rights to emit pollutants and the use of price mechanisms and economic incentives suitable to local conditions.

h) To explore the possibilities and scope for harmonizing environmental standards at the regional and international levels.

5.2 *Financing sustainable development*

The countries of Latin America and the Caribbean can only tackle the challenge of sustainable development through a net increase in the financial resources assigned for that purpose. The assignment and use of these financial resources depend on the specific criteria which are given below:

a) It is necessary to increase the financial resources. It would be quite unacceptable to the countries of the region if the external financing were provided through the "reallocation" of credits destined for economic development. Unless the external financing of sustainable development is an additional financing item, the recipient nation will suffer a net deterioration in its position.

b) The need to finance sustainable development must not be made an excuse for the imposition of new forms of conditionality. This is particular important in the areas connected with structural adjustments, proposals for institutional reforms, and the design of national investment programmes. If sustainable development is only attained at the cost of the application of exogenous conditionalities, there will be a net loss in the effectiveness and degree of execution of development programmes.

c) Projects directly linked with sustainable development should enjoy favourable financing terms. In particular, there are grounds here for the granting of soft credits, most of which, moreover, should not be repayable. The management of these funds could be based on an agreement on objectives, monitored through national monitoring and evaluation systems.

d) In addition to the national programmes already referred to in this document, consideration could be given to the creation of a *regional fund*. The purpose of this fund would be eliminate the gap between each nation's traditional sources of financing and international sources such as the Global Environment Fund. This regional fund could be managed by regional development bodies.

The environment projects eligible for financing should include at least the following four categories:

The first group would consist of *projects directly related with changes in production patterns, poverty and the environment*. These would include all the activities needed to ensure a substantial improvement in the aspects of natural resources and the environment directly linked with that sector. They would include projects on production, technological change, resource management and the improvement of social welfare in general.

The second group would consist of *environmental adjustment projects*. These are not always exclusively of an environmental nature, but involve changes in productive and social activities which are expected to bring direct benefits for the environment, such as changes in production patterns and the transfer and adoption of technology.

The third group consists of *projects for the conservation and improvement* of specific areas (national parks, flora and fauna reserves), specific natural resources, or biodiversity. These projects would also involve the reduction of contamination in general, measures to check the rate of depletion, and action to promote the recovery of natural resources or the environment.

Finally, the fourth group is made up of *national programmes for human resource development, institutional change and preservation of cultural patterns*, which form the basis for the effective and sustainable execution of the projects in the areas already mentioned. Such programmes include education, technical training, public sector reforms, research and dissemination of information, etc. All these aspects are directly linked with questions of the management and organization of sustainable development.

5.3 *Monitoring, evaluation and prevention of threats to the environment*

It is necessary to set up a broad and open world-wide system of environmental monitoring and supervision, and carry out a general overhaul of the legal and institutional regulations in this field. From the point of view of Latin America and the Caribbean, the matters which should be subject to this system include in particular:

a) movement of materials and wastes, especially of a toxic and hazardous nature;

b) relocation of industrial activities, especially those which are the most highly polluting;

c) accidents which can cause serious environmental damage, such as those in connection with the production and transport of hydrocarbons, atomic energy production, etc.;

d) the levels of generation of pollutants, by countries and by sectors of activity, especially in the case of those which have a direct influence in world problems (greenhouse effect, depletion of the ozone layer, marine pollution, loss of biodiversity);

e) recurrent or non-recurrent natural disasters due to the faulty location of some human activities (urban, industrial, mining and agricultural activities) which can directly or indirectly cause the loss of human life or irreparable damage to the environment; and, finally,

f) the environmental policies and standards which are already being applied in the various countries.

If backed up by a suitable system of financing and technical assistance, the countries of the region could promote the establishment of the national and regional components of such a system, taking due account of some requirements with regard to its establishment and operation, namely:

– It must provide for the easy and guaranteed access of any country, regardless of whether the latter is directly involved or not in the various aspects dealt with by the system.

– Its data bases must be homogeneous, so as to permit the consolidation of data and the compatibility of evaluation methods for all countries.

– It must allow the countries to gain timely and efficient access to the information needed to set in motion early warning and preventive action in respect of possible hazards, as well as enabling them to receive the benefit of such compensation schemes as may be established.

5.4 *Human resource development*

Promotion of human resource development is one of the objectives set forth in General Assembly resolution 44/228. For the region, this objective has been formulated in a way which recognizes that changing production patterns and sustainable development call for more than merely overcoming poverty: they also call for financial resources and for intensive training of human resources not only at the higher level but also at the basic, middle and technical levels. In this respect, priority must be given to the training of middle-level professionals. The essential elements for the region in this respect are the following:

a) Training in connection with operational aspects of the environmental management practiced by the social, economic and political agents in the public and private sectors;

b) Incorporation of the environmental dimension in the training of technicians and professionals;

c) Theoretical and practical technological training;

d) Training of middle-level human resources through intermediate technical courses;

e) Education of the population in general regarding environmental problems.

Horizontal co-operation and the strengthening of the many programmes and activities which have been carried out in this respect in the region form a strategic element of the highest importance which must be given full support. In this respect, it is also extremely important to increase the technical and financial assistance received by the region from abroad.

5.5 *Transboundary movement of hazardous wastes*

With regard to the specific problem of the transboundary movement of hazardous wastes, the 1989 Basel Convention on the Control of Transboundary Movements of Hazardous Wastes and their Disposal needs to be supplemented with regional agreements. These should include legal instruments covering the needs of each region, monitoring mechanisms, as already mentioned in previous pages, and systems of co-operation and co-ordination for the exchange of the relevant data; mechanisms and systems for the safe repatriation of materials which are hazardous, obsolete or banned in their countries of origin, and finally, promotion of co-operation and technical assistance to assist in the solution of urgent problems. In this regard, the mandate given to the regional economic commissions by General Assembly resolution 44/228 deserves special attention.

5.6 *International trade and the environment*

The countries of the region are interested in carrying out an ongoing monitoring of the negotiations and progress made in the field of international trade and the environment. This follow-up should be supplemented by region-wide national and sectoral studies which permit the identification in detail of potential changes in the current comparative advantages and which place special emphasis on those aspects where unacceptable environmental conditionalities may be imposed. The main objective of these studies is to evaluate the trading situation of the region and its possible future evolution in the light of the foreseeable changes in international trade deriving from environmental factors or considerations. Furthermore, these matters will be closely linked with the evolution of the debates and negotiations on development and the environment in international forums.

Within the context of the studies in question, the countries of the region —either as a whole, or assembled in subregional groupings— must define their trade strategies at the intraregional and extraregional levels. Some salient elements in these strategies are:

a) Significantly increasing the added value given to commodities in regional exports, in line with the trends of the world economy, so as to achieve at the same time better use of the opportunities available on world markets and relief of the pressures on natural resources in order to reduce their degradation.

b) Ensuring that trade within the region and between the region and the rest of the world does not include goods which are banned in their countries of origin for environmental reasons.

c) Establishing the principle that environmental problems cannot serve as a pretext for creating unjustified trade barriers.

d) Establishing a programme for the gradual reduction of dependence on outside technology for cleaner production processes in agriculture, industry and services and technologies for the control of noxious wastes.

e) Incorporating within established trade circuits a set of goods and services which are environmentally quite abundant in the region but which currently circulate outside those circuits, with the corresponding adverse effects on the countries in question.

5.7 *Information and technical assistance*

The regional position on the subject of technical co-operation should take as its fundamental criterion the need to improve and expand the basic environmental information systems of each and every one of the countries. Horizontal and international technical assistance must be used in order to transfer information from the countries with the greatest experience and knowledge of the various aspects of environmental management to the countries with the greatest needs in this respect.

Many specific questions connected with this topic are examined in this chapter in connection with other aspects. The aim is to continue gaining a more complete knowledge of the resources which exist in the region in terms of their potential, rates of utilization and levels of investment required for their maintenance, while at the same time improving the institutional and organizational bases and the information systems for scientific and technological research on these matters.

5.8 *Biodiversity*

Genetic diversity, considered as part of overall biodiversity, is a resource which is abundant in the region but scarce in the world as a whole. While it is quite true that genetic diversity is currently seen as a gift which is essential for the survival of the planet, this does not mean that it is a public-domain good available for everyone to exploit as he sees fit. Biodiversity, as an economically valuable ecological resource, constitutes a "tradable good" which belongs to the countries that possess it. In view of this, the following are some of the main elements which should form part of a regional strategy to analyse the problem of biodiversity and its possible loss:

a) The countries of the region will make a significant effort to protect and conserve the biodiversity existing in their ecosystems, since they are well aware that this constitutes an important factor for the sustainable development of each country and of mankind as a whole. This effort will be reflected in various actions, such as the evaluation and reformulation of the regional system of protected areas, in order that this system may take proper account of the concept of protection of biodiversity.

b) This protection and conservation effort will call for a substantial amount of financial, human and physical resources. Once the areas to be protected have been precisely defined and the resources needed for the execution of the programmes have been determined, efforts will be made to secure the support and collaboration of the more developed nations through the mechanisms mentioned in General Assembly resolution 44/228.

c) In international forums, the region must do everything it can to further the adoption of new legal instruments aimed at the protection of the genetic heritage and suitable regulation of the "trade" in it. Particular attention should be paid in this respect to the links between this trade and the access that the region can have to technologies based on bioengineering and genetic engineering.

5.9 *Oceans and seas*

With regard to the oceans and seas, the concern expressed in foregoing chapters is reflected in the action proposals already adopted in some subregions, such as the South-East Pacific, which could satisfy the concerns of the entire region, namely:

a) Incorporating, within the specific actions undertaken by the region to maintain the biodiversity of the planet, explicit attention to the long-term economic and social consequences of those measures;

b) Developing strengthened scientific and financial capabilities to organize and conduct research and analysis on the dynamics of marine resources and their interactions with other factors;

c) Promoting the adoption of approaches providing for the integrated management of coastal and marine areas and resources;

d) Applying the "precautionary" principle and "clean production" approach in order to prevent or minimize the generation, transport and disposal of toxic wastes;

e) Urging the international community to create co-operation machinery for the conservation and optimum utilization of living marine resources which come within the areas of sovereignty and jurisdiction of two or more coastal States within the area of sovereignty and jurisdiction of one country or in the open sea, and, finally,

f) Stressing the need for a global agreement on the protection of marine resources from land-based sources of pollution.

5.10 *The legislative and institutional order*

To the extent that there is an improvement in the current economic conditions, the countries of the region will be able to strengthen their capacity for environmental planning and management so as to ensure the effective execution of the programmes and projects for environmental protection, rehabilitation and improvement prepared for this purpose. In view of the enormous diversity of institutional arrangements observed in the region, however, this also involves the need to make thoroughgoing reforms in some cases, minor rectifications in others, and the strengthening of many aspects in practically all cases.

Among the institutional measures which are suggested as criteria for a regional position, special mention may be made of the following:

a) Formulation or improvement of environmental legislation, regulations and standards and rules for the management of natural resources in each country. It may be noted that programmes of this type are under way in practically all the countries of the region;

b) Establishment or strengthening of flexible and highly operational systems of environmental information aimed particularly at ensuring that decisions on these matters are based on a full knowledge of the facts;

c) Establishment or strengthening of stable machinery for participation by the population and civil organizations in the environmental management of each country;

d) Training of human resources engaged in activities directly or indirectly connected with environmental matters, in respect of issues relating to environmental management at the local, regional, state and national levels;

e) Improvement of national systems of co-ordination and co-operation among the different State, para-State and private institutions and bodies whose activities have a significant impact on the environment;

f) Strengthening of the institutions and instruments for regional horizontal co-operation on institutional matters.

6. Preparatory activities for the United Nations Conference

The Governments of Latin America and the Caribbean are engaged in a task of changing production patterns with social equity in which they must incorporate environmental variables in order to ensure the sustainability of development. The United Nations Conference on Environment and Development provides a number of opportunities with regard to this task, and the Regional Preparatory Meeting for Latin America and the Caribbean is only one of the stages in the road leading up to that Conference. There will be other occasions on which the Governments will meet within BCLAC,[6] and many opportunities for them to continue to build up a negotiating platform. Consequently, it is necessary to outline a programme of work covering the rest of 1991 and the beginning of 1992, in order to provide the Governments of the region with even better elements for decision-making, information and analysis.

Some actions can be begun immediately within the regional context, on the basis of the agreements reached at the Regional Preparatory Meeting in Mexico City. After that meeting the BCLAC secretariat will initiate consultations with the countries in order to prepare a *regional agenda of items of common interest*, embodying the concrete suggestions made with regard to issues and actions for the 1990s. In these consultations, the collaboration of all the international and regional bodies would be sought, as well as that of the relevant non-governmental organizations.

6.1 *Executive Notes*

During this preparatory period, it is important to promote an active exchange of information among the countries of the region, and to this end BCLAC plans to provide the countries with a series of *Executive Notes* which will report on the most important matters arising during the period of preparation for the United Nations Conference, which is expected to be a period of intense negotiations. The aim of these Notes will be to provide information, set forth points of view on specific matters, explain the bases and terms of the negotiations taking place, and discuss topics which the countries of the region may consider to be of importance for their own work programmes. They will deal, *inter alia*, with legal, institutional, scientific, technical, economic and social aspects related with the provisional programme of the United Nations Conference and will also give full details of the work programmes approved at the Regional Preparatory Meeting in Mexico City.

6.2 *Strengthening of institutions*

The *strengthening of institutions* is also of priority importance. The capacity for the planning and execution of environmental programmes

urgently needs to be strengthened, since within a relatively short space of time the available financing may exceed the absorptive capacity. Consequently, priorities must be fixed for institutional reforms within the structural adjustment programmes. Through these reforms, ways can be found of strengthening national sovereignty and increasing the bargaining capacity of the whole region. An important part of this strengthening of institutions consists of matters connected with environmental legislation, regulations and standards and the management of natural resources.

BCLAC could devote special attention to this issue by forming an interim committee on legal affairs within the secretariat which would function up to the end of the United Nations Conference. This interdisciplinary committee, supported by experts from the countries, could set about preparing a document to programme the studies to be effected and assist in the formulation of guidelines for the most important negotiations. Its function during this period could also include the provision of assistance and advice to the countries of the region on questions of legislation in this field.

With respect to the recommendations of a regional and international nature aimed at adapting the institutional legal basis to the needs of sustainable development, it would be desirable to analyse in greater depth the existing international and regional regulations concerning the management of natural resources and the environment. This would help to evaluate the desirability of the participation of the countries of Latin America and the Caribbean in these instruments, as well as to identify legal shortcomings of various kinds and seek the possible adoption of new agreements. The Environmental Perspective to the Year 2000 and Beyond and the Montevideo Programme for the Development and Periodic Review of Environmental Law seem to be appropriate lines to follow in seeking out such shortcomings. It would also be desirable to carry out an ongoing follow-up of the negotiations on the framework agreement on climate change and the draft convention on the conservation of biological diversity, as well as other instruments whose adoption may be discussed at the 1992 Conference.

6.3 *Training*

It is particularly important for the population to participate more actively in education and training on matters relating to natural resources and the environment. This participation should take place on all levels, and should include persons working in the public service as well as in the private sector. In preparing the relevant programmes, a substantial contribution could be made by the professional experience existing in each nation, since the education and training must be carried out in the light of real national conditions.

In this respect, consideration could be given to the establishment of an international centre for education and training in these matters. In order to put this idea into practice immediately at low cost, this centre could begin its work as part of a specific activity within an existing body.

The appropriate adaptation of the structure already available in the ECLAC system could contribute to the achievement of the desired objectives within the short term, especially through the collaboration of experts from the region itself possessing specialized knowledge in the fields of natural resources, the environment, economics and technology. The aim of this effort of adaptation would be to offer a training programme on environmental matters by making use of the capacity already existing in the region so as to take full advantage of the experience of the institutions already involved in the provision of training on these matters, such as universities, NGOs or training centres, as well as of enterprises carrying out environmental programmes or providing environment-related equipment or services.

The United Nations Conference on Environment and Development offers an opportunity to gain a better understanding of the magnitude of the challenge involved in achieving sustainable development in the countries of Latin America and the Caribbean. In order to face up to this challenge, it is necessary to outline an agenda of priority activities which will make it possible both to advance in the substantive incorporation of the environmental dimension into the process of changing production patterns with equity and to secure the full participation of the countries of the region in the United Nations Conference: in the preparatory activities for it, in the Conference itself, and in the subsequent activities to which it will give rise.

6.4 *Protection of the biological diversity of the region*

It is now becoming essential to prepare detailed programmes for the protection and conservation of flora, fauna and certain ecosystems which give the region its biological diversity. These programmes could centre upon the various aspects involved in this issue, such as the spatial, technical, economic, social and other dimensions. In view of the intraregional and international externalities involved, the countries of the region could take part in a biodiversity committee based in a regional organization (which could be ECLAC itself, for example), in order to take proper advantage of the existing physical and institutional infrastructure.

6.5 *Other issues*

6.5.1 *Basic and applied research*

With regard to *basic and applied research*, the level of empirical knowledge relating to the sustainable development is insufficient and past experience has been somewhat random. It is therefore necessary to establish or strengthen information systems at both the micro and macroeconomic level. This means carrying out basic and applied research and setting up national institutional structures in keeping with the above needs. It will therefore be necessary to concentrate on aspects such as the following:

a) Developing the capacity to carry out evaluation and monitoring action on natural resources and the environment at both the national and regional levels. Such capacity practically does not exist in the region, even though it is indispensable for the preparation and execution of development policies. Frequently, the region is not in a position to defend its interests simply because it does not know what it possesses, how much it possesses, how much it is using, and the relations which exist between these aspects.

b) Arranging regional and subregional agreements on specific research matters such as pest and disease control, management of international river basins, climate change, etc. These co-operation agreements will increase each nation's management and negotiation capacity, as well as furthering regional integration.

With regard to *technology and environmental sustainability*, since technological change will play a central part in the attainment of sustainable development, various activities in this area are therefore of particular importance. Among them are:

a) Studying the experience accumulated in the course of bilateral, multilateral and national technology transfer programmes in the public and private sectors, with the aim of defining criteria to increase the effectiveness of such programmes.

b) Increasing national and regional capacity to create, adapt, evaluate and transfer technology, and developing policies and institutions in this sphere.

c) Strengthening international co-operation in terms of technical assistance and resources. Such co-operation is indispensable for attaining the objective of developing the "clean technologies" needed for sustainable development.

With regard to *energy and the environment*, in view of the significant environmental impact of the energy sector and the financial restrictions affecting its expansion, it is important to further the following activities, among others:

a) Programmes for the efficient use of energy at both the industrial and household levels. This is an area where there is an enormous amount of experience available, both inside and outside the region, as well as possibilities for financial co-operation and technical assistance.

b) The exchange of experience and information on the environmental impact of the various energy sources in Latin America. Those participating in these activities could include energy sector enterprises, local and national authorities responsible for energy and environmental matters, and multilateral financial agencies.

Activities are also called for in the field of the management of *environment-related enterprises*. In view of the role that should be played by enterprises in the identification and application of environmentally sustainable production methods, either as promoters of environmental programmes connected with their own productive activity or as suppliers of environment-related equipment and services, it seems necessary to promote the following activities at the regional level:

a) Participation by the countries of the region in the projected sectoral study on efficient energy use to be carried out under the co-ordination of the International Chamber of Commerce with the sponsorship of the meeting of entrepreneurs held in connection with the Bergen Conference organized in May 1990 by the Government of Norway in co-operation with the United Nations Economic Commission for Europe (ECE);

b) Promotion of the exchange of experience and information between Latin American and Caribbean enterprises currently carrying out environmental programmes and the national authorities responsible for establishing standards and promoting investments in this field at the local, provincial and national levels;

c) Promotion of the exchange of experience and information between enterprises supplying environment-related equipment and services, national, regional and multilateral financing bodies, and the authorities responsible for establishing standards;

d) Closer contact at the national and regional level between users and suppliers of environment-related equipment and services. In the case of the smaller companies, it will be necessary to promote forms of organization that facilitate these contacts.

145

6.5.2 *Economic policies*

With respect to *region-wide economic policies*, the relation between these policies and resource use and the environment has not yet been sufficiently investigated. In this context, priority should be given to a limited number of questions, especially the following:

a) The past and present effects of the external debt, which, as already explained in the chapter on economic policies, has affected the human and natural environment in various ways.

b) The terms and instruments of financing, which represent a basic priority, involving the investigation of the different forms of domestic and external financing. The contrast between the nature of the programmes and the forms of financing will give the countries vital pointers regarding forms of negotiation and conditionalities.

c) The capacity for the execution of these programmes, which is a matter which not only involves financial aspects but also institutional and governmental dimensions.

d) Economic policies aimed at growth, equity and sustainability, which should be analysed in greater detail. The main purpose of this would be to provide the countries with a broader range of options in terms of economic and environmental policies, so that they could select those which are most viable for each country from the economic, social and political point of view.

The analysis presented in this document and the proposals made in preceding paragraphs seek to provide the region with a better knowledge of its own resources and options as regards sustainable development. This is essential in order to be able to negotiate on the basis of a position that is *truly* –not just morally– equitable in all forums, with the aim of seeking agreements with other countries on the use of the region's resources, financing and the transfer of technology.

Notes

[1] For a more detailed discussion of this principle, see chapter IX.

[2] *Ibid*.

[3] UNEP, *Final Report of the Seventh Ministerial Meeting on the Environment in Latin America and the Caribbean* (UNEP/LAC-IG.VII/4), Port of Spain, 23 October 1990.

[4] Latin American and Caribbean Commission on Development and Environment, *Our Own Agenda*, Washington, D.C., IDB/UNDP, 1990.

[5] There are many institutions in the region which have ample capacity to participate in the development and dissemination of new technologies. Among these, mention may be made, purely by way of example, of the State University of Campinas and the Technological Research Institute of São Paulo (Brazil); the Centre for Research and Advanced Studies of the National Polytechnic Institute and the Institute of Engineering of the National Autonomous University of Mexico (Mexico); the Institute for Technological Research and Technical Standards of Peru; the Statistical Research Centre for Experimental Agroindustrial Production (Venezuela); the Caribbean Industrial Research Institute (Trinidad and Tobago) and the Central American Institute for Industrial Research and Technology (Guatemala).

[6] It may be recalled that the twenty-fourth session of the Commission will be held in Santiago, Chile in April 1992; that is to say, only two months before the United Nations Conference.

ECLAC
publications

ECONOMIC COMMISSION FOR LATIN AMERICA
AND THE CARIBBEAN
Casilla 179-D   Santiago de Chile

PERIODIC PUBLICATIONS

C E P A L Review

CEPAL Review first appeared in 1976 as part of the Publications Programme of the Economic Commission for Latin America and the Caribbean, its aim being to make a contribution to the study of the economic and social development problems of the region. The views expressed in signed articles, including those by Secretariat staff members, are those of the authors and therefore do not necessarily reflect the point of view of the Organization.

CEPAL Review is published in Spanish and English versions three times a year.

Annual subscription costs for 1989 are US$16 for the Spanish version and US$18 for the English version. The price of single issues is US$10 in both cases.

Estudio Económico de América Latina y el Caribe			Economic Survey of Latin America and the Caribbean		
1980,		664 pp.	1980,		629 pp.
1981,		863 pp.	1981,		837 pp.
1982,	vol. I	693 pp.	1982,	vol. I	658 pp.
1982,	vol. II	199 pp.	1982,	vol. II	186 pp.
1983,	vol. I	694 pp.	1983,	vol. I	686 pp.
1983,	vol. II	179 pp.	1983,	vol. II	166 pp.
1984,	vol. I	702 pp.	1984,	vol. I	685 pp.
1984,	vol. II	233 pp.	1984,	vol. II	216 pp.
1985,		672 pp.	1985,		660 pp.
1986,		734 pp.	1986,		729 pp.
1987,		692 pp.	1987,		685 pp.
1988,		741 pp.	1988,		637 pp.
1989,		821 pp.			

(Issues for previous years also available)

Anuario Estadístico de América Latina y el Caribe / Statistical Yearbook for Latin America and the Caribbean (bilingual)

1980,	617 pp.	*1986*,	782 pp.
1981,	727 pp.	*1987*,	714 pp.
1983,	(1982/1983) 749 pp.	*1988*,	782 pp.
1984,	761 pp.	*1989*,	770 pp.
1985,	792 pp.	*1990*,	782 pp.

(Issues for previous years also available)

Libros de la C E P A L

1 *Manual de proyectos de desarrollo económico,* 1958, 5th. ed. 1980, 264 pp.

1 **Manual on economic development projects,** 1958, 2nd. ed. 1972, 242 pp.

2 *América Latina en el umbral de los años ochenta,* 1979, 2nd. ed. 1980, 203 pp.

3 *Agua, desarrollo y medio ambiente en América Latina,* 1980, 443 pp.

4 *Los bancos transnacionales y el financiamiento externo de América Latina. La experiencia del Perú,* 1980, 265 pp.

4 **Transnational banks and the external finance of Latin America: the experience of Peru,** 1985, 342 pp.

5 *La dimensión ambiental en los estilos de desarrollo de América Latina,* Osvaldo Sunkel, 1981, 2nd. ed. 1984, 136 pp.

6 *La mujer y el desarrollo: guía para la planificación de programas y proyectos,* 1984, 115 pp.

6 **Women and development: guidelines for programme and project planning,** 1982, 3rd. ed. 1984, 123 pp.

7 *Africa y América Latina: perspectivas de la cooperación interregional,* 1983, 286 pp.

8 *Sobrevivencia campesina en ecosistemas de altura,* vols. I y II, 1983, 720 pp.

9 *La mujer en el sector popular urbano. América Latina y el Caribe,* 1984, 349 pp.

10 *Avances en la interpretación ambiental del desarrollo agrícola de América Latina,* 1985, 236 pp.

11 *El decenio de la mujer en el escenario latinoamericano,* 1986, 216 pp.

11 **The decade for women in Latin America and the Caribbean: background and prospects,** 1988, 215 pp.

12 *América Latina: sistema monetario internacional y financiamiento externo,* 1986, 416 pp.

12 **Latin America: international monetary system and external financing,** 1986, 405 pp.

13 *Raúl Prebisch: Un aporte al estudio de su pensamiento,* 1987, 146 pp.

14 *Cooperativismo latinoamericano: antecedentes y perspectivas,* 1989, 371 pp.

15 *CEPAL, 40 años (1948-1988)*, 1988, 85 pp.
15 **ECLAC 40 Years (1948-1988)**, 1989, 83 pp.
16 *América Latina en la economía mundial*, 1988, 321 pp.
17 *Gestión para el desarrollo de cuencas de alta montaña en la zona andina*, 1988, 187 pp.
18 *Políticas macroeconómicas y brecha externa: América Latina en los años ochenta*, 1989, 201 pp.
19 *CEPAL, Bibliografía, 1948-1988*, 1989, 648 pp.
20 *Desarrollo agrícola y participación campesina*, 1989, 404 pp.
21 *Planificación y gestión del desarrollo en áreas de expansión de la frontera agropecuaria en América Latina*, 1989, 113 pp.
22 *Transformación ocupacional y crisis social en América Latina*, 1989, 243 pp.
23 *La crisis urbana en América Latina y el Caribe: reflexiones sobre alternativas de solución*, 1990, 197 pp.
25 *Transformación productiva con equidad*, 1990, 185 pp.
25 **Changing production patterns with social equity**, 1990, 177 pp.
26 *América Latina y el Caribe: opciones para reducir el peso de la deuda*, 1990, 118 pp.
26 **Latin America and the Caribbean: options to reduce the debt burden**, 1990, 110 pp.

MONOGRAPH SERIES

Cuadernos de la C E P A L

1 *América Latina: el nuevo escenario regional y mundial/***Latin America: the new regional and world setting**, (bilingual), 1975, 2nd. ed. 1985, 103 pp.
2 *Las evoluciones regionales de la estrategia internacional del desarrollo*, 1975, 2nd. ed. 1984, 73 pp.
2 **Regional appraisals of the international development strategy**, 1975, 2nd. ed. 1985, 82 pp.
3 *Desarrollo humano, cambio social y crecimiento en América Latina*, 1975, 2nd. ed. 1984, 103 pp.
4 *Relaciones comerciales, crisis monetaria e integración económica en América Latina*, 1975, 85 pp.
5 *Síntesis de la segunda evaluación regional de la estrategia internacional del desarrollo*, 1975, 72 pp.
6 *Dinero de valor constante. Concepto, problemas y experiencias*, Jorge Rose, 1975, 2nd. ed. 1984, 43 pp.
7 *La coyuntura internacional y el sector externo*, 1975, 2nd. ed. 1983, 106 pp.
8 *La industrialización latinoamericana en los años setenta*, 1975, 2nd. ed. 1984, 116 pp.

9 *Dos estudios sobre inflación 1972-1974. La inflación en los países centrales. América Latina y la inflación importada*, 1975, 2nd. ed. 1984, 57 pp.
s/n **Canada and the foreign firm,** D. Pollock, 1976, 43 pp.
10 *Reactivación del mercado común centroamericano*, 1976, 2nd. ed. 1984, 149 pp.
11 *Integración y cooperación entre países en desarrollo en el ámbito agrícola*, Germánico Salgado, 1976, 2nd. ed. 1985, 62 pp.
12 *Temas del nuevo orden económico internacional*, 1976, 2nd. ed. 1984, 85 pp.
13 *En torno a las ideas de la CEPAL: desarrollo, industrialización y comercio exterior*, 1977, 2nd. ed. 1985, 57 pp.
14 *En torno a las ideas de la CEPAL: problemas de la industrialización en América Latina*, 1977, 2nd. ed. 1984, 46 pp.
15 *Los recursos hidráulicos de América Latina. Informe regional*, 1977, 2nd. ed. 1984, 75 pp.
15 **The water resources of Latin America. Regional report,** 1977, 2nd. ed. 1985, 79 pp.
16 *Desarrollo y cambio social en América Latina*, 1977, 2nd. ed. 1984, 59 pp.
17 *Estrategia internacional de desarrollo y establecimiento de un nuevo orden económico internacional*, 1977, 3rd. ed. 1984, 61 pp.
17 **International development strategy and establishment of a new international economic order,** 1977, 3rd. ed. 1985, 59 pp.
18 *Raíces históricas de las estructuras distributivas de América Latina*, A. di Filippo, 1977, 2nd. ed. 1983, 64 pp.
19 *Dos estudios sobre endeudamiento externo*, C. Massad y R. Zahler, 1977, 2nd. ed. 1986, 66 pp.
s/n **United States – Latin American trade and financial relations: some policy recommendations,** S. Weintraub, 1977, 44 pp.
20 *Tendencias y proyecciones a largo plazo del desarrollo económico de América Latina*, 1978, 3rd. ed. 1985, 134 pp.
21 *25 años en la agricultura de América Latina: rasgos principales 1950-1975*, 1978, 2nd. ed. 1983, 124 pp.
22 *Notas sobre la familia como unidad socio-económica*, Carlos A. Borsotti, 1978, 2nd. ed. 1984, 60 pp.
23 *La organización de la información para la evaluación del desarrollo*, Juan Sourrouille, 1978, 2nd. ed. 1984, 61 pp.
24 *Contabilidad nacional a precios constantes en América Latina*, 1978, 2nd. ed. 1983, 60 pp.
s/n **Energy in Latin America: The Historical Record,** J. Mullen, 1978, 66 pp.
25 *Ecuador: desafíos y logros de la política económica en la fase de expansión petrolera*, 1979, 2nd. ed. 1984, 153 pp.

26 *Las transformaciones rurales en América Latina: ¿desarrollo social o marginación?*, 1979, 2nd. ed. 1984, 160 pp.

27 *La dimensión de la pobreza en América Latina*, Oscar Altimir, 1979, 2nd. ed. 1983, 89 pp.

28 *Organización institucional para el control y manejo de la deuda externa. El caso chileno*, Rodolfo Hoffman, 1979, 35 pp.

29 *La política monetaria y el ajuste de la balanza de pagos: tres estudios*, 1979, 2nd. ed. 1984, 61 pp.

29 **Monetary policy and balance of payments adjustment: three studies**, 1979, 60 pp.

30 *América Latina: las evaluaciones regionales de la estrategia internacional del desarrollo en los años setenta*, 1979, 2nd. ed. 1982, 237 pp.

31 *Educación, imágenes y estilos de desarrollo*, G. Rama, 1979, 2nd. ed. 1982, 72 pp.

32 *Movimientos internacionales de capitales*, R. H. Arriazu, 1979, 2nd. ed. 1984, 90 pp.

33 *Informe sobre las inversiones directas extranjeras en América Latina*, A. E. Calcagno, 1980, 2nd. ed. 1982, 114 pp.

34 *Las fluctuaciones de la industria manufacturera argentina, 1950-1978*, D. Heymann, 1980, 2nd. ed. 1984, 234 pp.

35 *Perspectivas de reajuste industrial: la Comunidad Económica Europea y los países en desarrollo*, B. Evers, G. de Groot and W. Wagenmans, 1980, 2nd. ed. 1984, 69 pp.

36 *Un análisis sobre la posibilidad de evaluar la solvencia crediticia de los países en desarrollo*, A. Saieh, 1980, 2nd. ed. 1984, 82 pp.

37 *Hacia los censos latinoamericanos de los años ochenta*, 1981, 146 pp.

s/n **The economic relations of Latin America with Europe**, 1980, 2nd. ed. 1983, 156 pp.

38 *Desarrollo regional argentino: la agricultura*, J. Martin, 1981, 2nd. ed. 1984, 111 pp.

39 *Estratificación y movilidad ocupacional en América Latina*, C. Filgueira and C. Geneletti, 1981, 2nd. ed. 1985, 162 pp.

40 *Programa de acción regional para América Latina en los años ochenta*, 1981, 2nd. ed. 1984, 62 pp.

40 **Regional programme of action for Latin America in the 1980s**, 1981, 2nd. ed. 1984, 57 pp.

41 *El desarrollo de América Latina y sus repercusiones en la educación. Alfabetismo y escolaridad básica*, 1982, 246 pp.

42 *América Latina y la economía mundial del café*, 1982, 95 pp.

43 *El ciclo ganadero y la economía argentina*, 1983, 160 pp.

44 *Las encuestas de hogares en América Latina*, 1983, 122 pp.

45 *Las cuentas nacionales en América Latina y el Caribe*, 1983, 100 pp.

45 **National accounts in Latin America and the Caribbean**, 1983, 97 pp.

46 *Demanda de equipos para generación, transmisión y transformación eléctrica en América Latina*, 1983, 193 pp.

47 *La economía de América Latina en 1982: evolución general, política cambiaria y renegociación de la deuda externa*, 1984, 104 pp.

48 *Políticas de ajuste y renegociación de la deuda externa en América Latina*, 1984, 102 pp.

49 *La economía de América Latina y el Caribe en 1983: evolución general, crisis y procesos de ajuste*, 1985, 95 pp.

49 **The economy of Latin America and the Caribbean in 1983: main trends, the impact of the crisis and the adjustment processes**, 1985, 93 pp.

50 *La CEPAL, encarnación de una esperanza de América Latina*, Hernán Santa Cruz, 1985, 77 pp.

51 *Hacia nuevas modalidades de cooperación económica entre América Latina y el Japón*, 1986, 233 pp.

51 **Towards new forms of economic co-operation between Latin America and Japan**, 1987, 245 pp.

52 *Los conceptos básicos del transporte marítimo y la situación de la actividad en América Latina*, 1986, 112 pp.

52 **Basic concepts of maritime transport and its present status in Latin America and the Caribbean**, 1987, 114 pp.

53 *Encuestas de ingresos y gastos. Conceptos y métodos en la experiencia latinoamericana*. 1986, 128 pp.

54 *Crisis económica y políticas de ajuste, estabilización y crecimiento*, 1986, 123 pp.

54 **The economic crisis: policies for adjustment, stabilization and growth**, 1986, 125 pp.

55 *El desarrollo de América Latina y el Caribe: escollos, requisitos y opciones*, 1987, 184 pp.

55 **Latin American and Caribbean development: obstacles, requirements and options**, 1987, 184 pp.

56 *Los bancos transnacionales y el endeudamiento externo en la Argentina*, 1987, 112 pp.

57 *El proceso de desarrollo de la pequeña y mediana empresa y su papel en el sistema industrial: el caso de Italia*, 1988, 112 pp.

58 *La evolución de la economía de América Latina en 1986*, 1988, 99 pp.

58 **The evolution of the Latin American Economy in 1986**, 1988, 95 pp.

59 **Protectionism: regional negotiation and defence strategies**, 1988, 261 pp.

60 *Industrialización en América Latina: de la "caja negra" al "casillero vacío"*, F. Fajnzylber, 1989, 2nd. ed. 1990, 176 pp.

60 **Industrialization in Latin America: from the "Black Box" to the "Empty Box", F. Fajnzylber, 1990, 172 pp.**

61 *Hacia un desarrollo sostenido en América Latina y el Caribe: restricciones y requisitos, 1989, 94 pp.*

61 **Towards sustained development in Latin America and the Caribbean: restrictions and requisites, 1989, 93 pp.**

62 *La evolución de la economía de América Latina en 1987, 1989, 87 pp.*

62 **The evolution of the Latin American economy in 1987, 1989, 84 pp.**

63 *Elementos para el diseño de políticas industriales y tecnológicas en América Latina, 1990, 172 pp.*

64 *La industria de transporte regular internacional y la competitividad del comercio exterior de los países de América Latina y el Caribe, 1989, 132 pp.*

64 **The international common-carrier transportation industry and the competitiveness of the foreign trade of the countries of Latin America and the Caribbean, 1989, 116 pp.**

65 **Structural Changes in Ports and the Competitiveness of Latin American and Caribbean Foreign Trade, 1990, 126 pp.**

Cuadernos Estadísticos de la C E P A L

1 *América Latina: relación de precios del intercambio, 1976, 2nd. ed. 1984, 66 pp.*

2 *Indicadores del desarrollo económico y social en América Latina, 1976, 2nd. ed. 1984, 179 pp.*

3 *Series históricas del crecimiento de América Latina, 1978, 2nd. ed. 1984, 206 pp.*

4 *Estadísticas sobre la estructura del gasto de consumo de los hogares según finalidad del gasto, por grupos de ingreso, 1978, 110 pp. (Out of print; replaced by No. 8 below)*

5 *El balance de pagos de América Latina, 1950-1977, 1979, 2nd. ed. 1984, 164 pp.*

6 *Distribución regional del producto interno bruto sectorial en los países de América Latina, 1981, 2nd. ed. 1985, 68 pp.*

7 *Tablas de insumo-producto en América Latina, 1983, 383 pp.*

8 *Estructura del gasto de consumo de los hogares según finalidad del gasto, por grupos de ingreso, 1984, 146 pp.*

9 *Origen y destino del comercio exterior de los países de la Asociación Latinoamericana de Integración y del Mercado Común Centroamericano, 1985, 546 pp.*

10 *América Latina: balance de pagos, 1950-1984, 1986, 357 pp.*

11 *El comercio exterior de bienes de capital en América Latina, 1986, 288 pp.*

12 *América Latina: indices del comercio exterior, 1970-1984, 1987, 355 pp.*

13 *América Latina: comercio exterior según la clasificación industrial internacional uniforme de todas las actividades económicas, 1987, Vol. I, 675 pp; Vol. II, 675 pp.*

14 *La distribución del ingreso en Colombia. Antecedentes estadísticos y características socio-económicas de los receptores, 1988, 156 pp.*

Estudios e Informes de la C E P A L

1 *Nicaragua: el impacto de la mutación política, 1981, 2nd. ed. 1982, 126 pp.*

2 *Perú 1968-1977: la política económica en un proceso de cambio global, 1981, 2nd. ed. 1982, 166 pp.*

3 *La industrialización de América Latina y la cooperación internacional, 1981, 170 pp. (Out of print, will not be reprinted.)*

4 *Estilos de desarrollo, modernización y medio ambiente en la agricultura latinoamericana, 1981, 4th. ed. 1984, 130 pp.*

5 *El desarrollo de América Latina en los años ochenta, 1981, 2nd. ed. 1982, 153 pp.*

5 **Latin American development in the 1980s, 1981, 2nd. ed. 1982, 134 pp.**

6 *Proyecciones del desarrollo latinoamericano en los años ochenta, 1981, 3rd. ed. 1985, 96 pp.*

6 **Latin American development projections for the 1980s, 1982, 2nd. ed. 1983, 89 pp.**

7 *Las relaciones económicas externas de América Latina en los años ochenta, 1981, 2nd. ed. 1982, 180 pp.*

8 *Integración y cooperación regionales en los años ochenta, 1982, 2nd. ed. 1982, 174 pp.*

9 *Estrategias de desarrollo sectorial para los años ochenta: industria y agricultura, 1981, 2nd. ed. 1985, 100 pp.*

10 *Dinámica del subempleo en América Latina. PREALC, 1981, 2nd. ed. 1985, 101 pp.*

11 *Estilos de desarrollo de la industria manufacturera y medio ambiente en América Latina, 1982, 2nd. ed. 1984, 178 pp.*

12 *Relaciones económicas de América Latina con los países miembros del "Consejo de Asistencia Mutua Económica", 1982, 154 pp.*

13 *Campesinado y desarrollo agrícola en Bolivia, 1982, 175 pp.*

14 *El sector externo: indicadores y análisis de sus fluctuaciones. El caso argentino, 1982, 2nd. ed. 1985, 216 pp.*

15 *Ingeniería y consultoría en Brasil y el Grupo Andino, 1982, 320 pp.*

16 *Cinco estudios sobre la situación de la mujer en América Latina, 1982, 2nd. ed. 1985, 178 pp.*

16 **Five studies on the situation of women in Latin America,** 1983, 2nd. ed. 1984, 188 pp.

17 *Cuentas nacionales y producto material en América Latina,* 1982, 129 pp.

18 *El financiamiento de las exportaciones en América Latina,* 1983, 212 pp.

19 *Medición del empleo y de los ingresos rurales,* 1982, 2nd. ed. 1983, 173 pp.

19 **Measurement of employment and income in rural areas,** 1983, 184 pp.

20 *Efectos macroeconómicos de cambios en las barreras al comercio y al movimiento de capitales: un modelo de simulación,* 1982, 68 pp.

21 *La empresa pública en la economía: la experiencia argentina,* 1982, 2nd. ed. 1985, 134 pp.

22 *Las empresas transnacionales en la economía de Chile, 1974-1980,* 1983, 178 pp.

23 *La gestión y la informática en las empresas ferroviarias de América Latina y España,* 1983, 195 pp.

24 *Establecimiento de empresas de reparación y mantenimiento de contenedores en América Latina y el Caribe,* 1983, 314 pp.

24 **Establishing container repair and maintenance enterprises in Latin America and the Caribbean,** 1983, 236 pp.

25 *Agua potable y saneamiento ambiental en América Latina, 1981-1990/***Drinking water supply and sanitation in Latin America, 1981-1990** (bilingual), 1983, 140 pp.

26 *Los bancos transnacionales, el estado y el endeudamiento externo en Bolivia,* 1983, 282 pp.

27 *Política económica y procesos de desarrollo. La experiencia argentina entre 1976 y 1981,* 1983, 157 pp.

28 *Estilos de desarrollo, energía y medio ambiente: un estudio de caso exploratorio,* 1983, 129 pp.

29 *Empresas transnacionales en la industria de alimentos. El caso argentino: cereales y carne,* 1983, 93 pp.

30 *Industrialización en Centroamérica, 1960-1980,* 1983, 168 pp.

31 *Dos estudios sobre empresas transnacionales en Brasil,* 1983, 141 pp.

32 *La crisis económica internacional y su repercusión en América Latina,* 1983, 81 pp.

33 *La agricultura campesina en sus relaciones con la industria,* 1984, 120 pp.

34 *Cooperación económica entre Brasil y el Grupo Andino: el caso de los minerales y metales no ferrosos,* 1983, 148 pp.

35 *La agricultura campesina y el mercado de alimentos: la dependencia externa y sus efectos en una economía abierta,* 1984, 201 pp.

36 *El capital extranjero en la economía peruana,* 1984, 178 pp.

37 *Dos estudios sobre política arancelaria,* 1984, 96 pp.

38 *Estabilización y liberalización económica en el Cono Sur,* 1984, 193 pp.

39 *La agricultura campesina y el mercado de alimentos: el caso de Haití y el de la República Dominicana,* 1984, 255 pp.

40 *La industria siderúrgica latinoamericana: tendencias y potencial,* 1984, 280 pp.

41 *La presencia de las empresas transnacionales en la economía ecuatoriana,* 1984, 77 pp.

42 *Precios, salarios y empleo en la Argentina: estadísticas económicas de corto plazo,* 1984, 378 pp.

43 *El desarrollo de la seguridad social en América Latina,* 1985, 348 pp.

44 **Market structure, firm size and Brazilian exports,** 1985, 104 pp.

45 *La planificación del transporte en países de América Latina,* 1985, 247 pp.

46 *La crisis en América Latina: su evaluación y perspectivas,* 1985, 119 pp.

47 *La juventud en América Latina y el Caribe,* 1985, 181 pp.

48 *Desarrollo de los recursos mineros de América Latina,* 1985, 145 pp.

48 **Development of the mining resources of Latin America,** 1989, 160 pp.

49 *Las relaciones económicas internacionales de América Latina y la cooperación regional,* 1985, 224 pp.

50 *América Latina y la economía mundial del algodón,* 1985, 122 pp.

51 *Comercio y cooperación entre países de América Latina y países miembros del CAME,* 1985, 90 pp.

52 **Trade relations between Brazil and the United States,** 1985, 148 pp.

53 *Los recursos hídricos de América Latina y el Caribe y su aprovechamiento,* 1985, 138 pp.

53 **The water resources of Latin America and the Caribbean and their utilization,** 1985, 135 pp.

54 La pobreza en América Latina: dimensiones y políticas, 1985, 155 pp.

55 *Políticas de promoción de exportaciones en algunos países de América Latina,* 1985, 207 pp.

56 *Las empresas transnacionales en la Argentina,* 1986, 222 pp.

57 *El desarrollo frutícola y forestal en Chile y sus derivaciones sociales,* 1986, 227 pp.

58 *El cultivo del algodón y la soya en el Paraguay y sus derivaciones sociales,* 1986, 141 pp.

59 *Expansión del cultivo de la caña de azúcar y de la ganadería en el nordeste del Brasil: un examen del papel de la política pública y de sus derivaciones económicas y sociales,* 1986, 164 pp.

60 *Las empresas transnacionales en el desarrollo colombiano,* 1986, 212 pp.

61 *Las empresas transnacionales en la economía del Paraguay*, 1987, 115 pp.

62 *Problemas de la industria latinoamericana en la fase crítica*, 1986, 113 pp.

63 *Relaciones económicas internacionales y cooperación regional de América Latina y el Caribe*, 1987, 272 pp.

63 **International economic relations and regional co-operation in Latin America and the Caribbean**, 1987, 267 pp.

64 *Tres ensayos sobre inflación y políticas de estabilización*, 1986, 201 pp.

65 *La industria farmacéutica y farmoquímica: desarrollo histórico y posibilidades futuras. Argentina, Brasil y México*, 1987, 177 pp.

66 *Dos estudios sobre América Latina y el Caribe y la economía internacional*, 1987, 125 pp.

67 *Reestructuración de la industria automotriz mundial y perspectivas para América Latina*, 1987, 232 pp.

68 *Cooperación latinoamericana en servicios: antecedentes y perspectivas*, 1988, 155 pp.

69 *Desarrollo y transformación: estrategia para superar la pobreza*, 1988, 114 pp.

69 **Development and change: strategies for vanquishing poverty**, 1988, 114 pp.

70 *La evolución económica del Japón y su impacto en América Latina*, 1988, 88 pp.

70 **The economic evolution of Japan and its impact on Latin America**, 1990, 79 pp.

71 *La gestión de los recursos hídricos en América Latina y el Caribe*, 1989, 256 pp.

72 *La evolución del problema de la deuda externa en América Latina y el Caribe*, 1988, 77 pp.

72 **The evolution of the external debt problem in Latin America and the Caribbean**, 1988, 69 pp.

73 *Agricultura, comercio exterior y cooperación internacional*, 1988, 83 pp.

73 **Agriculture, external trade and international co-operation**, 1989, 79 pp.

74 *Reestructuración industrial y cambio tecnológico: consecuencias para América Latina*, 1989, 105 pp.

75 *El medio ambiente como factor de desarrollo*, 1989, 123 pp.

76 *El comportamiento de los bancos transnacionales y la crisis internacional de endeudamiento*, 1989, 214 pp.

76 **Transnational bank behaviour and the international debt crisis**, 1989, 198 pp.

77 *Los recursos hídricos de América Latina y del Caribe: planificación, desastres naturales y contaminación*, 1990, 266 pp.

77 **The water resources of Latin America and the Caribbean - Planning hazards and pollution**, 1990, 252 pp.

78 *La apertura financiera en Chile y el comportamiento de los bancos transnacionales*, 1990, 132 pp.

Serie INFOPLAN: Temas Especiales del Desarrollo

1 *Resúmenes de documentos sobre deuda externa*, 1986, 324 pp.

2 *Resúmenes de documentos sobre cooperación entre países en desarrollo*, 1986, 189 pp.

3 *Resúmenes de documentos sobre recursos hídricos*, 1987, 290 pp.

4 *Resúmenes de documentos sobre planificación y medio ambiente*, 1987, 111 pp.

5 *Resúmenes de documentos sobre integración económica en América Latina y el Caribe*, 1987, 273 pp.

6 *Resúmenes de documentos sobre cooperación entre países en desarrollo, II parte*, 1988, 146 pp.

Impreso en los Talleres de
EDITORIAL UNIVERSITARIA